# Mark Twain and His Illustrators

## Volume II (1875-1883)

# Mark Twain and His Illustrators

## Volume II (1875-1883)

### Beverly R. David

Whitston Publishing Company, Inc.
Albany, New York
2001

To my husband, Dr. John David, who has been so patient while "seeing nothing but the back of my head" while I work at the computer for these many years. Thank you.

# Contents

# Acknowledgments

For help and generosity with information, materials, and permissions, I am grateful to the Mark Twain Project and to the Project editors, Robert Hirst and Victor Fischer, for their assistance with my research. I am also indebted to fellow scholars Mark Woodhouse of the Gannett-Tripp Library of Elmira College for his help in the investigation of *Sketches #1* and Barbara Schmidt for allowing me to use portions of her study of the illustrator True Williams.

My gratitude goes to the late Professor Les Crossman, my mentor and editor for twenty years, and to Professor Alan Gribben who has been a constant champion of my work. I am also indebted to Professor Roger Wallace for his help in reading final copy.

I wish to thank the Research Foundation of Western Michigan University for their generous grants allowing me to complete my research for Volume II in Germany and Switzerland.

I could not have written this book without drawing on the work of the many Mark Twain scholars. In the notes at the end of each chapter, I trust I have identified them and credited their work.

# Abbreviations

The following abbreviations and locations symbols have been used for citation in this volume:

BALII Jacob Blanck, *Bibliography of American Literature,* Volume II (New Haven: Yale University Press, 1957).

BMT Merle Johnson, *A Bibliography of the Works of Mark Twain* (New York: Harper and Brothers, 1935).

*Businessman* *Mark Twain, Businessman.*

CL1 *Mark Twain's Letters,* Volume I (1853-1866), ed. Edgar M. Branch, Michael B. Frank and Kenneth M. Sanderson (Berkeley, Los Angeles, London: University of California Press, 1988).

CL2 *Mark Twain's Letters,* Volume II (1867-1868), ed. Harriet Elinor Smith and Richard Bucci (Berkeley, Los Angeles, London: University of California Press, 1990).

CL3 *Mark Twain's Letters,* Volume III (1871-1874), ed. Michael B. Frank (Berkeley, Los Angeles, London: University of California Press, 1993).

David Beverly R. David, *Mark Twain and His Illustrators,* Volume I (Troy, New York: Whitston Publishing Company, 1986).

ET&SkI *Early Tales and Sketches,* Volume I (1851-1864), ed. Edgar Banch and Robert Hirst (Berkeley, Los Angeles, London: University of California Press, 1979).

Hamilton I Sinclair Hamilton, *Nineteenth Century American Book Illustration,* Volume I (Princeton University Press, 1958).

| | |
|---|---|
| Hamilton II | Sinclair Hamilton, *Century American Book Illustration*, Supplement (Princeton University Press, 1968). |
| MTBI | Albert Bigelow Paine, *Mark Twain: A Biography*, Volume I (New York: Harper and Brothers, 1912). |
| MTCH | *Mark Twain, The Critical Heritage*, ed. Frederick Anderson (New York: Barnes and Noble, 1971). |
| MT&EB | Hamlin Hill, *Mark Twain and Elisah Bliss* (Columbia: University of Missouri Press, 1964). |
| MTHL II | *Mark Twain-Howells Letters*, Volume II, ed. Henry Nash Smith and William M. Gibson (Cambridge: Harvard University Press, 1960). |
| MTLI | *Mark Twain Letters to His Publishers*, ed. Hamlin Hill (Berkeley, Los Angeles, London: University of California Press, 1967). |
| MTMF | *Mark Twain to Mrs. Fairbanks*, ed. Dixon Wecter (San Marino, California: Huntington Library, 1949). |
| MTP | Mark Twain Papers, The Bancroft Library, University of California. |
| N&J I | *Mark Twain's Notebookes & Journals*, Volume I (1855-1873), ed. Frederick Anderson, Michael B. Frank and Kenneth Sanderson (Berkeley, Los Angeles, London: University of California Press, 1975). |
| N&J II | *Mark Twain's Notebooks & Journals*, Volume II (1877-1883), ed. Frederick Anderson, Lin Salamo and Bernard L. Stein (Berkeley, Los Angeles, London: University of California Press, 1975). |
| N&J III | *Mark Twain's Notebooks & Journals*, Volume III (1883-1891), ed. Robert Pack Browning, Michael B. Frank and Lin Salamo (Berkeley, Los Angeles, London: University of California Press, 1979). |
| Sk#1 | *Sketches, Number One* (New York: American News Company, 1874). |
| SkN&O | *Mark Twain Sketches, New and Old* (Hartford: The American Publishing Company, 1875). |
| Welland | Dennis Welland, *Mark Twain in England* (Atlantic Higlands, New Jersey: Humanities Press, 1978). |

# Introduction

If I get only half a chance I will write a book that will sell like fury provided you put pictures enough in it.[1]

According to the Oxford English Dictionary, in the fourteenth-century the word *illustration* had the connotation of "spiritual enlightening" or "illuminating." It wasn't until the early nineteenth-century that the word came to signify "a drawing, plate, engraving, cut, or the like, illustrating or embellishing a literary article." Since that time it has been a standard assumption that pictures should merely mirror the text, and illustration has taken on a secondary role. Text-centered scholars still readily accept this concept. It is, however, impossible for an illustrator to say in pictures the same thing as an author does in words. There are major differences between linguistic and graphic perceptions. No illustration can simply "mirror" the text, though indeed it may recreate a part of the same world that the text has created.

Mark Twain knew the language and power of pictures. His books were published by subscription, and subscription books were packed with prints of every type and size; the pages were bound with brassy gold, image-stamped covers. In the subscription market illustration functioned as a major sales tool. The pictures quickly conveyed the sense of Twain's stories, outlining the scope and tone of the work. When his editor was writing a sales pitch for *The Prince and the Pauper*, Twain reminded him: "Don't forget to glorify the illustrations."[2] One can assume that Twain was familiar with the ancient Chinese proverb, that "one picture is worth more than ten thousand words."

Not only did Twain recognize the potency of pictures he

also acknowledged that his subscription readers expected his books to be "fully illustrated," 300 to 400 pictures per volume. Twain, therefore, involved himself in more than just the writing. He often chose the illustrators, approved the artist's sketches, edited or created the captions, and even directed the placement of the prints in the letterpress.

Perhaps unconsciously Mark Twain understood the psychology of visual perception that dictated his reader's response. An illustration is likely to be seen, be it upon the book's cover or in the frontispiece, before a person begins to read, making the text a belated adjunct to the picture. Readers viewing Twain in an alpine costume on the cover of *A Tramp Abroad* fantasize they will be joining him on a mountain-climbing expedition; seeing a crown and shield on the cover of *The Prince and the Pauper* they imagine entering a more royal world than their own.

When scanning a picture, a reader processes information differently than when reading the words on the page.[3] Looking at an image, the central nervous system instantly organizes the several parts of a picture into a whole and there is an immediate emotional reaction. The phenomenon is called mosaic formation. When reading lines of text, however, each word, line, phrase and paragraph builds slowly, separately, until a complete concept is established. This phenomenon is called linear processing. Readers going through the linear process carefully "assemble" ideas in their mind; each individual's assemblage creates his/her personal interpretation of the author's idea.

We all understand this process. Dickens scholars acknowledge that George Cruikshank compelled the imagining of Charles Dickens Tiny Tim: "No character any more will walk for the first time into our memory as we ourselves imagine him."[4] Austin Dobson, nephew of Lewis Carroll wrote:

> Enchanting Alice! Black and White
> Has made your charm perennial;
> And nought save 'Chaos and old Night'
> Can part you now from Tenniel.

In the same manner, E. W. Kemble's frontispiece of Huck, with his Irish grin in *Adventures of Huckleberry Finn,* continues to be an accepted version of Twain's hero no matter how the author envisioned him.

On a more monumental scale mosaic perception is the reason why seeing a character in a movie forever shapes our definition of that character when, later, we read the book. For anyone who has seen the 1939 movie *Gone With the Wind*, Scarlett O'Hara will always be Vivien Leigh whatever Margaret Mitchell's intentions may have been.

E. H. Gombrich writes that "we build [a picture] up in time and hold the bits and pieces we scan in readiness till they fall into place as an imaginable object or event, and it is this totality we perceive and check against the picture in front of us." It is this totality that we perceive as the "moment" of the picture.[6]

The introduction of a picture into a work of narrative art, however, also causes the reader to become aware of his own as well as the author's interpretive role. When an illustration appears on a page of text, it works to control the reader's interpretation of that text; the picture "bends" the message of the linear page-print. In *A Tramp Abroad*, a picture of a singing, straggly-haired crone captioned THE LORELEI appears opposite Twain's description of the Nymph of the Rhine as an "enchanting figure of the beautiful Lore" (141). Viewing the illustration alongside the text, it is a signpost not to take Twain's characterization seriously, the picture contorts his words.

Moreover, even if a landscape or portrait directly corresponds to the author's specific place or person, the placement and size of the illustration has a bearing on the reader's sensibility. If an illustration is inserted on a page prior to a related text it may blunt the impact of the narrative by revealing too much; if it is inserted in close proximity to a related text it can complement and reinforce an author's intention. If a picture occupies more space on a page than the letterpress, it is foregrounded and creates more of an impact than the corresponding print passage by itself.

To add to these many visual variations, an individual's previous optical experience can distort their final impression since our perceptions are formed by our visual memory.

The relationship of pictures to print has seldom been studied in adult literature, though it has been examined and codified for children's literature. Understanding this codification can add another layer to a reader's responses. Scholars of children's literature have defined many of the differences between an author's narrative style and an artist's idea for illustration; they have shown how a reader's perception can be augmented or distorted by the combination of a picture and prose. Some of these perceptual differences involve contradictions (where the artist draws the opposite of the author's stated intention); some involve supplementation (where the artist adds details not specified in the text); some involve neglect (where the artist omits details of the story line that might normally be expected). In some instances there is the matter of selection (where the artist chooses images he/she considers significant regardless of the importance to the author's narrative).[7]

Examples of these differences appear in the illustration of all of Twain's first editions. Contradictions are rare, and those that exist are usually deliberate. As example the picture in *Life on the Mississippi*, where Twain writes that he "calmly" descended below decks while an illustration provides a very frightened, bug-eyed author. Another illustrator supplied an intriguing personal touch when he substituted a classic Venus de Milo statue for a sculpture Twain had titled "America" in *Sketches, New and Old*. In *The Prince and the Pauper*, Twain has the Prince "snatch up and put away an article of national importance that lay upon a table" (65). The illustrator, however, either failed to include or deliberately omitted the "article of national importance"—presumably the Great Seal—in his drawing. It is apparent that the combination of literal and graphic ideas can and does add an extra dimension to an interpretation of Twain's work.

Mark Twain wisely took these and many other illustrative ideas into account as he wrote and edited his text. Often he would write suggestions, "don't illustrate this," or "Make a picture of him." He would draw images in the margins of his manuscript as clues for his illustrator. Twain realized that if the illustrators were as skilled in their task as he was in his, they could further explicate an ambiguous point, take the edge off an indelicate or violent passage, supply emblematic references not easily referred to in the text, and/or heighten the humor in a comical situation. Illustration, therefore, would serve as a counterpoint and accompaniment to his words; his narrative would become more than it would have been without illustration.

Guy Pene' Du Bois, when arguing the complementary association between picture and print, described it this way:

> On the relation of the illustrator to the author . . .
> the illustrator with his medium fills the gaps left
> by the restrictions of the author's. He supple-
> ments, enlarges, enriches. . . . Moreover, the
> majority of people read badly, which may be to
> say, unimaginatively. Words are elusive. As
> descriptive factors they are disarmed by want of
> precision. Incapable, they certainly are, to build
> pictures in unimpressionable or unimaginative
> minds. These minds are in the majority. Perhaps
> their main poverty is want of experience. It is this
> experience which illustrators must supply in
> order to give a decisive descriptive force to the
> work he illustrates. He is an interpreter. His
> genius may lift the level of a story, just as the
> actor's genius may lift the level of a play. His fire
> or energy or personality act in complement to the
> author's, but need never be subservient to the
> author's. It is unquestionable that there are illus-
> trators who are read. By this I do not mean that
> the stories which appear with their illustrations
> are read, but that, which is more important, their
> illustrations are read into the stories.[8]

Working their way through the problems which differen-
tiated painting from writing, the French painter Jacques Raverat
and the author Virginia Woolf decided that the difficulty came
down essentially to this: painting was *spatial*—ideas and images
could be expressed simultaneously. Writing on the other hand was
*linear*—that is a series of ideas and images followed one another in
*time* in *sequence*. Writing, therefore, did not naturally possess the
aesthetic force of *simultaneity*.[9]

The argument about whether illustration is of primary or
secondary importance will probably continue. Many literary
"purists" may still consider illustration as mere ornamentation,
believing that looking at pictures in literary works corrupts the
integrity of the printed text. It is time, however, for readers of
Twain to understand how illustration, so much a part of his first editions, illuminate and interpret as well as embellish his writings.
Only then can they fully appreciate Mark Twain's genius when
reading his books.

## Notes

[1] MTLP, p. 37.

[2] MTLP, p. 139.

[3] "A painter must compensate for the natural deficiencies of his art. He has but one sentence to utter, but one moment of exhibit. He cannot, like the poet or historian, expatiate." Sir Joshua Reynolds, *Discourse on Art*, ed. Robert R. Wark, rev. ed. (New Haven: Yale University Press, 1975), p. 60.

[4] Jane R. Cohen, *Charles Dickens and His Original Illustrators* (Cambridge: Ohio State University Press, 1980), p. 234.

[5] *The Annotated Alice*, ed. Martin Gardner (New York: Bramhall House, 1960), p. 352. Sir John Tenniel was widely known for his illustrations of Lewis Carroll's *Alice* books.

[6] E. H. Gombrich, "Moment and Movement in Art," *Journal of the Warburg and Courtault Institutes*, 17 (1964): 293.

[7] Joseph H. Schwartz, *Ways of the Illustrator: Visual Communication in Children's Literature* (Chicago: American Library Association, 1982), pp. 16-18, 93-94.

[8] Guy Du Bois, Introduction, *Five American Illustrators* (1917), n.p.

[9] October 3, 1924, *The Diary of Virginia Woolf*, Vol. III, 1925-1930. Ed. Anne Oliver Bell, assisted by Andrew McNellie. London: Hogarth Press, 1982.

# Chapter I

## Mark Twain's
## *Sketches, New and Old* (1875)
## and Other Stories

"You must illustrate it."[1]

Mark Twain's sketches were collected in various editions throughout the years. The first gathering featured "The Celebrated Jumping Frog" with twenty-seven other pieces and was unillustrated. By 1870 Twain wanted a more taking model and he declared to Elisha Bliss that "the sketch-book should be as profusely illustrated as the Innocents."[2] The proposed book was to contain thirty-eight of Twain's short stories, not including the "Jumping Frog," and to be illustrated by a semi-reformed alcoholic, Edward F. Mullen.[3] The collection was never published.

Later, after numerous piracies of his short sketches, Twain wrote to his friend Mrs. Fairbanks about another try at issuing a book of short works, "I am preparing several volumes of my sketches for publication, & am writing new sketches to add to them."[4] An accumulation of stories was sent to the American News Company, a small New York firm that published pamphlets sold on trains and news-stands. Now referred to as *Sketches #1*, the 32-page pamphlet illustrated by R. T. Sperry was published in 1874. It contained ten old sketches and three unpublished stories from an abandoned work on England that Twain had written in 1872 and 1873. Sperry drew twelve illustrations, including the circular vignette on the cover—a drawing of a spectacled frog contemplating the cover of the News pamphlet while smoking a cigar. The light green and black paper wrapper had an overall decoration of intertwined branches with two smaller frogs acting as supporters for a list of the "Contents of No. 1" (Fig. 1).

Fig. 1. Cover,
American News Company, 1874

The brochure was meant to be part of a series which was certainly implied by the No. 1 on the cover and "Number One" at the top of the title page; the artist was given credit at the bottom: "With Illustrations by R. T. Sperry." Sperry created a vignette for this title page, a circled bevy of babies industriously erecting a wig-wam with several quill pens acting as poles. Inside the structure an ink pot sits on a scroll (Fig. 2).

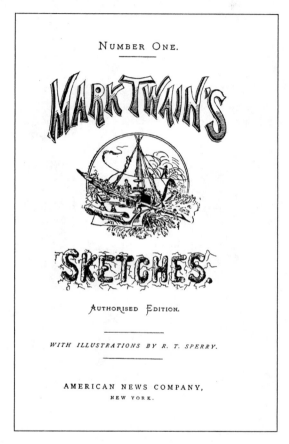

Fig. 2. Title Page

At Twain's direction, the pamphlet included his own Map of Paris, reproduced from the print page in the *Galaxy*. Twain's original Map of Paris had accompanied an editorial he had written for the *Buffalo Express* on the Franco-Prussian war. After writing the column, he added a diagram of his proposed campaign, laboring two days (so he says) with a pen-knife on a wood block to produce a "Fortification of Paris" map to be printed with his war report. His bizarre military comments and "mirror-image" map combined to form a journalistic burlesque of the actual Parisian battle plans. In his editorial Twain explained the manufacture of his strange *carte du pays*:

> By an unimportant oversight I have engraved the map so that it read wrong-end first, except to left-handed people. I forgot that in order to make it right in print it should be draw and engraved up-side down. However, let the student who desires to contemplate the map stand on his head or hold it before her looking-glass. That will bring it right. The reader will comprehend at a glance that the piece of river with the 'High Bridge' over it got left out to one side by reason of a slip of the graving-tool which rendered it necessary to change the entire course of the river Rhine or else spoil the map. After having spent two days in digging and gouging at the map, I would have changed the course of the Atlantic Ocean before I would have lost so much work (Fig. 3).[5]

Fig. 3. Fortifications of Paris

Twain was enthusiastic about his comical mock-heroic Map of Paris and was convinced that it should be reprinted as a market-ing gimmick for *Innocents*. He wrote Elisha Bliss urging him to reproduce it:

> My map is attracting a deal of attention. We get letters requesting copies from everywhere. Now what you need is something to make the postmaster and the public *preserve* your posters about 'Innocents' and stick them up and if you would put that map and accompanying testimonials right in the centre of the poster and the thing is accomplished, *sure*.[6]

Bliss ignored Twain's proposal.

The Map of Paris, which was to have been included in the 1870 edition of sketches, appeared now as the ninth story in the new small pamphlet. The first line of Twain's story directs the reader to his drawing: "*To the Reader*. The accompanying map explains itself" (26). Twain's war story, therefore, leads off with a tongue-in-cheek suggestion since the full-page map on the accompanying page is anything but self-explanatory. A layout that has the rivers Seine and Rhine and the Erie Canal running into the fortification wall of Paris, while the cities of Omaha and Saint Cloud are located to the western edge and Podunk, Jersey City and Vincennes to the east of the French capital, would be difficult to fathom even if Twain's map had not been printed as a mirror image on the page.

The first of the stories for the book, "A Memorable Midnight Experience," was reproduced from Twain's "Unpublished English Notes" and featured a Sperry headpiece depicting the royal tomb of Queen Elizabeth in Westminster Abbey. As in Twain's text, Sperry's queen was "dressed in the royal robes, lying as if at rest . . . ; the cat with stupendous simplicity, was coiled up and sound asleep upon the feet of the Great Queen!" (7) (Fig. 4).[7] Twain had made no mention of the docile lion, also dozing near the queen's feet—obviously Sperry's personal whimsical touch. The illustrator's second print, for which Twain had undoubtedly drawn the details, represented an in-

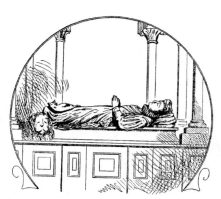

Fig. 4.
"A Memorable Midnight
Experience"

scription on a floor slab in the Poet's Corner of the Abbey. Sperry duplicated Twain's words, chiseling: "THO: PARR of Yᵉ COVNTY of SALLOP BORNE Aᵒ: 1483," onto blocks, the illustration placed just below Twain's text, "you can read the inscription" (5) (Fig. 5).[8] The other Twain-suggested drawing from his manuscript Sperry re-

Fig. 5.   "A Memorable Midnight Experience"

produced as a kind of graffiti supposedly to be found near the monument to Mary, Queen of Scots. On a wall this "bit of curiosity" read, "Wᵐ WEST TOOME SHOWER 1698" (Fig. 6). Twain left both William West and his "tomb-shower" to the reader's imagination,

Fig. 6.
"A Memorable Midnight Experience"

ignoring the man and his toilet in the story as Twain continued on his midnight stroll through the great burial place of England's honored dead.

A third sketch, again originating in Twain's unpublished "English Notes," was titled "Rogers." Sperry's drawing for the headpiece centered on a shabbily dressed English-man in a topsy-turvy room, the illustrator meticulously incorporating all the details of the setting from Twain's text. It seems that the British Rogers was giving an American, presumably a half-seen Twain, advice on where to shop for English finery. The threadbare Rogers had invited his guest to "take a bottle champagne and cigars" at his apartments; Sperry's tail piece of a spider-webbed porridge bowl clearly sums up the paradox of Twain's story (Figs. 7 & 8).

The next illustration was for a very short tale, "Back from 'Yurrup." Sperry's half-page headpiece features a group of American travelers just returned from a year abroad: a bored father, a grumpy mama, and the three exasperating youngsters. This family shares a railroad car with the narrator—Twain, though again not recognised—who records his memory of the foibles of these *nouveau riche* American tourists with their name-dropping pretensions and fractured French affectations. A Sperry tail piece adds a gleefully "nahsty" end to Twain's prose, puncturing the pompous family of snobs by giving them their own coat of arms: a shield emblazoned with

Fig. 7. "Rogers"

a pair of gabbling geese surmounted by a long-eared jackass (Figs. 9 & 10). In these and other tail pieces, Sperry's selective impulses in his art work act as footnotes to Twain's text.

Fig. 8. "Rogers"

Several of the shorter pieces in *Sketches #1*: "Breaking It Gently," "The Widow's Protest," "Property in Opulent London," "The Undertaker's Chat" and "Misplaced Confidence," were unillustrated.

None of the four illustrated sketches would be included in the subsequent 1875 American Publishing Company edition of Twain's collected sketches. He had debated about including all four but, in the end, scratched out the titles in his manuscript for the "table of contents."[9]

Fig. 9.
"Back from 'Yurrup'"

The paper-wrapped version of his sketches did not please Twain and it did not sell. The next year he advised Dan De Quille, "Hang it, man, you don't want a *pamphlet*—you want a book—600 pages 8-vol. illustrated. There isn't a single cent of money in a pamphlet."[10] A number two in the series, therefore, was never published. The pamphlet, however, had a rather ignominous end. On learning that there would be no *Sketches #2*, Hutchings, owner of the house that had prined the pamphlet, wrote to Twain that he had been offered $300 to dispose of "the entire lot of 'Sketches' to the Aetna Life Ins. Co."[11] The insurance company wanted to print their advertisement on the back cover and circulate the pamphlets to prospective customers. Twain agreed and the collection ended as an insurance circular.

Many other stories from the pamphlet—"The Jumping Frog" "The Great Beef Contract," "Aurelia's Unfortunate Young Man," "Concerning Chambermaids," etc.—would be included in the 1875 edition. (A comparison of the Sperry illustrations with the Williams drawings will be discussed in the upcoming pages.)

With the disappointing sales of the pamphlet, Mark Twain was again

Fig. 10.
"Back from 'Yurrup'"

ready to compile stories for an illustrated volume which, in his words, would contain "all my sketches complete." Such a book could keep his name in the forefront of the publishing market while he completed work on *The Adventures of Tom Sawyer*. His most recent subscription publication, *The Gilded Age*, had not sold well, and he was dissatisfied, writing, "There is one discomfort which I fear a man must put up with when he publishes by subscription, and that is wretched paper and vile engravings."[12] For a brief time he thought of publishing his new collection in the "trade"—books sold only in bookstores. Elisha Bliss, however, reminded Twain that he still held a book contract which legally tied the author to the American Publishing Company. In the end, the author acquiesced, allowing Bliss to have *Sketches* to be "sold by subscription only." Bliss's only concession was that *Sketches* would be profusely illustrated. Twain's contract stipulated that he was to be paid a 7 1/2% royalty until 50,000 books were sold and an additional 2 1/2% when sales exceeded that level. There was, however, no written contractual agreement about illustration.[13]

Since Twain envisioned the book as a self-promotional tool, he was wise to settle for a subscription publication. Trade books, though considered more prestigious, were seldom filled with illustration, much less multiple likenesses of the author. *Sketches, New and Old* was Twain's fourth book—not counting the smaller volumes like the Webb's publication of the *Frog* and the pamphleted *Sketches #1*—and in it he was publishing material calculated to advertise himself, keeping his name and face before his readers.

The illustrator for *Sketches, New and Old*, chosen by Twain and Bliss, was True Williams. By this time in his publishing career Twain understood that illustration had a great many useful features. A competent artist could not only enliven his story but also interpret the humor, explicate a point (where explication seemed necessary), or clarify an idea. Furthermore, by placing the author's features front-and-center in a majority of the stories, the illustrator could act as one of the author's most valuable publicity agents.

From the beginning of talks on publishing *Sketches, New and Old*, there was no consideration of other artists; Twain and Bliss agreed that True Williams alone would have the commission for the illustration. It was a practical choice. As an American Publishing Company staff employee, Williams had worked on previous Twain books: *Innocents*, *Roughing It*, and *The Gilded Age*. Unfortunately, however, he has been remembered largely through anecdotes about his alcoholism, which to a great extent colored critical assessments of his work. Because a good deal of more complimentary biographical material about True Williams has been found in the last few years,[14] we now know much more about this most influential Mark Twain illustrator.

He was born in western New York in 1839, and spent his childhood in Watertown, New York. He served during the Civil War in the Union Army as an advance scout for Sherman in his march to the sea. Though Twain's and Williams' early paths led in different directions, they would intersect when each of them settled in the publishing capital of the east, Hartford, Connecticut. Self-taught as an artist, Williams began work as an apprentice and later became a staff illustrator for the American Publishing Company. Throughout the 1870s he illustrated many noteworthy travel and local color books, including those of A. D. Richardson and Thomas Knox.[15]

Williams' participation in so many of Twain's subscription books[16] ranks him as the most significant and consistent collaborator of Twain's work. With this book Williams was, as he had been in the past, in no small measure involved in the creation of Twain's public image. He had earlier drawn many of the caricatures of Mark Twain for *Innocents* and *Roughing It* and would continue in this mode with *Sketches*. His contributions to Twain's *Sketches*, however, go well beyond mere cartooned caricatures of the author. His pictures would often deliver the punch for the author's straight man, add immediacy to a long-drawn-out tall tale, or invent darkly humorous landscapes to augment some of Twain's blackest comedies. He would fulfill Twain's desire for a competent artist. Twain and Williams combined to successfully synergize the art of writing and the art of illustration.

The cover for *Sketches, New and Old* was very plain and would be almost identical to the binding for Twain's forthcoming *Tom Sawyer*. Perhaps the author conceived of selling the two books as a matching set.[17] In his advertisements, however, Bliss touted the cover as "dainty blue so tastefully adorned with fanciful designs in black."[18] In actuality the cover had a royal blue cloth field imprinted with *Sketches* in black on a gold ribbon. Appearing in larger embossed letters below, were the words "By Mark Twain." Bliss's "fanciful designs" were four circled gold stars placed at each side.

The spine of the first edition had a reversed title, SKETCHES, OLD AND NEW, lettered in black on a gold background, while the title page read SKETCHES, NEW AND OLD (Figs. 11 & 12).[19] This book, unlike Twain's other subscription books, had no illustration relating

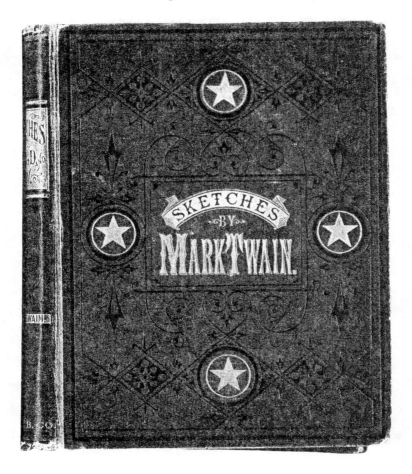

Fig. 11.   Cover and Spine
Hartford: American Publishing Company, 1875

to the text on the cover, no "List of Illustrations" preceding the usual "Contents" page (which would appear as an "Index" in this edition),

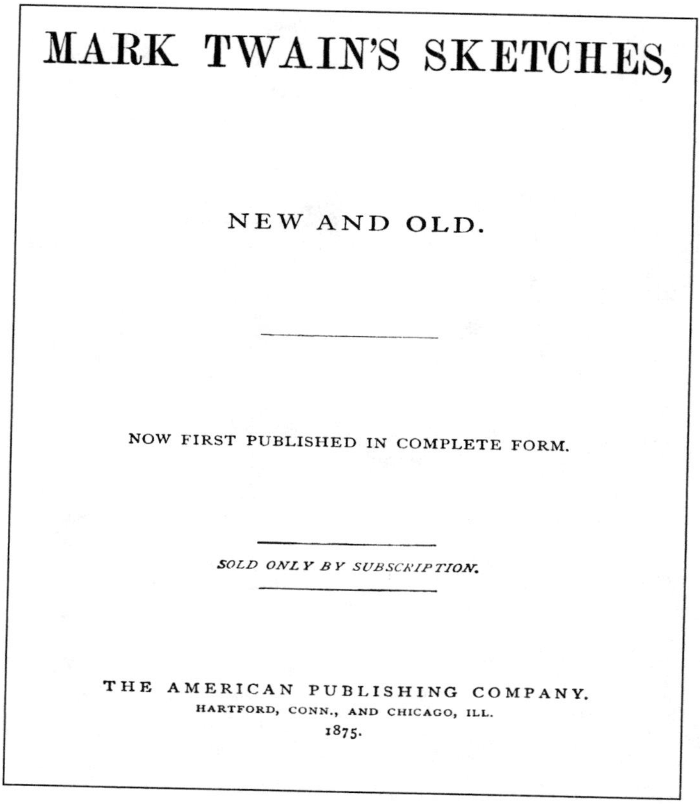

```
MARK TWAIN'S SKETCHES,


               NEW AND OLD.




         NOW FIRST PUBLISHED IN COMPLETE FORM.



              SOLD ONLY BY SUBSCRIPTION.



       THE AMERICAN PUBLISHING COMPANY.
            HARTFORD, CONN., AND CHICAGO, ILL.
                        1875.
```

Fig. 12.  Title Page, 1875

and no usual captions placed beneath the illustrations. For most of the stories, Williams' headpieces conjoined one or more overlapping illustrations and a hand-lettered title that did double-duty as a caption; at times, a "scripted" notation—sometimes in Twain's hand-writing—appeared as the caption.[20]

    Williams' frontispiece for the book centered a writer's port-folio boldly monogrammed with the initials M. T. Possibly in a nod to Sperry, a quill and an ink pot appear as desk top accessories. The Williams design, however, is far more detailed than Sperry's—and far more suggestive of what the reader is in for. In it, the central image of quill, ink pot, and writer's portfolio is surrounded by a whirlpool of characters—supposedly persons to be found in the sketches. Most of these images, however, are more generic outlines than specific individuals from the stories, though a few can be identified: "bad James" of the "Story of a Bad Little Boy," the helmeted young girl in "A Medieval Romance," the wide-eyed Chinese in "John Chinaman in New York," and the Indian (a ring in his ear and another in his nose) cast in "The Case of Geo. Fisher." No caricature of Twain appears among this frontispiece crowd (Fig. 13 ).

Fig. 13.   Frontispiece, 1996

Four of the tales illustrated by Sperry were also illustrated by Williams for *Sketches, New and Old.* The "Jumping Frog" one of the most popular, was placed as the third tale in the series. This version included all the transformations of Twain's celebrated "frog" through the several renditions in various publications and with all its extensions—as Twain puts it, "IN ENGLISH. THEN IN FRENCH. THEN CLAWED BACK INTO A CIVILIZED LANGUAGE ONCE MORE BY PATIENT, UNREMUNERATED TOIL."[21] The illustrations and additions lengthened the sketch to sixteen pages.

Williams' frog differs remarkably from Sperry's cover and headpiece for *Sketch #1.* In the pamphlet version the title for the sketch is "The Notorious Jumping Frog of Calaveras County"— Twain adding an asterisk to make sure that the county was "Pronounced Cal-e-*va*-ras." Sperry's cover-picture of a self-satisfied frog contrasts with the only other image, his headpiece where a woeful, sad-eyed, defeated Daniel Webster, his belly bulging with quail shot, looks dejectedly at the flying feet of his opponent (Fig. 14).

Fig. 14.
"The Notorious Jumping Frog,"
1874

Williams, on the other hand, creates six illustrations for the story. His pictures act as a visual narrative: Smiley and Wheeler seen at the beginning of the jumping contest, Twain listening to Wheeler's story, the fifteen-minute nag in the flying finish of a up-turning Daniel to let him belch out the double handful of shot. In the two frog close-up portraits—one in a side view and one in full face—Williams has the celebrated amphibian for the first time unmistakably a Daniel Webster look-alike. The illustrator more than completed his mission. His prints follow the story line, they expand Twain's tale, and they allow a reader to identify someone whose appearance is known to them in a totally different context

(Figs. 15 & 16). Williams' frog would end as the most famous emblem since the "gorgeous gold frog" on the cover of the Webb publication that had so pleased Mark Twain.

Fig. 15.
The "Jumping Frog,"
1996

Fig. 16.
The "Jumping Frog,"
1875

Williams correctly did not make Twain the principal player in this tale. That distinction is given to the "Frog," who had already gained sufficient stature as a public figure on his own. The artist did not completely ignore Twain, however; Twain appears in an insert with the "fat and bald-headed" Simon Wheeler, the garrulous old gentleman who tells the tale (Fig. 17).

Fig. 17.
The "Jumping Frog,"
1875

A second sketch illustrated by both Sperry and Williams is "The Great Beef Contract." For this semi-fictional tale in the pamphlet Sperry drew no headpiece, the only drawing being a tail piece of an unidentifiable gentleman in front of a columned building, a pack of dogs growling at his feet—a Sperry addition—while carrying a "Beef Contract" under his arm (Fig. 18).

Williams produced three drawings for this tale which stick closely to the narrative of the story. His headpiece features a busy governmental office with a harem of helpful young ladies; the next cut shows the murder (by tomahawk), of one of the several owners of the contract, John Wilson Mackenzie. In the third and last illustration the supplicant Mark Twain presents the contract to "the President of the United States" (103)—both Twain and President Grant

Fig. 18. "The Facts in the Case of the Great Beef Contract," 1874

easily identified.  A portrait of honest George Washington looks askance at the pair from a picture in the background (Figs. 19, 20 & 21).

Fig. 19.  "The Facts in the Case of the Great Beef Contract," 1875

Fig. 20.
"The Facts in the Case
of the Great Beef
Contract," 1875

Fig. 21.
"The Facts in the Case of the Great Beef
Contract," 1875

For "Aurelia's Unfortunate Young Man," in both the Sperry and the Williams headpieces the young man Caruthers was the grotesque target. In the "Aurelia" story, first published in the *Californian* in 1864 with the title "Whereas," Twain spins a tale of unresolved romance with "unfortunate" holding the key to his burlesque. Both Sperry's and Williams' initial drawings of Aurelia and her suitor broadcast the ridiculousness of the situation even before the reader takes in the first line. In Sperry's rendition Caruthers is bearded with a pock-marked face; little attention is given to Aurelia. Sperry also adds two side vignettes to his initial image: to the right an Indian fleeing with the scalp of Aurelia's admirer, to the left Caruthers' arm blown off by a canon (Fig. 22). No suspense, Twain's story is visually complete.

In Williams' headpiece a gracefully gowned young lady grasps the sleeve of her mustached lover who is in an advanced state of deterioration. Unlike Sperry, Williams has given Aurelia's peg-legged beau the upper hand with a slight grin on his face—and a malevolent cupid on a pedestal pointing his arrow at the mismatched pair. With this lone picture of the ill-fated duo, Williams does not tell all, and thus the uncertainty builds. Unfortunately as readers proceed in either version their empathy for poor Aurelia has already been strained beyond credulity since Twain's plot gives Caruthers no redeeming characteristics. Unlike Williams, however, Sperry adds his own final supplemental touch with a tail piece of a

Fig. 22. "Aurelia's Unfortunate Young Man," 1874

Fig. 23. "Aurelia's Unfortunate Young Man," 1875

Fig. 24.
"Aurelia's Unfortunate Young Man,"
1874

crying cupid beside a bound package of Caruthers' "spare parts." With either illustrator's interpretation, the combination of pictures and print gives Twain's satire of the nineteenth-century romantic yarn more bite than if it were read unillustrated (Figs. 23 & 24).

Sperry and Williams took entirely different tacks for Twain's story "Concerning Chambermaids." Originally titled "Depart, Ye Accursed!" this sketch was revised by Twain several times. In each successive revision he toned down his language. He changed the cursing chambermaids "in behalf of outraged bachelordom" to "I launch the curse of bachelordom," undoubtedly because of his now married status. Cuspidor was changed to spittoon, and though slop-tub was retained, slop-jar was switched to slop-tub. These minor modifications signal Twain's sensitivity to his new audience. This same audience would doubtless be offended by Sperry's drawing of the guest narrator—no resemblance to

Twain—returning to his room at midnight only to "proceed toward the window and sit down in that slop-tub" (32). The "low" subject of a gentleman's bottom in a "slop-tub" or "slop-jar," with all its connotations, had to be eliminated from both text and illustration for the new book. Williams' image dispelled all

Fig. 25.  "Concerning Chambermaids," 1874

controversy; his headpiece places an innocent young chambermaid preening herself before a mirror, a slop bucket at the bottom with a mop-handle determining its cleansing function (Figs. 25 & 26).

Fig. 26. "Concerning Chambermaids," 1875

Sperry was never commissioned to illustrate Mark Twain's work again. His illustrating career remains obscure. He did pedestrian service to Twain's sketches for this small pamphlet; his two-tone outline drawings religiously following the story line. He made no effort to caricature Twain as narrator, added no explication, nor did he add extra humor to the author's prose—the tail pieces for "Roger," "Back From 'Yurrup'" and "Aurelia's Unfortunate Young Man" being the only exceptions.

True Williams for *Sketches, New and Old* had a much more formidable challenge than Sperry. There were many more stories, sixty-six compared to the fourteen in the 1874 edition. Williams drew one or more illustrations for almost every tale, a total of at least one hundred and thirty drawings—more if you count the double headpiece prints as two and the tail pieces on pages 201 and 207, though it seems unlikely that these two tail pieces came from Williams' tail pieces pen.[22]

Williams' headpiece for the first story in the book, "My

Watch: A Little Instructive Tale," focuses on Twain as both author and narrator, an important initial image for this self-advertising volume. The book is full of first-person narratives; therefore this Williams sketch, as well as others in the book, underscores Twain's use of "I" in the text. The headpiece also fixes in the reader's mind the author's familiar features: piercing eyes, probing nose, rugged Western mustache, and a thick, unruly head of hair. This particular Williams rendition presents a well-dressed young Mark Twain attempting to dissuade a jeweler from tinkering with his watch (Fig. 27). In each of the next two inserted illustrations, the author becomes—as he does in the story—increasingly more bug-eyed, a feature Williams would over-emphasize in many of his drawings. The harried narrator, Twain, misses trains because he is unable to tell the correct time. He is further frustrated when dealing with a second watchmaker, a balding specimen pointing an elongated finger who is more taxing than the first (Fig. 28). With these opening pages Williams establishes Twain as a duped and bewildered "everyman" and reinforces the author's theme for the book of the vulnerable and beleaguered victim. It was a subject that Twain had used in his past work and one that he exploits over and over in these stories and would employ often in his future writings. Twain,

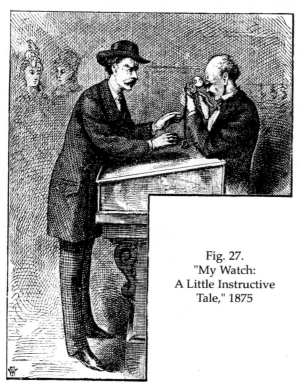

Fig. 27.
"My Watch:
A Little Instructive
Tale," 1875

with the help of his illustrator, identifies himself as a highly recognizable gent trying to grapple with the indignities lobbed at him by life. Without Williams' cleverly drawn cartoons, the narrator of this—and of so many of the other pieces—might have been seen by the reader as just any unlucky bungler, since the reader's only clue to the storyteller's identity is the author's name on the title page. Williams, however, made sure that the "I" in all the first-person narratives would be seen as Mark Twain himself. Roughly

Fig. 28. "My Watch: A Little Instructive Tale," 1875

one-fifth of the stories in *Sketches* are in the first-person and all of these are accompanied by broad interpretations of a Twain likeness.[23]

The second story in the collection is "Political Economy." Here the headpiece has Twain, dressing-gowned with a quill behind his ear, being flummoxed by the fancy talk of a loquacious lightning-rod salesman. The absurdity of this burlesque tale is instantly telegraphed to the reader as he views in the headpiece the multitude of rods sprouting from every chimney, every eave trough, and every roof line of the dangerously-wired mansion (Fig. 29). With this second portrait, the first-person narrator is again clearly recognized as the harried writer—which indeed Twain was at the time, performing "periodical dancing before the public" in both the *Galaxy* and the *Buffalo Express*. In 1870, the year "Political Economy" was first published, he was an editor, writer, and a bridegroom—he had married Olivia Langdon and had supposedly settled down to a genteel lifestyle in a magnificent Buffalo home similar to the one conceived by True Williams for this illustration. In *Sketches, New and Old* Twain's readers were introduced to the author, not as the tousled tourist of *Innocents* or the rowdy westerner of

*Roughing It,* but as a confused but sartorially splendid gentleman.

Fig. 29.
"Political Economy," 1875

In "Journalism in Tennessee," a more youthful Twain as narrator tells of the battles he experienced between dueling frontier jouralists while serving as a visiting associate editor in the South. This chronicle, written in 1869 for the *Buffalo Express,* is offered as comedy, but it reflects Twain's deep frustration with newspapers and their inflamed rhetoric in the late 60s. With the text cleansed of the strong language from its first publication, this black imaginative tale has a raccoon-eyed Mark Twain seen as the naive newsman in three inserted illustrations, the last one showing him as a brick-bashed, shot, and scalped correspondent as he lies recuperating in a "hospital apartment." With the drawing of Williams' ACCIDENT WARD sign on the sickbed wall, the vicious attacks of the story turn into mere misadventures; the whole episode goes a fraction over the top (Fig. 30). This pattern of Twain as plagued by scoundrels and sharpers from Buffalo to Tennessee, continues in his next tale of "Niagara."

As expected, Twain is again the primary, sharply hilarious image in the headpiece. Seen smoking a pipe and baiting a fishhook, he is sitting dangerously near the edge of the precipitous 160-foot drop of the falls (Fig. 31). Twain had visited the Falls before and after his marriage to Olivia.

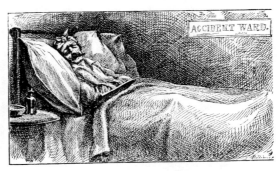

Fig. 30. "Journalism in Tennessee," 1875

(They would live just 15 miles from this most famous honeymoon attraction.) He wrote the original Niagara sketch for the *Buffalo Express* in 1869 and would allude to the beauty and Eden-like atmosphere of the Falls in many of his later writings. In this story, in illustration as well as narration, one meets the guileless, romantic tourist, the kind and genuine being who so appealed to Twain's readers in his former best seller *Innocents Abroad*.

Fig. 31.
"Niagara," 1875

In the Niagara story, one line of dialogue identifies Twain's noble Red Man as neither noble nor red: "An'is it mesilf, Dennis Hooligan, that ye'd be takin' for a dirty Injin"

(68) (Fig. 32).   It is Williams' slouch-hatted, shillelagh-toting Irishman, however, who resolves any confusion with Twain's punchline.

Fig. 32.  "Niagara," 1875

In the next few paragraphs the author writes of greeting "a gentle daughter of the aborigines." He questions this buckskin maiden: "Is the heart of the forest maiden heavy?" (69).  When she replies in dialect that her name is Biddy Malone, and when, simultaneously the reader observes Williams' middle-aged, stout, lantern-jawed Irish damsel, the comic effect of Twain's dialogue is instant (Fig. 33). The conspiracy in this story turns on the incongruity of a tourist's naive assumptions about red men and aborigines who come from "Limerick," and the tale is given greater spice when the disparity between truth and presumption are bolstered by Williams' admittedly stereotyped Shanty-Irish characters. In all three illustrations, True Williams, who had a puckishly outrageous humor similar to Twain's, reinforces the author's wry humor and gives it an extra sting not fully apparent unless his drawings are present accompanying the text.

In "John Chinaman in New York," Williams' two pictures of

Fig. 33.  "Niagara," 1875

the pseudo-Chinese "John" preempts the joke in Twain's story. This John Chinaman, who is advertising a brand of tea for a New York merchant, is found to be no Chinaman at all but an Irish immigrant getting by on four dollars a week. Williams goes along with the gag, a calligraphic title and his headpiece depicting Twain talking to (and apparently offering sympathy to) this "friendless mongol" with his long, braided queue—undoubtedly a fake—dangling behind him. But in an overlapping drawing the artist gives us a peek at the cunning face of the clay-pipe smoking rogue who matches Twain's dialogue, "Divil a cint but four dollars a week and find meself [i.e., to pay all my own expenses]; but it's aisy, barrin the troublesome furrin clothes that's so expinsive" (232) (Fig. 34).

Of Twain's stories about the three McWilliamses only the first episode appears in *Sketches*, the "Experience of the McWilliamses with Membranous Croup." Scholars have suggested that this and  subsequent sketches about the couple are thinly disguised portraits reporting on the domestic life of the newly-married couple, Samuel and Olivia Clemens. True Williams must have had similar suspicions for his depictions for the headpiece and other prints has a dapper and pop-eyed Mortimer McWilliams favor his

Fig. 34.
"John Chinaman in
New York,"
1996

other Twain caricatures throughout the book. Williams' less well drafted Caroline McWillliams cannot be similarly identified as a true rendition of Olivia— though the high forehead and expression of wide-eyed innocence could be hers (Fig. 35).

Providentially, Twain and Williams travel parallel farcical lines in the *Sketches* with their continuing portrayal of Twain as a nineteenth-century Chaplin figure. In "To Raise Poultry," Williams' tail piece has Twain as a chicken thief, himself

Fig. 35.
"Experiences of the McWilliamses
With Membranous Croup,"
1996

caught in the steel trap (Fig. 36). In "How the Author was Sold in Newark," the Williams illustration—looking remarkably like his drawing for the prospectus of *Roughing It*—has the author/lecturer hurling jokes at a "deaf and dumb, and blind as a badger" old man seated in a front row (Fig. 37). In "Mr. Bloke's Item," one of the illustrations has the now familiar, wide-eyed, frizzle-haired Mark Twain, as sub-editor of the Virginia City *Territorial Enterprise*, trying to make sense of an utterly incomprehensible stop-press "item" involving a run-away horse, an injured pedestrian, a disastrous fire, someone's fondness for the "flowing bowl," and other vaguely related matters—all represented in some way by the figures that Williams has shown swirling around the head (and even the feet) of the confused and harassed sub-editor Twain (Fig. 38). And for "Lionizing Murderers," the skeptical cat's eyeballs in the Williams' illustration rival the protuberant stare of the author

Fig. 36.
"To Raise Poultry,"
1875

Fig. 37.
"How the Author Was Sold
in Newark,"
1875

Fig. 38.
"Mr. Bloke's Item,"
1875

(Fig. 39). Twain was more right than even he knew when he later said of Williams and his art work, "He takes a book of mine, & without suggestion from anybody builds no end of pictures just from his reading of it."[24]

Fig. 39.
"Lionizing Murderers,"
1875

There are a number of famous personages featured in *Sketches,* and Williams produced faithful likenesses of all of them. "The Late Ben Franklin," first published in the *Galaxy* in 1870 and next in Thomas Nast's *Almanac* in 1872—with Nast illustrations (Fig. 40)—was now illustrated with a new twist. Williams' inventor

*NAST'S ALMANAC FOR 1872.*

**THE LATE BENJAMIN FRANKLIN.**
BY MARK TWAIN.

Fig. 40.
"The Late Ben
Franklin,"
*Nast's Almanac for
1872*

Franklin, who supposedly lived "wholly on bread and water," is armed not only with a kite but also has a tell-tale jug at his feet (Fig. 41) (275). Inveterate practical joker Artemus Ward (the popular

Fig. 41.
"The Late Ben Franklin,"
1875

humorist Charles Farrar Browne) appears in "First Interview With Artemus Ward" (Figs. 42 & 43) (283); and the previously mentioned President Grant, and George Washington are added Williams'

Fig. 42. "First Interview With Artemus Ward," 1875

Fig. 43.
Artemus Ward,
Don C. Seitz,
*Artemas Ward*, 1919

touches for "The Facts of the Beef Contract" (103). All of these distinguished persons are recognizable in Williams' caricatures.

A few of the stories do not find Twain as narrator. Yet even these Williams' illustrations add a fillip to Twain's at times socially conscious prose. In "The Judge's 'Spirited Woman,'" taken from reports of the trial of Prince Pierre Napoleon Bonaparte, the central image in Williams' headpiece creates immediate intrigue for the tale. A lovely mantilla-covered Mexican woman is seen holding a Colt 45 on a cringing Spanish desperado (Fig. 44). In this skimpy sketch, Williams' picture of a gun attaches strength to the judge's already forceful statement, "Why,

Fig. 44. "The Judge's 'Spirited Woman,'" 1875

she turned on that smirking Spanish fool like a wild cat, and out with a 'navy' and shot him dead in open court" (122). For the uninitiated reader, Williams' picture defines Twain's "navy."

In "The Capitoline Venus," Twain combines his ridicule of the plunder of the European art scene—one of his major themes in *Innocents*[25]—with a Barnum "there's-one-born-every-minute" admonition. This tale is, of course, another "art hoax," written shortly after the Cardiff Giant deception (Twain's "Note" as a postscript to the story pointing out that fact). The story also resembles Twain's earlier sketch "The Petrified Man."

Williams' designs for the Venus story are both narrative and interpretive. He took his lead from Twain's title "The Capitoline Venus," drawing a statue closely resembling in coiffure, posture, drapery, and demeanor the famous dismembered statue, the Venus de Milo (Fig. 45). Williams plays wittily with the framing by having the reality of a "fully-armed" Venus discreetly posed as a subsidiary image on the margin of the headpiece. Williams' celebrated look-alike supplies an extra dimension to Twain's mocking of the commercialism of trafficking in "found" antiquities. When a reader

Fig. 45.
"Venus de Milo,"
Louvre, R.M.N. Paris,
1989

recognizes the de Milo his/her thoughts are immediately infected with allusions to the Louvre's celebrated goddess (Fig. 46). Two distraught young lovers are centered in a circle of the headpiece, a bust of an incomplete work-in-progress, originally titled "America" in the text, is barely seen in the shadowed background. An extended, lower portion of this drawing recounts the activities of the second chapter of this condensed novel; the novice sculptor, hat in hand and head bowed, is shown being discharged by his lady's market-conscious father.

By the final drawing, supposedly ten years later, Willliams presents the same artisan as a now corpulent braggart with a giddy but fashionable wife. The completed but patched Capitoline Venus, still in the de Milo pose of the Greek statue, is only lacking her hands (Fig. 47). Williams' designs for this story work in tandem with Twain's themes of the gullibility of Italian art merchants and the materialism of American businessmen. Yet with his rendition of

Fig. 46.
"The Capitoline Venus,"
1996

the Venus as the classic de Milo, not the "America" of the text, the illustrator makes an allusive connection that lifts Twain's tale to a level far above an obscure, contemporary "art hoax."

The virtuoso Williams also remedied any possible misinterpretation with his illustration for another Twain hoax, "The Petrified Man." This story had first appeared in the *Territorial Enterprise* and was reprinted in several California and Nevada newspapers.

Twain had had two motives for writing his "petrified man" hoax: First he believed it was time to strike a blow against the growing mania for petrifaction but he also felt it was the perfect opportunity to skewer all self-proclaimed experts—most pointedly a certain judge, G. T. Sewell, with whom Twain may have tangled over a "blind ledge" mining right while he was prospecting in Nevada. Twain had been both delighted and disappointed that many editors had received his satire "in innocent good faith." When the piece

Fig. 47.   "The Capitoline Venus," 1875

was to be illustrated for *Sketches*, he wrote instructions for the artist in the margin, "Make a picture of him [the petrified man, that is]."[26]

Williams' headpiece finds Twain presumably pleading with Sewell—though the man is unnamed and only identified as the "new coroner and justice of the peace of Humboldt." A rowdy crowd of silver miners are seen about to free the stone figure from his place in the wall, Williams placing a keg of blasting powder at the base of the illustration. More importantly he followed Twain's instruction and made a picture complying with Twain's text; positioning the fossilized man's hands with his left thumb "hooked into the right little finger; the fingers of the left hand . . . spread like those of the right." Any innocent belief in Twain's satire was permanently dispelled.

Two subsequent prints for the hoax served to annoy the pesky Justice Sewell: In one he is seen mounted on a mule and in the other, a tail piece, he is shoveling out the door a pile of newspaper copies of the hoax that Twain had sent him (Figs. 48, 49 & 50). At the time of the initial writing Twain was candid about his attitude toward the justice. "I got it [the hoax] up to worry Sewell. Every day, I sent him some California paper containing it."[27] In the three

Fig. 48.
"The Petrified Man,"
1875

Fig. 49.
"The Petrified Man,"
1875

Fig. 50.
"The Petrified Man," 1875

pictures Williams unfolds the plot, explodes the hoax of the ossified remains, identifies the gullible silver-mining official, and parodies the mining mania of the times.

"The Killing of Julius Caesar 'Localized,'" an 1864 sketch formerly published in the San Francisco *Californian*, describes the assassination of Caesar as it might be reported by a nineteenth-century newspaper. The strength of this account lies in the disjointed, tongue-in-cheek imitation of Act III of Shakespeare's *Julius Caesar* that Twain salted with contemporary political jargon—for which he had such a good ear. The Williams illustration (Fig. 51) follows the text showing Caesar with his back to Pompey's statue, his mantle loose about his shoulders, trying to defend himself with bare fists (strictly "a Twainism" and in defiance of Shakespeare). Williams' Caesar has bloodied a nose or two, but the sandal-shod conspirators in Roman garb—one of whom could be the knife-wielding "George W. Cassius (commonly known as the 'Nobby Boy of the Third Ward')"—are closing in for the kill. One could only wish that Williams had drawn the features of the perpetrators of this dastardly crime distinctly enough to enable us to identify some of them as the "pols" of the day as he had done so ably for Twain's *The Gilded Age*.

Twain's "A Medieval Romance" is likewise a costumed period piece. However, this tale has a rather tangled background. Issued first as "An Awful Terrible Medieval Romance" in the *Buffalo Express* in 1870, the story next appeared as part of a book entitled,

Fig. 51. "The Killing of Julius Caesar 'Localized,'" 1875

*Mark Twain's (Burlesque) Autobiography and First Romance*, published by Sheldon and Company in 1871—a book that had running through its pages a series of irrelevant, full-page cartoons of politicians not noted for their virtue.[28] For this new publication of the "Medieval Romance," Williams' headpiece stuck closely to the story line with a central image of gloomy castle towers and adjoining circles of wailing maidens, a Rapunsel-like damsel, a stern father, and knights clad heel to head in mail (Fig. 52). In the only other illustration, Williams, much like Twain, declined to resolve the dilemma of this tongue-in-cheek tale of Constances and Conrads. Instead he produces a straightforward scene where the pretty princess points to a gender-confused Conrad, the grim old father, Lord Klugstein swoons at the fateful news, and a distraught hero (or heroine) faces an uncertain future (Fig. 53). After writing this leg-pulling, logical

Fig. 52.
"A Medieval Romance,"
1875

tale, Twain ends with "I thought it was going to be easy enough to straighten out that little difficulty, but it looks different now" (179). After straining credulity to the limit—like the writers of medieval romances—Twain then says "Fooled you," and walks away. Williams agreed with the author and played it straight, the son-daughter, hero-heroine problem was unsolvable.

For "The Siamese Twins," Williams added his ideas to the twins certain characteristics not in the text of Twain's original dark burlesque nor in his subsequent versions in "Those Extraordinary Twins" or in *Pudd'nhead Wilson*. The conjoined twins were supposedly identical. (The term Siamese a popular term for the phenomenon.) Twain was inspired to write his first twin story by reading

Fig. 53. "A Medieval Romance," 1875

newspaper accounts of the celebrated "Chinese" twins, Chang and Eng Bunker, who were born in Siam with separate bodies but joined by a ligament connecting them at the chest. Twain's original story was published in the 1869 *Packard Monthly* entitled "The Personal Habits of the Siamese Twins." The piece was selected to appear in *Sketches* the year the twins died. Williams' three-quarter page illustration, placed above the title, displays the twins correctly attached at the rib cage. Chang, the twin who falls in love and gets the girl, is, however, a good deal darker than Eng. In fact, Williams has given Chang distinctly negroid features, whereas the stouter and more full-faced Eng has chiefly Caucasian features. Neither has a hint of Chinese and both appear with darkened complexions in the tail piece. Obviously Williams threw fact to the wind when he scanned the ridiculous sketch before beginning his drawings. On reading the ending where Twain had pronounced "the ages of the Siamese Twins are respectively fifty-one and fifty-three years" (212)

(Figs. 54, 55 & 56), the illustrator undoubtedly felt fully justified in supplying his own innovations.

Fig. 54.   "The Siamese Twins," 1875

Fig. 55.
Chang & Eng Bunker
[1811-1874]
*Collier Encyclopedia*

Another story in *Sketches*, one that highlights a living black woman, is, of course, "A True Story. Repeated Word For Word As I Heard It."[29] For years the tale has been touted as an original inspiration for Twain's use of dialect. Williams faithfully fashioned Aunt Rachel—in reality Auntie Cord, who was the Negro cook at Quarry Farm—just as she was in real life, "age 62, turbaned, very tall, very broad . . ." (see her portrait in "A True Story Just as I Heard It" in my *Sketches*.[30]

Fig. 56.
"The Siamese Twins," 1996

His depiction was also true to the way she emerged in Twain's tale—"of mighty frame and stature; she was

Fig. 57.
Aunt Cory
*Courtesy, Mark Twain Memorial,*
*Hartford*

sixty years old, but her eye was undimmed" (Fig. 57) (202). Twain himself starts out as narrator of this story, but as soon as Aunt Rachel is "seated respectfully below our level," he gives over that authority as he asks Aunt Rachel the crucial question about her troubles. The focus for both the story and the illustration is on Aunt Rachel; there is no likeness of Twain in the pages. Williams' striking portrait of her, turbaned and with a determined scowl and piercing eyes, covers nearly half a page and appears at the very beginning of the sketch. At the bottom of this Williams illustration are the words (almost certainly in Mark Twain's handwriting) that are of prime importance to the story Aunt Rachel relates: "I's one o' de ole Blue Hen's chickens, *I* is." In the conclusion of Rachel's narration, Williams depicts

Fig. 58.
"A True Story," 1875

Fig. 59.
"A True Story,"
1875

her in a similar no-nonsense pose at the "black regiment's ball" (Figs. 58 & 59). It is, of course, Rachel's African-American speech patterns, not her formidable form, that long ago established this legendary character in the Twain canon. Williams did her justice in making her presence "tower" above all.

Williams was also most helpful in providing the necessary bulk for some of Twain's perhaps too brief texts. For example, in "A Fashion Item" Twain is observed in the headpiece quizzically examining an elaborate dress with "a good deal of rake to it—to the train, I mean" (153) (Fig. 60). Williams' picture faithfully exaggerates the unwieldy

fashion, his plumped-up, double-tucked bustle and flowing train ridiculing the style in a way Twain's words would not. Taking up fully a third of the page, the elongated print expanded this minuscule piece of writing to subscription book size, quantity large enough to be acceptable as a valid piece for the *Sketches*.[31] For seventy per cent of the sketches Williams' L-shaped headpieces take up more space than the print on the same page.

Bliss's lack of enthusiasm for the collection, coupled with Twain's eagerness to get on with the writing of *Tom Sawyer*, may account for some omissions and a few flaws in *Sketches, New and Old*. There are no authentic visual counterparts for some of the real characters, Charles J. Langdon, Dan Slote, and Jack Van Nostrand in Twain's "Cannibalism in the Cars." Apparently Williams (or Twain or Bliss) over-looked the already available portraits of at least two of the three people in the story. Williams himself had earlier produced a facsimile of Dan Slote and Jack Van Nostrand from their *cartes de visite* for *Innocents Abroad* (Figs. 61 & 62).[32] Charles Jervis Langdon was, of course, Clemens' brother-in-law. Unfortunately,

Fig. 60.
"A Fashion Item," 1875

Rear Elevation of Jack

Jack

Fig. 61.  Jack Van Nostrand, *Innocents Abroad*

Dan

Fig. 62.  Dan Slote, *Innocents Abroad*

for the "Cannibalism" piece, Williams created only a headpiece of the ill-fated, snowbound train with the desperate passengers waist-deep in snowdrifts. Overlaid in a smaller insert—and a poorly worked one at that—Twain is seen listening to the monomaniac "stranger" from the Capital telling his grotesque tale (Fig. 63). What sport if Williams had inserted illustrations of Twain's three fellow passengers from the *Quaker City* voyage into this cannibalistic adventure.

Fig. 63.
"Cannibalism in the Cars,"
1875

Work on the printer's copy had begun and the book was "on the point of issuing" by April 1874, Twain having pruned indelicacies such as expectorating in "About Barbers" and diminishing a "naked" to only "half the clothes torn off" in "Niagara." The final selection of the stories had been decided jointly by Bliss and Twain, their choices "clearly affected by unforseen problems like the need to fill out a page, the cost of illustrations, and even accidents at the printing house."[33]

"The Widow's Protest," and three other short pieces,[34] were appended to other sketches in a strange fashion, apparently under Bliss's orders. For example, for the "Protest," when the editor was confronted with a minor problem in "The Killing Of Julius Caesar 'Localized,'" . . . [and] they were left with an unsightly blank on two-thirds of the last page,"[35] in a *horror vacui*, they clipped a page proof of the widow story to the end of "Caesar" as instruction to the printer to add the story. For a subscription book it was heresy to have "white space."

Bliss made several judgments for aesthetic rather than logical reasons, such as shortening words in "The Fashion Item" to adequately facilitate the combination of text and picture. Unfortunately, several of the sketches contained no illustration, presumably because Williams was finished with his task before all the "culled and sifted" selections had been made by Bliss and Twain.[36] Time was running short and after picking and pasting, Williams' illustrations still had to be engraved and electroplated before any type could be set or any proofs read.

Well before the date that proof was ready, Twain wrote some advertising copy and sent it to Bliss. The copy suggests both the author's aspirations and his anxiety about the quality of the book:

> The American Publishing Company of Hartford will shortly issue Mark Twain's Miscellaneous Sketches, complete—both old & new. The book will be a handsome quarto, daintily & profusely illustrated by True Williams. An inspection of the work will show that the growing excellence of subscription-house typography & binding has made one more stride forward in this book. This will be the first complete edition of Twain's Sketches which has appeared, on either side of the water.[37]

Few of the desired refinements appeared in the final volume. Nevertheless, when Twain finally saw the completed book he thought the *Sketches* was "exceedingly handsome."

Twain's confidence in Williams had been well placed. The artist had made judicious use of space, often incorporating sectioned headpieces for designs allowing him to chronicle in overlapping drawings of the several plot lines into the stories. His illustrations were larger than usual in proportion to the text, even by subscription standards. At times in a two-page sketch his headpiece would take up as much room as the prose—a blessing since the book was only a little over three-hundred pages long, and subscription publications usually ran nearer the five-hundred page range. Moreover, the book was far from the "complete" collection promised in Twain's advertising copy. The Hotten piracy in 1873-1874 had published many more of Twain's sketches and that book was almost twice as large. However, when writing to Howells Twain had declared, "I destroyed a mass of sketches, & now heartily wish I had destroyed more of them."[38]

Howells, who had been given advance sheets earlier, wrote a glowing review for the *Atlantic Monthly* praising Twain's new "growing seriousness of meaning." Thomas Nast wrote that the edition was "very well got up and makes a very attractive book," while Oliver Wendell Holmes likewise pronounced it a "very handsome volume."[39]

Williams' one hundred and thirty plus illustrations were hailed as a major selling point. The extravagant advertising prospectus, probably written by Elisha Bliss with a cue from Twain's earlier advertising copy, gave almost as much room to touting the illustrations as it did to applauding Twain's text:

> Artist has vied with the Author in the preparation of this book, and the result is a volume of rare beauty; THE MOST ARTISTIC ILLUSTRATIONS are profusely scattered over its pages, and the reader will often hesitate which to first enjoy—the sparkling humor of the Pen or of the Pencil. Printed on super-calendared, delicate tinted paper, in the most perfect manner—with its large, open, honest pages, its dainty blue cover so tastefully adorned with fanciful designs in black, and pure gold, its profusion of *Superb Illustrations* and the almost inexhaustible wealth of its text—this book is without doubt a model one, unequalled in it combinations by any in print.[40]

This strange collection of old newspaper articles, short speeches, and condensed novels achieved many of its original objectives. Twain's name was kept before his public and his features became a well-recognized commodity. Unlike R. T. Sperry, True Williams was more than just the dutiful illustrator faithfully documenting his author's text. Twain's attitude, whether comic or dark in this jumble of literary prose, was matched and often extended by Williams' similar point of view. Twain's burlesques reached their greatest potency when combined with True Williams' cartooned, slap-stick wit; Twain's despondency dropped to the depths when coupled with Williams' empty socketed skulls and gloomy graveyards. In many of these sketches both Twain's text and Williams' drawings opted for the easy and obvious baroque hyperbole. Too often the travesty is over the top. In the cause of storytelling both men would exploit their art, sometimes skillfully and sometimes ham-handedly. But the marriage of words and illustration in this small book reveals a kinship between Twain and his illustrator, a kinship that would continue through many more of Twain's works.

Sales for *Sketches* were slim, never reaching the 50,000 number. Twain never received his extra 2 1/2%. Both author and artist had succeeded, however, in their mission of making Mark Twain a household name and his pop-eyed, hawk-nosed features a lasting trademark.

\* \* \* \* \*

A small book entitled *A True Story and the Recent Carnival of Crime*—a rather rare collector's item in the Twain canon—was published by James Osgood and Company two years after *Sketches, New and Old* was issued by Bliss's American Publishing Company. The tiny pocket book was printed for Osgood's Vest-Pocket series, a series which included short works by both American and English authors. It would be the first time Osgood would act as publisher for a Twain work. Their second publishing venture would be the unillustrated *The Stolen White Elephant* in 1882, where the second tale in this two-story volume, "The Facts Concerning the Recent Carnival of Crime in Connecticut," would surface again.[41]

The thin book contained a very odd pairing of stories which are related only by the fact that both had originally appeared in *The*

*Atlantic Monthly,* "A True Story" in November 1874 and "Facts Concerning the Recent Carnival of Crime" in June 1876. Neither *Atlantic* publication was illustrated.

Osgood's 96-page volume was illustrated and issued in one printing, though there are two states of the binding. In a first state Osgood's "JRO" monogram is found blind stamped on the front cover; in a second state Houghton/Osgood's "HO" monogram is in its place. Both bindings were offered in terra cotta, green, and maroon. The front covers are stamped A TRUE STORY with MARK TWAIN below in gold (Fig. 64). The spine reads the same with the title and author's name enclosed in a decorative box. There is no evidence of priority between the colors or monograms on the bindings.

Fig. 64. Cover,
*A True Story and the Recent Carnival of Crime*

An American flag is printed in black on the title page and a page with an illustration of a single forget-me-not separates the two tales. There is a frontispiece and three other, full-page illustrations. The frontispiece recreates a scene from the last section of "A True Story," the unknown illustrator using True Williams' Aunt Rachel in *Sketches, New and Old* as a model with an identical dress, turban and plaid apron (Fig. 65). For this illustration, however, the artist added a kitchen scene background with Rachel's "pan of biscuits on the

"Den I goes for his forehead and push de hair back."

Fig. 65. Frontispiece, "A True Story"

floor." Though the scene is more accurate to the text than in the Williams picture, with a lack of facial features Aunt Rachel's stature is diminished. The reader sees motherly compassion but no sense of the strength in the woman. The caption for the illustration is from Rachel's speech as she identifies her son by his scar, "Den I goes for his forehead and push de hair back." Unfortunately for the reader, this first glimpse of the mother-and-son pair pre-empts the critical moment in Mark Twain's story. Even before the reader begins this former slave's sad tale, he/she knows that in the end the grown son will be recognized by and be reunited with his mother.

The second illustration inserted into the text of Aunt Rachel's story (Fig. 66), is fashioned in setting and costume closer

Fig. 66.
"A True Story"

to the Williams illustration in *Sketches, New and Old*, with a sternly postured Aunt Rachel, fists on hips, eyeing her son and "yellow wench" partner dancing at the ball. Other than the aggressive stance, Rachel's attitude about the couple is lost since the facial details for both mother and son are blurred. Williams had Rachel's eyes spitting fire; here the eyes and any other expression are simply a black smear. Also, where Williams' illustration had no caption, this illustration's caption reads "An' roun' an' roun' dey went," a flat line from the text.

In both of these renditions for "A True Story," though Aunt Rachel wears Aunt Jemima-like clothing, her character appears much less formidable than in the Williams illustrations. Her features, as well as those of her son, lack the essential details—no visible scar on the son, no take charge "Old Blue hen chicken" attitude for the mother. The strength of Mary Ann Cord, the Quarry Farm cook, is lost in this Aunt Rachel.

The second story listed on the title page of Osgood's publication reads "The Recent Carnival of Crime," while the head-title for the story reads, "FACTS CONCERNING THE RECENT CARNIVAL OF CRIME IN CONNECTICUT."[42] The story itself is a strange fantasy-burlesque in which a 40-year-old "unnamed" writer-narrator confronts his conscience, a "mold-covered and deformed dwarf." The first illustration for the story allows the reader to identify the anonymous narrator. He is, of course, Mark Twain, the cigar-smoking figure having the profile and generous mustache of the now well-known author. The reader, therefore, can assume that the I-narrator is Twain, a real person behind the page. With this the story's protagonist takes on a confusing coloration. Superimposed on the story is the readers' perception of the Mark Twain they have read about in the newspapers and magazines. The reader is pulled in several directions and the story takes on a satirical twist. Surely the jovial Mark Twain would never turn away a tramp or break a young writer's heart—or would he?

The dwarf in the illustration deviates in description from both text and caption, "Straightway the door opened, and a shrivelled, shabby dwarf entered." This tiny, dapper man in the picture is neither shriveled nor shabby—though he is a miniature size (Fig. 67). Twain the narrator, however, perceives "similarities" between the dwarf and himself.—each one exhibits rude behavior and each has an exaggerated drawl. Since the illustrator was unable to picture movement or speech, he took Twain's cue of "similarities" and made the dwarf-Conscience a diminutive of Twain the man, each figure sporting a mustache and costumed in a dark coat with light trousers.

"Straightway the door opened, and a shrivelled, shabby dwarf entered."

Fig. 67.
"Recent Carnival of Crime,"
*A True Story and the Recent Carnival of Crime*

"He was already perched on the top of the high bookcase."

Fig. 68.
"Recent Carnival of Crime,"
*A True Story and the Recent Carnival of Crime*

In the final picture the spokesman Twain is about to hurl an object at the dwarf who has flown up to the top of a book case and remains perched with his "thumb at a point of derision" (Fig. 68). Though Twain only hints at Conscience's indecent hand position, the illustrator picked up the cue but unfortunately neglected to make explicit the location of the tiny man's thumb. Even an alert reader might miss the rude gesture in the text, but if it had been augmented with a drawing of a nose-thumbing dwarf, the message would have been clear. Twain was toying with his reader in the same way he had played with his readers' gullibility many years before in "The Petrified Man," hoax where the statute's thumb was similarly placed.[43]

The tale goes on to tell how the narrator was finally able to destroy his conscience and lead a blissfully happy life without this burden. The protagonist would subsequently murder a tramp and thirty-seven other old enemies, burn down a house that obstructed his view, and become a swindler of orphans and widows. If readers identify Twain as I-confessor, they would rebel at taking the tale seriously. Moreover, when the body count reaches thirty-eight and the widows are penniless, the story becomes a cynical comedy. Twain has turned the story about morals on its head and one wonders at Olivia's response to the amoral tone (she would resist several pictures of Twain in unfavorable situations in *Life on the Mississippi*) if she envisioned her husband fitting into the narrator's shoes. Years later in a 7 January 1897 notebook entry, Twain concluded that his approach to conscience in "CCC" [Carnival of Crime] was wrong and that the conscious self and the separate interior must always be strangers to one another.[44]

In this cynical story Twain's imagination had run amok. Yet it does reveal the early conflict with conscience that would erupt more fully in the author's later writings: Huck in *Adventures of Huckleberry Finn*, Hank Morgan in *A Connecticut Yankee*, and the Fischer/Feldner dream self in "The Mysterious Stranger." Osgood's unknown illustrator had little graphic skill, and therefore couldn't take full pictorial advantage of the many visual possibilities in these two Twain tales. But he identified Twain as the narrator, in the same way Williams identified him in several of the stories in *Sketches*, and added a dimension with which reader's had to deal. Either they could join in the joke or remake their image of Mark Twain.

## Notes

1 ET&Sk. I: 572.

2 SLC to Bliss, 22 December 1870, ET&Sk. I: 573, n. 112.

3 Mullen had been suggested by Twain for his *Burlesque Autobiography* and his earliest collection of sketches. He did, however, complete several cuts for *Roughing It*. See David, *Illustrators*, I: 132-133.

4 SLC to Mrs. Fairbanks. 25 February 1874, MTMF, pp. 183-184. Some sketches had been pirated and published by Hotten in England. To prevent further piracy, Twain prepared a similar collection, which was copyrighted and published in 1872 by Routledge, his British publishers.

5 *Contributions to the Galaxy*, 1868-1871, ed. Bruce R. McElderry, Jr. (Gainesville, Florida: Scholar's Facsimile & Reprint, 1961), pp. 87-88.

6 MTLP, p. 39.

7 Sk. #1, p. 7. My thanks to Mark Woodhouse, Gannett-Tripp Library, Elmira College, Elmira, New York for providing a copy of *Sketches #1*.

8 The "Y" is actually a thorn and pronounced "th" as in The, not "Ye." The "A" would indicate the month of August. Sk. #1, p. 5.

9 The Doheny table of contents, ET&Sk. I: 624-632.

10 ET&Sk. I: 616.

11 ET&Sk. I: 616.

12 SLC to Thomas Bailey Aldrich, 24 March 1874, MTLP, p. 81.

13 Selected illustrations from Mark Twain's SkN&O were treated in David, *Illustrators*, I: 207-218. In that volume it was demonstrated how Williams' illustrations provided enduring caricatures of the author and how the artist's work in SkN&O influenced his illustrations in *The Adventures of Tom Sawyer*. Also noted and documented were suggestions that Twain made to Williams about illustrations for four of the pieces in the book. Since the publication of the Oxford University Press inexpensive reproduction of the first edition of SkN&O is now available, it seems prudent to comment further on the interrelationships of Twain's sixty-three little stories and Williams' over one hundred and thirty illustrations in this collection.

14 Thanks to Barbara Schmidt for information on True Williams which she will publish in a forthcoming article. See Beverly R. David and Ray Saperstein, "Reading the Illustrations in Tom Sawyer," *The Adventures of Tom Sawyer* (New York: Oxford University Press, 1996), pp. 28-30.

15 Elisha Bliss's use of many of the illustrations from books authored by Richardson and Knox for Mark Twain's *Roughing It* is discussed in David, *Illustrators*, I: 134-145.

16 True Williams had been an illustrator for the first editions of *Innocents Abroad, Roughing It, The Gilded Age*, and *Sketches, New and Old*. Later he would illustrate the first editions of *Tom Sawyer* and *A Tramp Abroad*.

17 Twain had suggested a similar ploy for selling sets of *Adventures of Huckleberry Finn* and *The Adventures of Tom Sawyer* with matching bindings

and cover designs.

[18] Advertising copy from the American Publishing Company prospectus. ET&Sk. I: 438.

[19] BMT, p. 26.

[20] True Williams would often truncate Twain's lengthy titles if they would not appear as an aesthetically pleasing design in his combined title/headpieces. For example, "A Visit To Niagara" became "Niagara," "The Facts in the Case of George Fisher, Deceased" became "The Case of Geo. Fisher," "An Item Which the Editor Himself Could Not Understand" became "Mr. Bloke's Item," "Personal Habits of the Siamese Twins" became "The Siamese Twins," "Legend of the Capitoline Venus" became "The Capitoline Venus," and "A True Story Repeated Word for Word As I Heard It" became "A True Story Just As I Heard It."

[21] SkN&O, 1996, p. 28.

[22] These two tail pieces are probably stock cuts used to fill white space. Neither print is in Williams style nor do the cuts relate to the accompanying sketches.

[23] "My Watch" was first published in the Buffalo *Express*, 26 November 1870.

[24] MTHL, I: 121.

[25] Twain also had alluded to a similar Vatican acquisition when he wrote of the Jupiter statue in *Innocents*: "When a man digs up an ancient statue in Campagna, the Pope gives him a fortune in gold coin." *Innocents*, 1996, p. 305. He would later write a similar "art hoax" story in 1893, "Is He Living or Is He Dead?"

[26] ET&Sk. I: 641.

[27] SLC to Orion Clemens, 21 October 1862, ET&Sk. I: 155.

[28] The book and its illustrations are discussed in David, *Illustrators*, I: 69-106.

[29] Listed in the "Index" as "A True Story Just As I Heard It," the title on the story page is "A True Story. Repeated Word For Word As I Heard It."

[30] Clemens to Howells, August 1877, MTHL I: 195.

[31] Another sketch, "A Fine Old Man (158)" has, like "A Fashion Item," more picture than prose.

[32] Mark Twain was aware of his character's real identity and had made corrections for Van Nastrand, deleting the "a" and adding an "o," on a proof page. ET&Sk. I: 639.

[33] ET&Sk. I: 641.

[34] ET&Sk. I: 646-647. A few of the other stories: "Johnny Greer," "The Petition Concerning Copyright" (179), and "'After' Jenkins" (253) also appear as if pasted to an incomplete page of a Twain story to fill white space.

[35] ET&Sk. I: 644.

[36] The following sketches contain no illustration: "Johnny Greer," "Disgraceful Persecution Of A Boy" "The Facts Concerning The Late Senatorial Secretaryship," "Speech At The Scottish Banquet At London," "The

Undertaker's Chat," "'After' Jenkins," and "The Facts Concerning The Recent Resignation."

37 ET&Sk. I: 645.

38 SLC to Howells, 14 September 1875, MTHL, I: 99.

39 ET&Sk. I: 649.

40 Advertising copy from the American Publishing Company prospectus. ET&Sk. I: 439.

41 "The Facts Concerning The Recent Carnival Of Crime In Connecticut" would also be collected in the 1896 publication of *Tom Sawyer Abroad, Tom Sawyer, Detective and Other Stories*.

42 In the *Atlantic Monthly* publication the title would not specify "in Connecticut." Twain used the words "Facts Concerning" in his titles for seven other stories in the late sixties and early and middle seventies.

43 See the Williams drawing for "The Petrified Man" in Fig. 46.

44 Andrew Jay Hoffmann, "Facts Concerning the Recent Carnival of Crime in Connecticut," *The Mark Twain Encyclopedia* (New York: Garland Publishing Company, 1993), p. 279.

## List of Illustrations

Illustrations from *Sketches #1*,
Courtesy Gannett-Tripp Library, Elmira College, Elmira, New York.

Illustrations from *Sketches, New and Old*
are taken from Oxford Edition of Sketches,
New York:Oxford University Press, 1996.

Illustrations from *A True Story and the Recent Carnival of Crime*,
Boston: James Osgood and Company, 1877,
Courtesy Gannett-Tripp Library,
Elmira College, Elmira, New York.

# Chapter II

## *A Tramp Abroad*

—WITH ALSO THREE OR FOUR PICTURES
MADE BY THE AUTHOR OF THIS BOOK,
WITHOUT OUTSIDE HELP![1]

Following the mismanaged and financially disastrous release of his last two works, *Sketches New and Old* (1875) and *The
Adventures of Tom Sawyer* (1876), Mark Twain decided to reenter the
tried and true subscription market and seek the profits produced by
his former travel books.  In public he blamed Elisha Bliss for the
commercial failures, though he privately realized that he himself
was largely responsible.  After all, it was he who had talked Bliss
into tossing aside the subscription formula.  Neither *Sketches* nor
*Tom* had reflected the bulk or literary content of a subscription "best
seller"—*Tom Sawyer* was a small novel of less than two hundred
pages while in *Sketches* fifty-six of the sixty-three selections had previously been  published in the *Galaxy Magazine* and the *Buffalo
Express*.  Twain needed to return to the subscription market's format: a travel narrative loaded with comic anecdotes, tall tales,
eccentric characters, and page after page of vivid and uproarious
illustrations—the author himself prominent in many of these.  With
determination and his eye on the dollar, Twain made plans for an
extended tour of Europe to gather the material for a new travel book
modeled on his earlier successes, *The Innocents Abroad* and *Roughing
It*.

To publish his new work Twain wanted to avoid a return to
his former editor, Elisha Bliss, and spent some time scouting for a
reliable alternative.  He soon learned that Frank Bliss, Elisha's son,

was planning to open his own break-away subscription house. On 8 March, barely a month before his ship sailed for Germany, Twain signed a secret agreement with Frank. The clandestine contract stipulated that Twain would provide "a manuscript of original matter in quantity sufficient to make a volume when published of size suitable to sell by agents as a subscription book."[2] Contract in hand, Twain boarded the *S. S. Holsatia* to begin his "tramp abroad."

The new publisher/editor, Frank Bliss would seem to be a perfect choice. He had worked on all of Twain's American Publishing Company books since *The Innocents Abroad*. He understood the subscription business, having been taught by the master, Elisha Bliss. Furthermore, Twain respected the son's editorial judgment as earlier he had the father's. Twain, however, had certain more compelling and Machiavellian reasons for signing with the younger rather than the senior editor. He calculated that he could more easily control the flow of dollars with an ingenuous Frank than with the wily Elisha.

The secret contract with Frank plainly reflected Twain's concern over the elder Elisha Bliss's business practices. Orion Clemens had previously alerted his brother to Bliss's double-billing for the pictures in *Roughing It*,[3] though Twain did nothing about the matter at the time. The wording of the new contract hinted at the author's desire to maintain control over production, design, and illustration costs for his new work. Two sections read:

> Section 3.     And the said [Frank] Bliss further agrees that he will keep a **true and correct** record of the cost of preparing the plates for said book both of text and engravings and of every article needed in order to be in a state of preparation to make the book, such as cover stamps &c—this to include the drawings and engraving of cuts [emphasis mine].

> Section 7.     From this gross amount shall be deducted the cost of making the plates and other articles necessary for making the book as before mentioned in Section 3.[4]

During these early contract days Twain waged a subtle campaign with Frank Bliss to shift the responsibility for the manufacture of the book from editor to author. In the correspondence that passed between the two men during Twain's tour through Europe, the author continued pressuring Frank, writing that it would be best if he (Twain) made all the major decisions on design, the selection of illustrators, print size and placement, approving all sketches, and contracting with European, not state-side, engravers. Frank strongly objected but wanting a Twain book for the launch of his new firm, he submitted to many of Twain's demands.

Mark Twain, unfamiliar with the production side of publication, would make several unfortunate decisions. When choosing an illustrator, he commissioned a young, relatively unknown illustrator/painter as the "principal artist." Because Twain was unschooled in the formula for the percentage of prints to text in a subscription book, Twain's early estimates—10 full pages, 25 half-page and 100 sixth-page cuts—were much too low. He also underestimated the costs charged by European engravers as compared with the rates for the hometown Hartford engravers—a miscalculation that would run up illustrating costs. Over time the younger Bliss was able to argue Twain out of many of his demands but he had little luck with other, more aggressive parts of the contract agreement.

Twain's arrangement with Frank Bliss was the reverse of the usual contract between a subscription publishing company and its author. He had persuaded Frank to mail money directly to him in Europe so that he could pay illustrating and printing costs. Frank had also agreed that his author would have final approval of all payments of bills, even the expenses in Hartford, plus have access to the company books. In Frank's early eagerness to get the contract, he had made concessions which not only compromised the production process on *A Tramp Abroad* but eventually had a negative impact on all future contract negotiations with Mark Twain.

In the meantime, Elisha Bliss remained oblivious to Frank's arrangement with Twain. As editor of the American Publishing Company he busied himself working out clever ways to persuade the author to again sign with the parent company. He wrote Twain flattering letters projecting enormous sales for a new travel book and dangling other interesting incentives: "Would you like to buy up (unintelligible word) the plates of your books? I expect to leave the Co. by & by & I have thought that perhaps the Co. would sell any of their plates." In this late-winter letter Elisha also briefly mentioned his son's activities in setting up his new publishing firm.

"Frank is not with the Co. and is doing nothing except organizing for future business, corresponding with agts, making General agencies &c, & getting his machinery in shape for work."[5]

By March of '79, however, rumors of the secret contractual agreement had begun to circulate around the small publishing town of Hartford and the news finally reached the senior Bliss. Frank, anxious to maintain friendly relations between himself and his father, wrote to Twain:

> It is beginning to get noised about that I am to publish your book; the rumor naturally excites a little anxiety on the part of some of the Company & [people] are asking me how it is. I tell them all, that, I shall try to get your book as it is my privilege to do. Should you say anything in your letters to any one here respecting the publication of the book please don't mention that our contract is not of recent date, as, while it is no one's business it may perhaps *keep things smoother* all around.[6]

From Paris two weeks later, Twain replied to Frank, "I never have mentioned your contract & mine to anybody unless it was Twichell, & I don't think I mentioned it to him. It was not a thing I would be likely to speak of."[7]

Though Frank Bliss was a competent editor and had served an excellent internship with his father, the late eighteen hundreds were shaky years in which to start a new publishing business. Subscription publication was depressed; sales were off even in the established houses. To compound these problems, young Bliss had launched his enterprise with an insufficient cash flow—a real dilemma in the dollar-eating, door-to-door publishing industry. Frank's fledgling firm would produce only one book, *The Life of the Hon. William F. Cody*, and that only with his father's help. To hold down expenses a compassionate Elisha Bliss lent his son the company illustrator, True Williams, to do the art work and also allowed him to insert engravings from plates that had been made for Twain's *Roughing It* and *The Adventures of Tom Sawyer* into the Cody book.[8]

By late November the elder Bliss's health had failed and the junior Bliss, running out of money, shut down his stillborn company. Frank returned to the American Publishing Company as chief editor and it was agreed by all parties, including Twain, that the "secret" Frank Bliss contract would be considered an official American Publishing Company document. Twain agreed to this new arrangement and in November 1879 he signed the papers:

> I hereby agree to the transfer by F. E. Bliss of the contract for a book now existing between him and myself, to the American Publishing Co., in case he makes satisfactory arrangements with sd. Co. for such transfer.[9]

To avoid any possible changes in the financial agreement when transferring back to American, Twain demanded that his lawyer, Charles Perkins, inspect the final contract. He instructed Perkins to examine the papers to make sure they are "in good and clear form" or "please reword it." Twain wanted the American to be "strictly bound" by his contract with Frank Bliss.[10]

Twain's concerns were well founded. Now that E. Bliss and his directors were back in the picture, they would undoubtedly question the peculiar arrangements spelled out in the transferred contract. In fact, young Bliss spent his days in constant fear that Sidney Drake, the powerful chair of the Board (or someone else from the Board of Directors) would hear of the unusual terms of the contract—principally, the fact that Frank was sending money for illustration directly to Twain. However, in the many months since the transfer had been made to the American Publishing Company, many of Twain's atypical provisions had already been put in place.

With Perkins overseeing his interests, Mark Twain felt confident that all contractual problems were settled and that he was in control of production and design of his new book. He felt free, therefore, to explore a few of his own unique and as yet untested illustrating theories. For over a decade Twain had considered publishing an author-illustrated book. He was under no illusion that he had artistic talent but he was convinced that there could be promotional possibilities in such a publication.

Appleton Publishers had first put the notion in his head as early as 1870 when they contacted him about writing "expanded legends" for a humorous picture book. He wrote about such an undertaking to Elisha Bliss: "What do you think of it? I thought that in as much as half the public would think I made the engravings as well as did the letter-press, it would be a unique and splendid advertisement wherewith to boost the 'Innocents.'"[11]

For *A Tramp Abroad*, Twain determined to take the chance. In his new book he would add his own comical crude drawings— the sketches in his travel journals providing a veritable shopping list of penciled memorabilia. He'd accompany the pictures with a text full of arty, technical gibberish to rationalize their existence. Uncertain as to how his readers might view this new role, Twain first revealed his intentions to his friend Joseph Twichell, a Hartford minister who would later become an important contributor to *A Tramp Abroad*:

> I shall make from 10 to 20 illustrations for my book with my own [almighty rude and crude] pencil, and shall say in the title page that some of the pictures in the book are from original drawings by the author. I have already made two or three which suit me. It gives me the belly-ache to look at them.[12]

Apparently Twichell approved and the more Twain thought about the idea, the more intrigued he became with the idea as a marketing ploy. Previously promotional ads and agents' prospectus books which had featured him as the gullible, plaid-panted traveler in *Innocents* and the sincere but bumbling lecturer in *Roughing It*, had helped sell his books. He reasoned, therefore, that if similar, self-ridiculing anecdotes were part of the narration in *A Tramp Abroad*, and the words were combined with his own crude cartoons, the verbal-visual marriage might work as an advertising gimmick. Moreover, his ludicrous art work would also serve to picture for his readers his mocking of European pretensions and American naiveté. The more unpolished his illustrations the more absurd the expansive explanations in his narrative.

On one of his whirlwind trips back to the States, Twain alerted his public to his plan. In an interview in early spring with the *New York World*, he was asked about the content of his current book. He drawled:

> It is a gossipy volume of travel, and will be similar to the "Innocents Abroad" in size, and similarly illustrated. I shall draw some of the pictures for it myself. However, that need not frighten anybody, for I shall draw only a few.[13]

With his author-illustrator concept launched, Twain's next major move should have been the hiring of a principal illustrator. This decision, however, languished until Spring 1879 when Twain was working on his manuscript in Paris. While in France he was introduced to an Ecole des Beaux Arts student named Walter Francis Brown (1853-1929). In a cautious, preparatory note to Frank, Twain put forward Brown's qualifications:

> I've got an artist, here, to my mind,—young Walter F. Brown; you have seen pictures of his occasionally in St. Nicholas and Harper's Weekly. He is a pupil of the painter Gérôme, here, and has greatly improved, of late.[14]

Twain's letter stating Brown's previous and present occupations was accurate. Though still in his early twenties, Brown had been a sometime contributor to several American magazines, principally *St. Nicholas* and *Harper's*. By 1876, however, he had resolved to give up illustration and become one of the many students studying painting with the reputed Parisian "king of art," Jean Leon Gérôme. It was deemed an honor to be accepted as a pupil into Gérôme's select group. However, the distinction paid not a *sou*. Housed in a shabby garret on the Boulevard de Clichy, Brown continued to send art work to *Harper's* to cover his living expenses. In one full-page drawing depicting the daily routine of A PARISIAN ART SCHOOL (Fig. 1), Brown displayed both a talent for caricature and a wry sense of humor. In another double-page illustration, a cosmopolitan melange captioned OUR ARTIST'S DREAM OF THE CENTENNIAL RESTAURANTS (Fig. 2), he proved his compositional skill and drafting ability.

After meeting and talking with Twain—and in need of a more steady source of cash—Brown agreed to divide his creative talents: mornings he would sketch in Gérôme's *atelier*, afternoons he would draw illustrations for Twain's new book. With a background in illustration, albeit more lampoon than literary, and a contract stipulating his duties and commission, Brown seemed a reasonable candidate to illustrate *A Tramp Abroad*.

In a long letter to Frank Bliss, Twain wrote of how he had cleverly managed to expand Brown's artistic duties (though not his fee). With money again the prime concern, Twain informed Frank about the arrangement:

Fig. 1.   A Parisian Art School

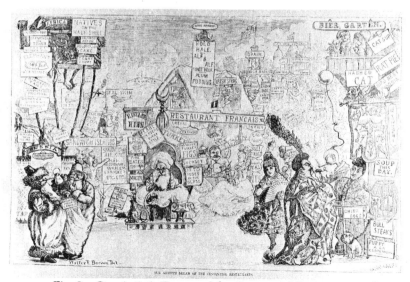

Fig. 2.   Our Artist's Dream of the Centennial Restaurants

> He [Brown] is willing to make the pictures for my
> book about as cheaply as the photo-people here
> [Paris] will put them on the plates. . . . Brown
> agrees to submit all pictures to me and re-draw
> them till I approve of them. He also agrees to
> superintend the process business and see that the
> work is properly done. . . . If you agree, ship the
> money along, and I will pay for the artist's work
> and the plates from time to time as they are ap-
> proved and delivered into my hands. The best
> way will be for you to hand the money to Geo. P.
> Bissell & Co. and let them send me ordinary *letter
> of credit* for the amount.[15]

Twain, always penurious when it came to paying artists for
their work, took full advantage of the young man. Brown's part was
to act as a Jack of all trades: do the illustrating, oversee the printing,
and perform all tasks remotely related to the illustrating process.
For his part, Twain would supervise.

Back in Connecticut, Frank's major concerns were about the
circuitous route for shipping money and Twain's lack of real experience in book production. Realizing they would need hundreds of
pictures to make the book subscription size, in a postscript of a 30
May letter Bliss diplomatically pleaded with Twain to "leave room
for a few cuts" to be drawn by Hartford artists.

Through the months Bliss had also become increasingly dis-
enchanted with Brown's illustrating capabilities. In trans-Atlantic
letters he quarreled with Brown's ideas for sketches and filled pages
with instructions on illustrating technique. Through it all, Twain
remained committed to Brown as the principal illustrator for *A
Tramp Abroad*.

To add to the disagreements about whether the bulk of the
illustrations should be drawn by Brown or by Hartford artists, there
were also arguments about which company should engrave the
plates. Fay and Cox had worked on most of Twain's former books.
Frank Bliss and Twain had often voiced their impatience with Cox
and Company, but no alternatives had ever been proposed. Twain,
of course, wanted to move the engraving process out of Hartford
altogether and have all the work done in Europe; Frank wanted the
process to remain in or near Hartford but be placed in more capable
hands. In Europe, Twain continued to push his preference for the
plates to be engraved overseas.

With Twain dictating the design of the book from abroad, the illustrating process became confused.  To fill the pages of his new travel book with engravings of tourist sites, historical personages and geographical locations, Twain complained it cost him "more days to *get* material than to write it up."[16]  He kept busy gathering picture postcards, brochures, and travel books for illustrators to copy.  As the publication deadline approached many pictures were not finished and Bliss had to rush in Hartford artists as reinforcements.

When Twain's first edition was off the presses it would include a majority of the illustrations by Brown, a few of the author's and some by Harris (drawn by either Twichell or Twain), caricatures and locations by the ever faithful True Williams, illustrations submitted by a crew of Hartford professionals (who spent time copying European scenes into the final chapters), and a good many pictures pirated from other books and artists.

After the "secret" contract was signed, and before the heated exchange of correspondence with Frank Bliss on illustration began, Twain gathered together his family—Olivia, Clara, and Susy—for the long European trip.  Olivia invited her friend Clara Spaulding and the children's tutor, Rosina Hag, to join them.  On 25 April 1878, the traveling troupe boarded the *S. S. Holsatia* for the Atlantic crossing, stopping first in Hamburg, then making their way to Frankfurt and on to Heidelberg.

The Clemens family's longest residence in Germany was in Heidelberg where they lived for three months.  They stopped only one night in the heart of the city, but their stay was duly noted in the local paper: "*Familie Clemans [sic] aus New York im Hotel Schrieder.*" They soon "left the valley and took quarters at the Schloss Hotel, on the hill, above the castle (24)," settling in for a protracted stay.[17] Twain was so enchanted with the place he had a full-page cut drawn to include in his book.  Captioned SCHLOSS HOTEL, HEIDELBERG (Fig. 3), the picture would be drawn by a Hartford artist and was probably copied from postcards or advertisements mailed or brought home by Twain (see far right in Fig. 4).

Since Twain addressed his travel books toward middle-American readers—an audience that had neither traveled abroad nor had access to pictures of European scenes, illustrations of verbally described German architecture and Rhineland landscape became essential.  In Twain's narrative the hotel is described in minute detail:

Fig. 3.
Schloss Hotel,
Heidelberg

Fig. 4. Schloss Hotel, Heidelberg

> The building seems very airily situated. It has the
> appearance of being on a shelf half way up the
> wooded mountain side; and as it is remote and
> isolated, and very white, it makes a strong mark
> against the lofty leafy rampart at its back.    (27)

It was impossible, however, to describe in words alone, the sight of
the famous hotel perched above the wandering Neckar River with a
medieval tower on the shore to a reader who had never been outside Missouri. Mark Twain publishing in the subscription market,
therefore, routinely used pictures to complement and extend his
descriptions for his readers.

A feature that enchanted Twain about the Schloss was the
"glass-enclosed parlors *clinging to the outside of the house*" (27). He
had Walter Brown sketch the hotel's hanging parlors—Twain called
them "bird cages"—so that his reader would appreciate the unique-
ness of his German accommodation. The picture was placed in an
early page of the first edition.

In Brown's rendition, the cigar-smoking author is seen
viewed from the back in black in one of his "cages," allowing his
image to push forward in relief. The effect forces both the reader—
and the author—to observe the "fine sight (28)" at the base of the
castle. This view through the cage windows accurately reflects the
scene in Twain's description, however, Brown's background detail
takes artistic license and defies any actual view from hotel. The
Schloss, as can be seen in previous illustrations atop one of the highest hills in Heidelberg, has no straight, eye-level view of the
Heidelberg Castle or the Neckar River bridge from the bird cages
(Fig. 5).

Fig. 5.
In My Cage

The old Heidelberg Castle positioned much below the hotel, has a steep path which leads directly into the castle grounds, a path that was often trod by Twain on his afternoon walks. The fourteenth-century fortress was—and still is—the pride of the city and in his book the author wrote lovingly of the battered old building with its evening illumination show, considered one of the not-to-be-missed sights in all of Europe. Several pictures of the famous fortress were included in the first edition: HEIDELBERG CASTLE; HEIDELBURG [sic] CASTLE, RIVER FRONTAGE; THE CASTLE COURT; and the GREAT HEIDELBERG TUN. Two of the prints are signed by Hartford illustrators: True Williams for an incorrectly captioned HEIDELBURG CASTLE, RIVER FRONTAGE; Benjamin Day for the GREAT HEIDELBERG TUN. Obviously Twain had acquiesced to Frank Bliss's admonition to have "other artists" do some of the art work.

Pictures of many of these German scenes—and in later chapters Alpine towns and mountain peaks—were inserted as full-page illustrations with blank verso or recto. The blank pages not only added bulk to the book but also gave Twain's subscription buyer the ability to slice out the print without deleting text. This bonus permitted persons never able to travel out of their home town to frame prints of the Rhineland and Swiss Alps to decorate the walls of their living rooms.

The Heidelberg Castle designs that were used as models by Day and Williams have authentic and intriguing chronologies. In 1842, only thirty-odd years before Twain's "tramp" through Germany, the city fathers of Heidelberg had commissioned a series of lithographs of the ancient town and its famous castle. They hired three artists for the project—a local professional named Theodore Verhas, and two French artists, Nickolas Marie Joseph Capuy and Charles Claude Bachlier, the latter an artist/engraver. These three men completed their drawings and the *Album von Heidelberg* was published in August 1844.[18] Subsequently, the engravings were reproduced on postcards, in guidebooks, and on all manner of souvenir bric-a-brac. Even today these "old Heidelberg" scenes are found on many tourist mementos.

Of the prints included in *A Tramp Abroad*, three are copies from this 1844 album. The original *Der Altan des Schlosses zu Heidelberg* had been drawn by T. Verhas and engraved by Bachlier. The Verhas lithograph featured an afternoon scene with strolling couples on the castle terrace and a view of the Neckar Valley in the distance. The True Williams version, captioned HEIDELBURG [sic] CASTLE, RIVER FRONTAGE, was a cropped and altered variant of the Verhas original. Williams darkened the background to simulate a moonlight night and included only two solitary strolling couples; Williams also chose to omit the view of the valley below (Figs. 6 & 7).[19]

Fig. 6.  *Heidelberg, Schloss Altan*

The original *Der Schlosshof zu Heidelberg* had been both drawn and engraved by Bachlier. This early engraving had groups of figures in the courtyard and a marvelously detailed view of the building's Renaissance facade which featured a series of huge statues depicting rulers dating from Charlemange to Frederick IV, for whom the building was named.  Ben Day was probably the Hartford artist who copied this Bachlier print for his illustration captioned THE CASTLE COURT. He, too, recomposed the original design, changing the composition to permit a pleasing but less ornate view of the facade of the structure. Hurried, or bored with the intricate detail of the original litho, Day added foliage to the front of the Frederick edifice, which eliminated the need to draw in

Fig. 7.
Heidelburg [sic] Castle, River Frontage

all the statues, architectural curlicues and scrolls (Figs. 8 & 9).

Fig. 8.   *Heidelberg, der Schlosshof*

Fig. 9.   The Castle Court

It was also Ben Day who drew a replica of the Great Tun for the first edition (Fig. 10). The most famous lithograph of *Das Grasse Fass* had first been drawn by T. Verhas and engraved by Karl Lindeman in 1850 (Fig. 11). This print continues to be reproduced as the poster/postcard version of this monumental vat. There is, however, one detail of the Verhas original print, included in most past and contemporary reproductions, that is germane to the history of the tun but was omitted from Day's illustration for *A Tramp Abroad*.

The Heidelberg Tun has a fascinating history; Twain devoted Appendix B to a detailed discussion of the castle and its giant vat. Included in this appendix was Day's modified version of the Verhas lithograph. Twain's text goes on at length about the vat's dimensions ("the size of a cathedral"), and its function ("to collect several milkings in a teacup, pour it into the Great Tun, fill up with water, and then skim off the cream from time to time as the needs of the German Empire demanded") (591-592). An important person, however, is missing from both Twain's text and Day's print. Most reproduced versions of the Tun, new or old, feature a red-headed dwarf named Perkeo, Court Fool of the ruler who restored the castle, Karl Theodore. According to legend, one of Perkeo's official duties was to guard the giant vat, and tradition has it that he died after drinking a glass of water instead of his customary daily ration of wine.

Not to include Perkeo in Day's print seems strange until we learn more about this dwarf jokester. Perkeo's full name was "Clemens Perkeo," a name inscribed on his official portrait housed in Heidelberg's *Kurpfalzisches* Museum (Fig. 12). Apparently, Mark Twain was either unaware of Perkeo's full name (doubtful) or he decided if he capitalized on the humorous possibilities of this strange coincidence, the negatives would outweigh the positives. An auburn-haired clown (Twain's original hair color), noted for his excessive drinking (Twain's capacity was also legend), and having the first name Clemens—well, this might not be the image Twain wanted his readers to dwell on in his new travel book. Whatever the reason, Perkeo, the guardian of *Das Grass Fass*, is not seen in *A Tramp Abroad*.

Twain borrowed liberally from many of the available sources he found in Heidelberg. In the first pages of *A Tramp Abroad*, he recalled his first days in Germany and acknowledged

Fig. 10.
Great Heidelberg Tun,
B. Day

Fig. 11.
*Das Grosse Fass*

Fig. 12.
Perkeo

one of the books he would use as prototype for a number of anecdotes for his book:

> In one of the shops I had the luck to stumble upon
> a book which has charmed me nearly to death. It
> is entitled "The Legends of the Rhine from Basle
> to Rotterdam, by F. J. Kiefer; translated by L. W.
> Garnham, B. A."                                    (19)

In the opening pages of *A Tramp Abroad*, a reader enters into
Mark Twain's travel world with a description of the family's arrival
in Frankfort. Three pages later, there is an abrupt detour, and we
find ourselves in the legendary world of medieval knights when
Twain transfers a Rhine legend, "The Knave of Bergen," from
Kiefer's work and places it in his own book.

The only changes to Kiefer's unillustrated story, were three line drawings by W. F. Brown (Figs. 13, 14 & 15). Brown's drawings

Fig. 13.   The Black Knight

relate directly to the text and demonstrate his close attention to the details of the story. The first cut finds the hero knight clothed in black armor and dancing with the Queen of the festival; the last illustration finds the Emperor "glowing with rage" (21). Both of these cartoon-like drawings are unbordered, which relegates them to a minor status being "let in" alongside a narrow column of continuing text.

In Brown's illustration for the sec-

ond print, OPENING HIS VIZIER, he uses perspective in lines from a vaulted ceiling as a framing device to draw attention to the armored knave surrounded by a bevy of swooning

Fig. 14.   Opening His Vizier

Fig. 15.
The Enraged Emperor

ladies. The picture is centered near the bottom of the page and enclosed in an arched border to give it greater emphasis. Through careful composition Brown forces a reader's attention to the most critical moment in the story, the unmasking of the guests at the ball.

A most fascinating question, however, is the caption for Brown's "vizier" illustration, a word taken straight from the text. The dictionary definition of vizier is a "high state official or minister, one vested with regal authority"; a visor (sometimes spelled vizor) on the other hand, is "the front part of a helmet covering the face." The dark knight does have a visored helmet hiding his features. However, it is the word "vizier," not visor, that appears in the text, the caption and in the "List of Illustrations." Could it be that Twain missed the error in reading proof? Or could he be allowing the caption to foreshadow the elevation of the disguised executioner, endowing him with regal authority even before he is knighted at the story's end?

The borrowed fable augured a poor opening for a hoped-for bestseller and was a harbinger of the textual jumble that was to follow. The book would have no strong narrative line and the shift from personal narrative to historical legend would continue throughout the pages. *A Tramp Abroad* would contain a hodgepodge of colorful legends, a few arresting anecdotes, and some personal experiences as the author happened upon them in his travels.

Twain continued borrowing legends from European published texts for any number of his tales in *A Tramp*. For some of these he copied the text word-for-word, as he had with Kiefer's "Knave." More often, however, he would paraphrase, restructure, and/or elaborate on an original story. At times he included correct citations for his sources; other times he offered no acknowledgment. Pirating from already published works was not an unusual procedure for nineteenth-century travel books, and Twain certainly understood the peculiar ethics of travel literature. He rationalized his lack of documentation for these German legends to his audience by informing them in the text that "all tourists *mention* the Rhine legends ... but no tourist ever *tells* them. . . ; in my turn, I intend to feed my reader, with one or two little lunches from the same larder" (19).[20]

Twain served up another of his little German lunches when he reconstructed the famed Lorelei legend to add to his book. Titling his Lorelei "The Legend"—and apprising his readers of the correct pronunciation—he again copied the entire text from the Kiefer book. This time, however, he embellished the Kiefer account with several Twainian touches. He reproduced two pages of the original musical score of Heine's song *Die Lorelei* (including three stanzas of German lyrics),[21] added his own personal English translation of the Heine work (in poetic form), and interjected a humorously faulty translation of the tale by L. W. Garnham (author of the poor translation of "The Knave of Bergen"). He also had inserted into the letter-press, a "crude and rude" drawing, perhaps drawn by Twain (it resembles Twain's other art contributions in style).

Twain first created a drawing of *Die Lorelei*, the original of which is housed at the Mark Twain Papers, modeled on the engraving found in the Kiefer book (Fig. 16). This drawing has many

Fig. 16.   Die Lorelei

of the requisite elements: a disdainful maiden with flowing locks looking down on a potential lover. In Twain's version Lorelei has a comb not a harp (Fig. 17) and is pointing at a figure in a boat (presumably Hermann), who is smiling like a fool with his arms raised above his head. In the margin is penciled in Twain's hand:

> That young fellow has not a bonnet on, he is
> merely clasping his hands over his head. This is
> to indicate despair. The apparent joy in his face is
> a typographical error.[22]

Fig. 17. Die Lorelei

On another sheet of manuscript Twain continues with what seems to be either a suggestion to an illustrator or his comment on seeing proof of the Lorelei in the first edition: "The pictures make her a washerwoman, with breasts which suggest that her right place in life is purveyor to a foundling hospital—or she is grooming her mane with a rake."[23]

Fig. 18.   The Lorelei

The two illustrations of the Lorelei printed for the first edition, however, mock the beauty of this celebrated water siren. The first picture is a most unflattering Lorelei figure, in modern dress, anorexic in shape with big feet and spindly arms, despite the fact that both Kiefer and Twain's text had the Rhine sprite as an "enchanting figure" (Fig. 18). This damsel is combing her flowing hair with a rake-like comb, plucking a two-stringed harp (a musical symbol of stress and suffering), while behind her rest two skulls (the symbols of death). This first Lorelei, however, neglects to position Hermann, the joyful lover, into the lower half of the drawing. Hermann, the lovesick victim—with the beckoning Lorelei in a silhouette above—is in a second inserted picture. True to the text, this Hermann plays a guitar, has a feather in his hat, and an assistant in the back of the boat. The lovesick lad, as far as can be seen, is not "in despair" (Fig. 19).

Though the illustrations in the first edition seem to contradict Twain's words, in actuality, they lend credence to his many cynical twists. The words used in his description of the siren's song, "Clang of a wonderfully charm-

Fig. 19. The Lover's Fate

ing voice," and the legend's reputation, "will remain a favorite always, maybe" are subtle hints planted in Twain's text. The two illustrations are true to the facts of the translated legend—Lorelei perched on a cliff, Hermann strumming his guitar—truer than in Twain's original drawing. The symbolic skulls and pathetic harp foretell the fate of Lorelei's victim. An added tail piece, probably a stock cut, is coincidentally appropriate to the tale. Three allegorical figures are viewed as lamenting the lot of the young lover (Fig. 20).[24] The three first-edition illustrations fortify Twain's not-too-subtle critique of the Lorelei legend making his actual meaning abundantly clear.

Fig. 20.   Tail Piece

These various "borrowed" legends supplied the necessary bulk for Twain's book, the Lorelei with its many forms stretching to ten pages. Also filling the pages of *Tramp* were six appendixes.[25] In Appendix D, "The Awful German Language," Twain wrote a 7,530 word essay railing about convoluted German grammar and the illogic of gender in the language. In his account: "In German a young lady has no sex, while a turnip has" (607). He continued with "some German words are so long that they have perspective" (612). To add credence to this linear perspective, Walter Brown supplied an illustration. Captioned A COMPLETE WORD, Brown's drawing features letters that meander through a panoramic German landscape and end at the vanishing point of a distant castle door (Fig. 21). Though an exaggeration, the point is made.

Fig. 21.
The Complete
Word

In another appendix—there are six in all—"The College Prison," Twain describes the *Karzer* (or Student Prison) and the experience of some of its former inhabitants. As he would note in his journal, this unique prison contained a gold mine of material for his new book. He wrote with delight to Frank Bliss about his find:

> I have been gathering a lot of excellent matter here [the *Karzer*] during the past ten days [*stuff which has never been in a book*] and shall finish gathering it in a week more.[26]

The prison, visited by Twain—and a tourist attraction even today—held student captives from 1712 to 1914. During this period Heidelberg University acted in *loco parentis*; town authorities judging the campus off limits. Students were regarded as a university problem. The school's incarceration system was a unique form of punishment that fascinated Twain. In his manuscript he noted the mandatory "list of laws" governing the prisoners of the *Karzer*:

> For every day spent in the Carcer [Twain's incorrect journal spelling for the prison], prisoner must pay 50 pf. . . . You send out for your dinner & supper. . . . Dreadful old straw tick, no sheets or anything. But you are privileged to bring your own bedding.[27]

When noting these curious prison rules for his Appendix C, Twain gave the 1879 American exchange rate for the German *phennig*, "for every day spent in prison, 12 cents" (597).

Apparently for German students, being in the *Karzer* was deemed more a badge of honor than a penance. Of the hundreds of names scrawled on the walls (Fig. 22), Twain took particular note of one, "F. Graf Bismarck (sign of his corps) <-IIII '74> - 27-29-IIII '74." In his detailing of the prison inmates he gave a background for this regal captive: "Count Bismarck, son of the great statesman, was a prisoner two days in 1874" (597). Brown's accompanying illustration shows a young, well-dressed gentleman, minimal profile, from a side angle, erasing the need for an exact portraiture. A crude lettering of the Count's name, F. Graf Bismarck, is relegated to an upper right corner. The prisoner is not inscribing his name but the word RACHE (597), thereby drawing attention to this German

Fig. 22. Student's room in the Karzer with candle-soot graffiti

word. Brown's picture acts as an interesting transition, a segue way for the reader into Twain's "little mystery" about RACHE! on the next page (Fig. 23). Without the caption, BISMARCK IN PRISON, the identity of the man as a son of German royalty could only be inferred.

Fig. 23. Bismarck in Prison

The *Karzer* was founded late in the college's history, Heidelberg University being the third oldest in Germany, established in 1386. The school was and remains a major force in the town. At the time of Twain's residence there were seven hundred and fifty students in attendance. Twain became interested in these young men and their curious customs, especially the two-hundred-year old tradition of dueling—a sport that kept the *Karzer* cells filled. Twain would often meet these university-capped students

while strolling in the castle grounds, or while indulging in a *kneip*—
a beer-drinking ritual—at the historic beer hall known as Seppl's
(Fig. 24). The dueling corps, a minor but powerful branch of the
student body, distinguished each of their groups by color-coded
caps—Frankonia in red, Vandalia in blue, and Prussia in white.
Twain noted in his journal that the faces of many of the students
were "dreadfully scarred" and added rather cynically, "Here you
can't tell whether a man is a Franco-Prussian war hero, or merely
has a university education."[29]

Fig. 24. Seppl's, the student pub, with original signs and old photos

Twain actually visited one of the *afaire d'honneur* rooms in
the Hirschgasse Inn.[30] He probably obtained a photograph of the
hall—many hang prominently on the walls of Seppl's—and had
Brown copy the scene for the chapter AT THE STUDENTS' DUEL-
ING GROUND. In Brown's variant the dueling pair are in proper
attire: mummy-like padding from neck to ankle, iron goggles, and
jaunty hats. The illustration stands just below, "the combatants
were watching each other with alert eyes" in the text (54) where
Brown focuses on the squared-off dueling schoolboys. He sketched

in just enough background to anchor the scene yet allow the central duelists to give immediate impact to the unfolding spectacle. The picture, captioned THE FIRST WOUND, contains historically correct details of the "dueling room," with its planked floors and high ceilings, the room where proud contestants fought and, after "blood was flowing," were "patched up with lint and bandages." Even the postures of the contestants and their seconds mimic the postures of the duelists in an 1850 photograph (Figs. 25 & 26).

Fig. 25. The First Wound

Fig. 26. Dueling Room, Hirschgasse Inn 1850

Twain, intimately involved in the process of illustration for the book, found in this early dueling chapter an appropriate spot for one of his own drawings. On his visit to the dueling hall he asked to borrow a section of a broken sword. Twain then drew his own sketch, entering these words to direct his reader in his narrative, "I will now make a 'life-size' sketch of it by tracing a line around it with my pen (68)." Captioned simply PIECE OF SWORD, the picture was roughly "life size" since his 4 by 1/2 inch drawing was traced from a "6-inch piece of sword, broken . . . [that] was 2-edged, & wonderfully whetted up & sharp." By verbally recording that sword play can be a "fearful spectacle," while visually showing a toy-like broken blade, Twain furnishes his readers a sense of both the peril and the folly in these traditional student games (Fig. 27).31

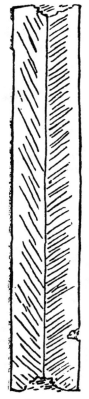

While the Clemenses were in Heidelberg, Joseph Twichell, Congregational minister and family friend from Hartford, arrived as Twain's guest. The plan was to have the two men travel together through southern Germany, Switzerland, and Italy—the rest of the Clemens family remaining in less transitory accommodations in Germany. Twichell's role evolved into much more than mere touring companion. While Twain was writing his manuscript, the minister emerged as the anxious, imaginary literary agent named Harris, the butt of many of the jokes and always in the shadow of the narrator, Mark Twain. Twichell appeared as agent Harris in four-hundred and forty pages of the book, although the friends actually only toured together for thirty-nine days. Twain would often note in his journal that Twichell's companionship proved to be a rich source of inspiration for *A Tramp Abroad*.

The Twichell/Harris character also became the source of some of the book's stories. For example, the dentist yarn was an actual experience Twichell had included in a letter he wrote to his friend. Twain slipped this hair-raising portrayal of pulling teeth on the battlefield into the pages of *A Tramp Abroad*, accompanied by a True

Fig. 27.
Piece of Sword

Williams' drawing captioned GENERAL HOWL (Fig. 28). Williams' picture lent credence to the text and visually explained why the army surgeons chose "open-air dentistry" over "tent surgery"—the poor patient being humbled in front of his comrades and would remain mute while every one of the rest of the rascals would "howl with all the lungs he had!" (223).[32]

Fig. 28. General Howl

Even more than an inspiration and a source for stories, photographs of the bespectacled minister were used by W. Fr. Brown as models for the Harris character. He copied Twichell's features in thirteen illustrations. Brown's Harris/Twichell image is found very early in the book. The genial minister is shown as HARRIS ATTENDING THE OPERA (Fig. 29), a contradiction to Twain's narrative since the author has the King arriving "solitary and alone" as the "one individual in the vast solemn theatre for audience" (97). The Twichell/Harris character, who appeared in the first two chapters, would not actually appear again until much later. Perhaps Twain thought it prudent to introduce Harris visually with an

almost photographic likeness before the reader saw him in caricature in the subsequent pages.

Fig. 29.
Harris Attending the Opera

Twichell was a natural
for caricature, with his lanky
stance and his pince-nez or
wire-rimmed glasses giving
him an ever-present, blank-
eyed stare. The Hartford
artists carried through with
the Twichell-as-Harris model
for the last chapters of the
book—Ben Day drawing
seven poses and William
Wallace Denslow, one of

Frank Bliss's "late artist hires," sketching
four not-too-flattering likenesses.[33]

Though silhouettes are often
considered a short-cut form of illustration, Walter Brown drew several for
Chapters XXXVII and XXXVIII. In one
black-and-white outline Brown presents
just enough detail, is just concrete
enough to capture the image of Twichell
as Harris climbing a "hook rope" (Fig.
30). The placement of the picture, let-in
along the right-hand margin, is a fine
example of how illustration can combine
with print to expand the descriptive
words of the author. Just below the
illustration, the narrator explains how
"Harris started up it [the hook rope]
hand over hand" (427). Upon reading

Fig. 30.
The Hook

these modest words, the reader turns to Brown's silhouette and his eye follows Harris's image as he "struggles" to climb the rope "hand over hand." With a snip and a clip, Brown has communicated both the sensation of a difficult climb and a sense of the ridiculous, picturing this conservative soul, dressed in a swallow-tailed coat and bow-tied dress shoes, fighting his way up a knotted rope. The English were so charmed with Brown's silhouettes they included one, a line of mangled men on crutches captioned TWENTY MINUTES WORK, as part of the cover design for the unillustrated British edition (Fig. 31).

Fig. 31. Twenty Minutes' Work

During their month-long tour Twain and Twichell were inseparable. The role of the imaginary agent/fellow-artist Harris—in reality Twichell—expanded to include Harris as art apprentice making crude attempts at self-portraiture. In this way Twain took a further step in his droll author-illustrator idea, cartooning not only himself but his traveling companion in several illustrations. Harris as amateur artist enlarged the comedy of Twain's description of both men's as students of "high art," a theme that continued throughout the book.

In one of these efforts, OUR START (BY HARRIS), Twain drew an exaggeration of the costuming required for a pedestrian trek along the Neckar River to Heilbronn. The drawing details the asinine attire and cumbersome gear required for the journey: leather gaiters buttoned from knee to toe, knapsacks, slouch hats, sun umbrellas, and alpen-stocks. The outlandish paraphernalia corresponded precisely to that described by Twain's text, yet the illustration heightens the absurdity with Twain and Harris seen reeling under their unwieldy loads (Fig. 32).

Fig. 32.
Our Start (by Harris)

By contract, and with the author's not-so-subtle persuasion, Frank Bliss was trapped into accepting illustrations after they had been supervised and approved by Twain. When a batch of thirty-five arrived in the Hartford office, some by Brown, a smattering by Twain, and some signed "Harris," Frank, assuming the Harris sketches were drawn by Twain, grudgingly accepted all the drawings. He wrote back, "I shan't offer any suggestions about the pictures of MT or Harris. *They* are all right & will pass muster."[34] The Harris and the Twain illustrations were placed in the first edition.[35]

When Twain first decided to add his own sketches to his book, he confided to Howells his motive for inflating his text with his amateur attempts: "I have a notion to put a few hideous pen & ink sketches of my own in my book, & explain their merits & defects in the technical language of art."[36] And indeed, Twain's comic "art-school" lessons remained as a running subplot in his narrative. In an early illustration, PAINTING MY GREAT PICTURE, Twain is seen in Moorish dress, seated at his easel and busy dabbing paint on his version of the "Heidelberg Castle Illuminated." On the wall are hung some of Twain's early efforts: a dog in the Twain style, a pro-filed head (the model for the head that would appear in a Brown/Twain illustration in a later chapter captioned BEAUTY AT

THE BATH), and a donkey which would appear in a "paste-up" Matterhorn picture in a Swiss chapter (Fig. 33).

Fig. 33. Painting My Great Picture

While tramping along the Neckar, Twain and Twichell passed near the small town of Wimpfen. When Twain described the town's famous military tower in his narrative, he also supplied a drawing. The actual tower (Fig. 34) does not "lean" but it does, as Twain specifies, have "more windows." Twain accompanies his unpolished drawing with a lengthy exposition on the merits of his artistic technique, as a sample of his "art/text" theory. He rambled on in amateur-artist, elitist jargon—as he had told Howells he would—at the same time steering his reader's gaze toward his humble effort (Fig. 35):

Fig. 34.  Wimpfen                    Fig. 35.   The Tower

> I made a little sketch of it [the tower]. I kept a
> copy, but gave the original to the Burgomaster. I
> think the original was better than the copy,
> because it had more windows in it and the grass
> stood up better. . . . I composed the grass myself,
> from studies I made in a field by Heidelberg in
> Hammerling's time. The man on top, looking at
> the view, is apparently too large, but I found he
> could not be made smaller, conveniently. . . . I
> composed the picture from two points of view;
> the spectator is to observe the man from about
> where that flag is, and he must observe the tower
> itself from the ground.   This harmonizes the
> seeming discrepancy.[37]                    (104-105)

Twain's laughable depiction of the listing tower, with its
ludicrous ratio of a 115 foot high structure to a "normal" man
perched on top (the man would have had to be at least forty feet
tall), adds to the wordy, comic sequence.  While Twain verbally
rationalizes his art work in pedagogical terms, he escalates the non-

sense by visually demonstrating his inept craftsmanship. As he did in *The Innocents*, he is entertaining his reader at his own expense, while also puncturing some of the foolish pretensions of inept artists.

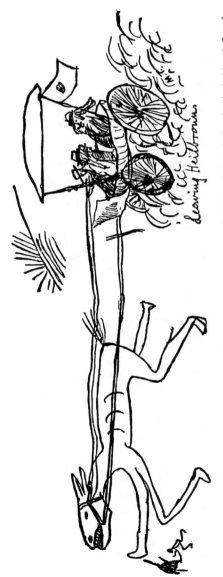

In another drawing Twain produces a picture of a carriage ride captioned "Leaving Heilbronn." In this illustration the reader is made visually aware, as he/she has been throughout the text, that Twain and Twichell literally never "tramp"—the tramp being both a pun and a ruse for the book. In this instance Twain's combined sketch and narrative served several purposes: to draw attention to the his non-pedestrian mode of transportation, to continue his sub-plot of mocking technically incompetent artists, and to extend the nonsense in his semi-serious narrative. With a pompous Work (always capitalized), study, and perspective, Twain apologizes for his artistic flaws by saying the piece is only a "study." He then compounds the farce by touting the "study sketch" as one being "exhibited in a Paris Salon" (Fig. 36). Finally he guides his reader from the text to his "crude and rude" design:

Fig. 36.
Leaving Heilbronn

> I made a sketch of the turnout. It is not a Work, it
> is only what artists call a 'study'—a thing to make
> a finished picture from. This sketch has several
> blemishes in it; for instance, the wagon is not
> traveling as fast as the horse is. This is wrong.
> Again, the person trying to get out of the way is
> too small; he is out of perspective, as we say. The
> two upper lines are not the horse's back, they are
> the reins;—there seems to be a wheel missing—
> this would be corrected in a finished Work, of
> course. That thing flying out behind is not a flag,
> it is a curtain. That other thing up there is the
> sun, but I didn't get enough distance on it. I do
> not remember, now, what that thing is that is in
> the front of the man who is running, but I think it
> is a haystack or a woman. This study was exhib-
> ited in the Paris Salon of 1879, but did not take
> any medal; they do not give medals for studies.[38]
> (122-123)

Twain's out-of-proportion sketch italicizes the descriptive
passage and visually lifts pedantry to a comic height that would
have been impossible with the narrative alone. As an added devil-
ish touch, Twain's drawing is printed as it was in ATA—vertically
on the page, running flush to the inside margin, which demanded
that the reader swivel either the book or his neck for a proper view.

Still another Twain narrative-drawing combination plays
with the art school tenets of "foreshortening" and "color." For this
example the author drew a lopsided circle (so much for foreshortening), in black and white (so much for color). In his text he
claimed the image represented a pedigreed, museum-quality Henri
II plate, not the "false Henri II ware" found in antique shops (Fig.
37). As usual, he draws his reader's attention to his asymmetric
design:

> See sketch from my pencil; it is in the main cor-
> rect, though I think I have foreshortened one end
> of it a little too much. . . . Of course the main pre-
> ciousness of this piece lies in its color; it is that old
> sensuous, pervading, ramifying, interpolating,
> transboreal blue which is the despair of modern
> art. The little sketch which I have made of this
> gem cannot and does not do it justice, since I have

been obliged to leave out the color. But I've got
the expression, though.                    (185-187)

An article similar to the Henri plate, an ancient Etruscan
tear jug, was also drawn by Twain for his reader's pleasure (Fig. 38).
Combining in pictures and print a pedigreed plate and an ancient
jug, Twain could ridicule the inflated attitude of the *artiste* and also
poke fun at the typical nineteenth-century American tourist with a
penchant for what the author in his notebook called "crippled"
treasures. If Twain's tongue-in-cheek tale about tourist souvenirs
had not been united with his childish drawings, much of the fun of
art-lesson episodes would be lost.

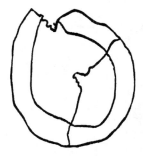

Fig. 37.
Henri II Plate

Moreover, Twain actually turned
the joke on himself, for despite his protes-
tations about crippled bric-a-brac, even
he had not been immune to the attraction
of "antiquarian rot." While on his 1867
*Quaker City* trip he had purchased a four-
hundred dollar "tear jug"—the Italian
salesman assuring him that the relic was
4000 years old and found near an
Etruscan city near Civita Vecchia. Years
later his changing attitudes about antique
traveler trash would be jotted down in his
notebook, "antiquarian shops—my pet
detestation . . . I do hate this antiquarian rot, sham, humbug."[39]
Nevertheless, even on this trip he and the family spent their days in
Italy, wandering the shops and buying "treasures" to furnish their
home in Hartford.

Fig. 38.
Etruscan Tear-Jug

Another "prize picture" drawn by
Twain for his first edition—though the
actual piece was not to be found in his
personal collection—was a pen-and-ink
outline of a cat smiling at a mouse.
Captioned OLD BLUE CHINA, the original porcelain piece, according to Twain's
text, belonged to the fanciful "Chung-a-
Lung-Fung" dynasty—Chinese relics
being the rage in Victorian times.
Twain's eloquent language when

describing the design of this exquisite old Chinese work appears not in regular type face but in large, handwritten script, identifiable as Twain's own handwriting. The grinning Cheshire-cat-like drawing is inserted into the upper left corner of the page. Scripted text and picture comprise a full-page for the first edition, another imaginative way of Twain (or Frank Bliss) supplying the needed bulk for the subscription book (Fig. 39).[40]

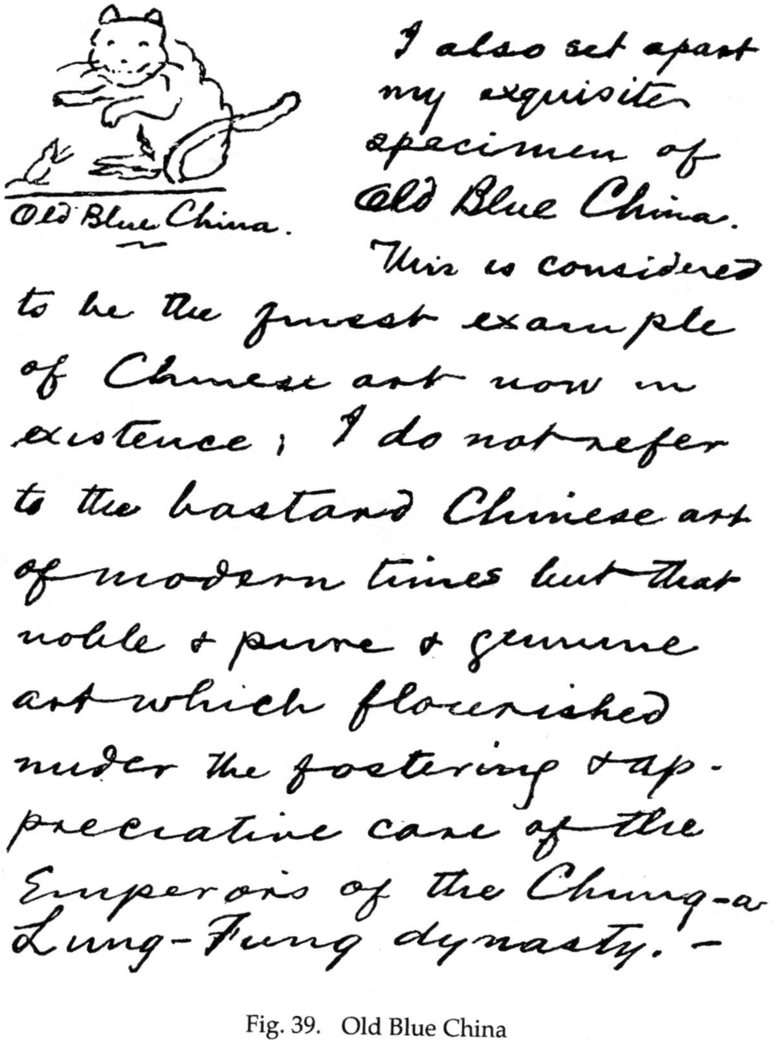

I also set apart my exquisite specimen of Old Blue China. This is considered to be the finest example of Chinese art now in existence; I do not refer to the bastard Chinese art of modern times but that noble & pure & genuine art which flourished under the fostering & appreciative care of the Emperors of the Chung-a-Lung-Fung dynasty.—

Fig. 39. Old Blue China

A similar instance of padding and parody on artistic theory is contained in Twain's full-page drawing of an imaginary river trip, RAFTING THE NECKAR (Fig. 40). Here the author again combines a coarse line drawing with parenthetical, handwritten notes in which he apologizes for the imperfections in his amateur "work in progress." Twain's scripted notices on the cut: "Bird waiting for a Fish," "Perspective of Bird not Correct," and "merely a study not a

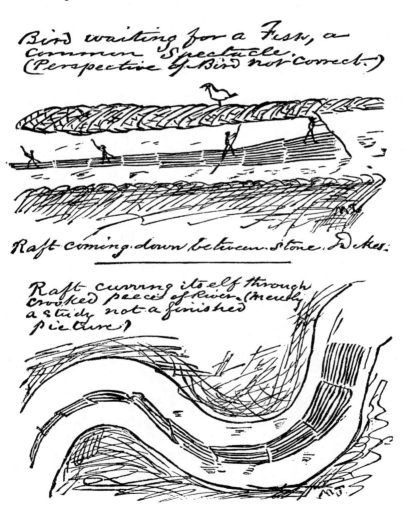

Fig. 40. Rafting the Neckar

finished picture" are relevant only to his sub plot, an explanation on the "defects in technical art"; they have no relevance to his narrative in the chapter. There seems little typographical reason for the raft-trip image to be placed as this chapter's second tail piece; it would have been more appropriate as a tail piece for the previous chapter seven pages earlier where Twain extols the jubilant music of the birds and the joys of the meandering down the river. Unfortunately, if Twain had wanted any correlation between leisurely rafting and inept art, the relationship was botched by the poor placement of the picture.[41]

In another of Twain's artistic endeavors the author allowed himself a bit of revenge. An annoying woman, a ticket-seller in the lobby of the Frederichsbad baths, had cheated Twain. He transferred his frustration into a portrait of the disagreeable woman, Twain responsible for her beak nose and chinless profile while Brown clothed the upper half of her body. An extra touch of sarcasm was supplied by the cut's caption, BEAUTY AT THE BATH (Fig. 41).

While in Germany, Twichell and Twain continued their daily forays into the small towns surrounding Heidelberg. In early August the two men took a day cruise down the Neckar River from Heilbronn to Hirschorn, stopping numerous times en route to drink beer and to watch "joyous groups of naked children" bathing in the river. Turning a bend, "a slender girl of twelve years . . . had not time to run . . . but did what answered just as well; she promptly drew a lithe young willow bow athwart her white body with one hand" (129).[42] The caption for the Williams illustration, "WHICH ANSWERED JUST AS WELL," is from the text but the illustrator's hand outfitting the girl and her three willow-shrouded com-

Fig. 41.
Beauty at the Bath

panions in charming innocence, blunts any thought of voyeurism for Twain's passage (Fig. 42).

Fig. 42.   "Which Answered Just As Well"

Fig. 43.   Our Advance on Dilsberg

During this leisurely raft trip Twain and Harris also stopped at the tiny town of Dilsberg. In a letter to Howells, Twain admits that he "invented quite a nice little legend for Dilsberg Castle."[43] His invention, however, was grounded in recorded fact.

Twain found the spark for his story in the fascinating history of the ancient town. Inspecting the sketches, OUR AD-VANCE ON DILSBERG, an illustration signed Harris (Fig. 43), and DILS-BERG, a sketch signed

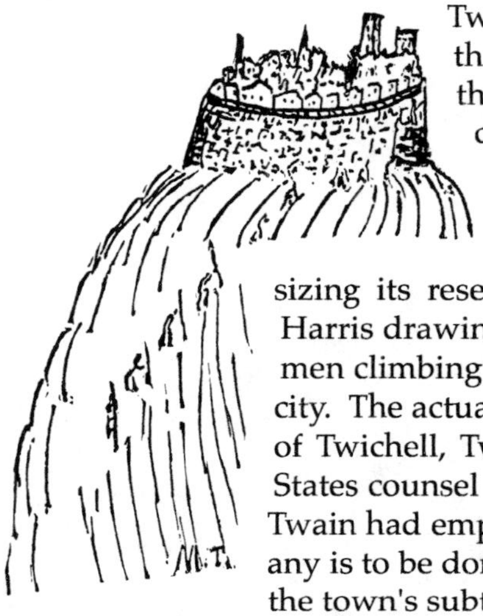

Twain (Fig. 44), supports the notion that the author was enchanted by the quaint town with its "king's crown" architecture, an architecture that is Dilsberg even today (Fig. 45). Twain drew the walled-town's roof line, emphasizing its resemblance to a royal coronet; the Harris drawing presents four mountain-geared men climbing a steep ascent to a more box-like city. The actual group of climbers was made up of Twichell, Twain, Edward Smith (the United States counsel at Mannheim), and a hired agent Twain had employed to "do the real work when any is to be done."[44] Twain's later description of the town's subterranean well and an ancient linden tree, along with detailed drawings of these two principal artifacts, confirms the fact that either all four men actually climbed up to visit the town or Twain's agent made the ascent and collected remarkably accurate anecdotal information.

Fig. 44.   Dilsberg

Fig. 45.   Dilsberg

The two illustrations, like the silhouette of Twichell fighting his way up the hook rope, are particularly good examples of how a precise placement of illustration into a page of text can complement the meaning of what is being written in the narrative. The two pictures are inserted in such a way that the resulting shape of the letter-press seems to move up the page from left to right in a steep, step-like fashion. The climbing figures in both drawings follow the path of type. The sketches form a counterpart to the author's description of the "narrow steep path" ascending the "instantaneous hill" which rises "abruptly out of the dead level of the surrounding green plains" (171). Thus, illustration and text are cleverly united in a physical way and allow the reader a sense of the elevation of the "crown-perched" town.

Through the ages, Dilsberg had remained a tiny, heavily fortified hamlet, the stronghold of an eleventh-century count of Elgengnau. The town was famous for having resisted the armies of the imperial general Tilly during the Thirty Years War. Twain probably first read about these skirmishes in his ever-handy Baedeker and later used the guidebook as reference for this section when working on manuscript in Paris. Folklore—not Baedeker—has it that the reason Dilsberg was never captured was that it had a secret supply route leading from the hilltop crown of the town to the Neckar River below. Supposedly, access to this hidden tunnel was down the town's courtyard well. In his description of the Dilsberg Castle grounds Twain remarks that "the principal show" of the town was "the ancient and empty well in the grass-grown court of the castle" (175). True Williams' sketch of THE OLD WELL, shows Twain and Twichell peering down the well-head as the children make smoke disappear through an underground exit to prove that a supply tunnel exists (Fig. 46).

A medieval map housed in the village archives locates the town well exactly as Twain described it, in the castle courtyard (Fig. 47), and present-day inhabitants of Dilsberg still point out the well to passing tourists—though they belittle Mark Twain's idea of a "subterranean escape route." Townsfolk suggest that Twain's underground fable be attributed either to his abundant imagination or his gullible acceptance of ancient old wives' tales.

Twain did invent a legend about Dilsberg, a tragic tale of two young lovers buried beneath a four-hundred-year old linden tree. The couple in this Romeo and Juliet love story are a product of

Fig. 46.   The Old Well

Twain's imagination. Records in the Dilsberg archives, however, verify that indeed an ancient gigantic linden was felled by a terrific storm in 1923. Twain, in developing his romantic Dilsberg tale, may have remembered seeing the giant courtyard tree. Combining a picture of a devastated young maiden UNDER THE

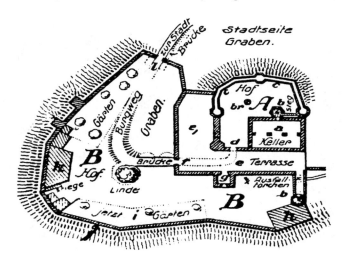

Fig. 47.   *Stadtseite Graben*

LINDEN with Twain's Shakespearean narrative adds an extra pulse of pathos to this tale of unrequited love (Fig. 48).[45]

Another tale, "The Legend of the Spectacular Ruin," contained a smattering of fact and a lot of fantasy. Twain worked his

Fig. 48.
Under the Linden

"ruin" idea into a "Spectacular Ruin"
and cited it as another authentic
German legend. The story, however,
was undoubtedly inspired not by any

Fig. 49.
The Unknown Knight

Fig. 50.
Rev. Joseph Twichell

ancient legend but by personal
observation. The key to this
tale was a play on the word
"spectacular." In Twain's journal notes he records his interest in German spectacles: "Is
half Germany near-sighted,"
he asks, "or do they wear
glasses for style?" A few pages
later he returns to the subject
again:

> Would like to have 2
> monopolies [—] umbrel-
> las in England & specs
> here. I would rather be
> a spectacle-maker in
> Germany than anything

else.—These people . . . might possibly get along without clothes, or Bibles, or even beer, but they've got to have spectacles.[46]

Taking his cue from his journal notes, Twain invented a character he calls Sir Wissenschaft (which means science in German), who triumphs in the story of the "Spectacular Ruin" by slaying a fire-eating dragon. He then flouts tradition by asking the reigning monarch to make his reward a monopoly on Germany's "spectacle concession"—custom has it that the usual prize is the hand of his daughter.

Twain, of course, was traveling with the very near-sighted Joseph Twichell, a man who was never without his spectacles. In the illustration captioned THE UNKNOWN KNIGHT, the fire-extinguishing hero of the "Spectacular Ruin," is a caricature of Joe Twichell shown as a pitiable knight, his armour in shreds (Figs. 49 & 50).[47] Joe is armed with all the necessary paraphernalia for a fight with a fire-eating dragon: an umbrella and a knapsack-packed fire extinguisher. Twain's interest in spectacles—and all modern inventions—and his friendship with Joe Twichell furnished him with the inspiration for this delightful "Legend." Twichell's portrait adds zest to this comic tale (and a laugh for those who recognize Twichell). The episode also reflects an early examination of the blessings of modern technology that Twain was to explore more thoroughly in A Connecticut Yankee. With or without the whimsical illustration, a reader would hardly mistake the fire-extinguisher tale for an authentic German legend.

After the book's publication Twain presented Twichell with a special copy of the first edition carrying a personal inscription which explained the placement of another caricature of Twichell. In the picture, drawn by Brown, there is little doubt as to the identity of Twain's pastor-crony. However, this section of the text recounts the meeting of a young, very verbal American Twain had run into on a steamer in Switzerland. In Twain's journal he identified him as "The Yale cub who asked so many questions on the lake steamer."[48] In his manuscript Twain turned the student into a Harvard wanabee and Brown drew a meticulous picture—narrow-brimmed straw hat, patent leather shoes, tied with black ribbon, and cigarette stuck in a meershaum holder. The confusion comes in an illustration a few pages later where Twain's Yalie is still expounding on the correct choices of ships, hotels, and language. At this point Twichell is seen caricatured as the CONSTANT SEARCHER (Fig. 51) and student, guidebook in hand. The Twichell/Harris character, however, had not been involved in the chapter at all. Twain explained the confusion to his friend:

> You'll find reminders of things, all along, that happened to us, and of others that didn't happen. . . ; At 281 is 'Harris [Twichell],' and should have been so entitled, but Bliss has made a mistake and turned you into some other character.[49]

Fig. 51.
The Constant Searcher

In Twain's use of both real and concocted "German" legends—and his writings about Heidelberg and the surrounding regions—it seems essential to explain why Twain included the several scattered allusions to a German hero, Gotz von Berlichingen, in the pages of the book. While touring the Rhineland and thumbing through his Murray and Baedeker handbooks, Twain could hardly avoid reading the story of Gotz. He may even have read about the infamous man with the "iron hand" in the Goethe play, *Gotz von Berlichingen*, based on the same character.

Twain refers to the "iron-fisted" warrior on five separate occasions in *A Tramp Abroad*, the longest reference being an improvised account of the sixteenth-century knight's life (107-108). These numerous dispersed and seemingly irrelevant references form an interesting pattern. In each instance when Twain refers to the hero—during a stay at an inn, on a hack ride to Weibertreu, on a proposed walk to Heidelberg, and rafting down the Neckar—there is no real reason to mention this Robin Hood-like thief. Twain's objective, however, is more calculated than just name-dropping.

The key to Twain's name repetition lies in a famous line acknowledged by Gotz in his memoirs, repeated by Goethe in his play, and well known throughout Germany. According to the play, when Gotz finds himself and his army surrounded and is asked to surrender, he sends this ribald message to his enemy, *Er kann mich im Arsch lechen.* The colloquial English equivalent of the line would be, "Kiss my ass." This quote has become part of the German vernacular and whenever the name Gotz is heard in Germany it brings a knowing smile to a Rhinelander's face.

Twain certainly must have savored Gotz's colorful rebuttal and he created a clever strategy to have the classic allusion work to his own ends. Twain would tweak his readers by off-handedly dropping the name Gotz von Berlichingen in his text. The name would alert and amuse German readers; most Americans wouldn't have a clue. Berlichingen was Twain's way of avoiding the censorship of family, friends or editors while also mocking his less-learned stateside readers. With an off-hand, "If you believe I stayed at the inn, went on a hack ride to Weibertreu, etc., you can 'von Berlichingen,'" Twain slips in a reference that only Twain and a few scholars steeped in German history would understand and find laughable.

Unfortunately, the accompanying full-page illustration, THE ROBBER CHIEF, did not advance Twain's little stratagem. The bearded peasant in the picture bears no resemblance to the well-known von Berlichingen portraits, not even those of his more youthful days. The portrait also omits a most critical item, the famous "iron-fist," which had become the knight's distinguishing trademark (Figs. 52 & 53).[50] With so many images of this notorious gentleman available, it is curious that Twain didn't demand his publishers furnish an accu-

Fig. 52.  The Robber Chief

rate picture. The full-page illustration has no signature nor is it in the style of any of the known *Tramp* artists. Frank Bliss in Hartford probably cribbed this illustration from a source unidentifiable at this time.

By late summer 1878, Twain and Twichell had moved on from Germany to Switzerland. In his first mention of the region the author has a bit of fun with their custom of hunting the celebrated chamois. In an introduction to the "hunting" chapter, the reader encounters a full-page print of the "conventional chamois" in all his grandeur (Fig. 54). On the facing page Twain takes over the narrative and characterizes the venerated mountain quarry as "not a wild goat . . . not a horned animal. . . . The chamois is a black or brown creature no bigger than a mustard seed" (241). This "mustard seed" size is the first clue to the nature of the pursued prey and throughout the sequence the word "flea" is never mentioned. The identity of the lauded animal is only fully comprehended when the reader sees the inserted picture on the following page where we see Twain toting weapons of a boot-jack, a gun, and a dagger in hot pursuit of

Fig. 53.  Gotz von Berlickingen

a gigantic flea, a ubiquitous pest found in all Swiss hotels (Fig. 55). Twain reveals that "the best way to hunt this game is to do it without any costume at all"; the illustrator, however, found it prudent to clothe him in a nightshirt. With Twain in the illustration ON THE WILD CHAMOIS TRACK! pursuing a gargantuan flea, the author has turned the perilous hunt for the fabled mountain goat into a harmless bedroom skirmish. The chamois chase sequence concludes with another full-page picture where an anonymous

Fig. 54.   Traditional Chamois

Fig. 55.   Hunting Chamois—The True Way

hunter is dressed in the customary, picturesque Alpine costume
HUNTING CHAMOIS (AS REPORTED) (Fig. 56).  Without the pictured flea, readers might be confused by all Twain's talk of a haz-
ardous chamois stalk; with it the reader can laugh at and with the
author in his pursuit of this ferocious beast.

Twain and Brown would sometimes collaborate on drawings for *A Tramp Abroad*.  One, the aforementioned BEAUTY AT

Fig. 56.
Hunting Chamois (as reported)

THE BATH and in another, NEW AND OLD STYLE, where the two "artists" teamed up to illustrate some typical Swiss architecture. Twain's outline drawing featured a three-storied house fashioned in the new manner, "a prim, hideous, straight-up-and-down thing"; Brown drawing detailed the picturesque "old style with gabled ends, quaint windows, and elaborate carvings" (324) (Fig. 57). Twain's pictured rough design prejudices his readers against the new style while Brown's colorful authentic design reinforces a partiality for old. Both prints were initialed by the artists.

The most interesting of the "composite cuts," however, finds Twain collaborating not with Brown but with the engraving skills of a famous engraver-artist, Edward Whymper. The composite was used in the chapter detailing Twain's visit to the famous Matterhorn. This illustration, along with others in the Alpine section of

Fig. 57. New and Old Styles

the book, has a very complicated background.

Twain found what he would presume to be a Whymper original drawing in Whymper's book, *Scrambles Amongst the Alps*. Twain appropriated from *Scrambles* the illustration originally captioned THE MATTERHORN, FROM NEAR THE SUMMIT OF THE THEODULE PASS, and playfully superimposed his own crude cutout of a donkey over the Whymper scene. In a note at the bottom of the first-edition page containing the picture, Twain explained the merger to his readers:

> I had the very unusual luck to catch one little momentary glimpse of the Matterhorn wholly unencumbered by clouds. I leveled my photographic apparatus at it without the loss of an instant, and should have got an elegant picture if my donkey had not interfered. It was my purpose to draw this photograph all by myself for my book, but was obliged to put the mountain part of it into the hands of the professional artist because I found I could not do landscape well.
>
> (448)

Liberal side-cropping and Twain's "pasted" donkey nearly obliterated the venerated image of the Matterhorn while also deleting the English engraver's signature. The Whymper caption was changed appropriately to read MY PICTURE OF THE MATTERHORN. The donkey-doctored print, with a batch of thirty-five others, was sent on to Hartford where Frank Bliss wrote a humorless response that dealt only with the technical problems of Twain's effort:

> It doesn't seem to me that I like the sky of the Matterhorn picture exactly, seems as if it was too flat & dark for the rest of the picture. I wonder how it will print on a printing press. It appears to me as if that stipple work would be likely to fill up with the ink & make a bad mess of the thing. Perhaps you could have it put on a power press & run say 50 copies on book paper & see how the thing acts. You see the white spaces in the process work is [sic] apt to be rather shallow & where the black lines or dots are very close together there is a danger of their filling up.[51]

Twain took Frank's advice and ran a few copies of the picture. On scanning the results he reversed his notion about using "stipple work" in illustration. He wrote back to Bliss: "I don't like those stipple processes half as well as I thought I should and am glad the plates are not to be made here. Pen and ink on plain paper looks much cleaner and stronger."[52] By this time Twain had obviously also changed his mind about the engraving plates being processed in Europe.

Receiving a final drawing of the composite in Hartford, the practical Frank accepted the print but made a suggestion in his reply: "I'll go over that donkey you sent and make the lines black so he'll take, as you used 'mauve' ink—*India* is the stuff to use."[53] Twain's Matterhorn donkey with an explanation for its appearance was placed in the first edition (Figs. 58 & 59).

It was in Zermatt that the author gathered much of the information for his mountain-tramping anecdotes. Twain found the town and the area breathtakingly beautiful and took copious notes so that he could later re-record the information into his book. From the townsfolk he learned about the shocking loss of life for climbers challenging the Matterhorn. His interest was especially piqued when he stopped by the mountain-climbers' cemetery and read the inscriptions on the gravestones. He registered his visit in his journal: "Saw the graves of a young English Lord (19) a young clergyman, who, with 3 guides, were killed on the . . . Matterhorn July 14, '65. See Baedeker."[54]

Twain's facts were faulty, three English climbers and one Swiss guide were killed. Further reading and questioning of several Zermatters revealed more facts surrounding the tragedy that had taken place on the Matterhorn over a decade before. Twain realized he had found a mother lode: a compelling adventure story, a "royal" victim, and incidentally, a treasure trove of illustrations.

The Matterhorn episode had become famous world-wide through the writings of the aforementioned Edward Whymper, one of the surviving participants. After the death of the four young men, Whymper published an account of this first ascent from the east face to the crest of the Matterhorn and the Swiss mountain town ironically blossomed into an English tourist attraction. Guides who were formerly smugglers *cum* mountain-climbing escorts, became full-fledged, certified mountain guides. Thrill-seeking visitors (men and women) bought hob-nailed boots, alpen-stocks, and ice axes, to ready themselves for their conquest of the slopes. Women (and men) unable to make the trek on foot were conveyed up the steep slope in a cushioned box between two long poles, "carried by relays of strong porters" (387). The "Alpine litter" ride cost four francs per carry. William F. Brown sketched one of

Fig. 58.   My Picture of the Matterhorn

Fig. 59.
The Matterhorn from near the Summit of Theodule Pass

these unique conveyances for Chapter XXXV, a barely recognizable Twain appearing as the back porter (Figs. 60 & 61).

Fig. 60.   The Alpine Litter

Twain and Twichell had arrived in the small mountain town in August of 1878. An unsigned picture in *A Tramp Abroad* captioned ARRIVAL AT ZERMATT, was probably copied by the illustrator from a postcard

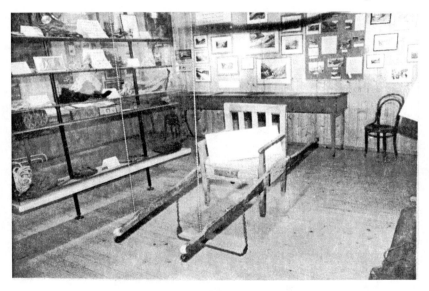

Fig. 61.   *Les Moyens de Transport*

or a tourist brochure purchased by Twain during his stay (Figs. 62 & 63). The pair settled into the Cervin Hotel[55] and while gossiping with several of the shopkeepers found that the ill-fated Whymper climb was a continuing topic of conversation. Pictures of the opti-

Fig. 62.   Arrival at Zermatt

Fig. 63.   Zermatt, Anno 1865

mistic band of climbers (the survivors, Edward Whymper and two
guides, Taugwalder senior and junior; the deceased, guide Michael

August Croz, the Englishmen Rev. Hudson, Lord Douglas, and Douglas Hadow) were displayed in the hotel lobby and in every shop window (Fig. 64). Twain, intrigued with the continuing speculation surrounding the mysterious deaths, noted in his journal:

Fig. 64.  *Erstbesteigung des Matterhorn, 14 Juli 1865*

> It is whispered that the survivors *cut* the rope—
> which I believe.  I lay an hour last night trying to
> imagine how it could break—or how the sur-
> vivors could by any possibility haul the others
> up.[56]

Edward Whymper was in no small part responsible for keeping the story alive.  His first description of the catastrophic conquest of the Matterhorn appeared in a letter to the London *Times* on

8 August 1865, less than a month after the accident. In 1871 he followed up with a book, *Scrambles Amongst the Alps*. The book went through multiple editions and, though flawed (most Alpine scholars agree that Whymper's descriptions of his mountain-climbing adventures were filled with personal promotion and picturesque invention), it is still considered an outstanding contribution to mountain literature.[57]

Whymper, only twenty-five at the time of the event, rose in one year from an unknown artist/engraver and amateur mountain climber to international celebrity. As a consequence of the publication of *Scrambles*, Zermatt became the nineteenth-century mountain-climbing capital of the world. Whymper took full advantage of his international reputation, exploiting his participation in the misadventure for the rest of his life through subsequent books and world-wide lecture tours.

Major discrepancies about the particulars of the ascent have come to light since Whymper's original version of the climb documented in his *Times* letter and his 1871 book. In both Whymper accounts he had written as though he had initiated the plans for the team's climb. In reality, Charles Hudson (a much more experienced climber), Lord Douglas (who first commissioned the fated Michael Croz as guide), and Edward Whymper had each independently dreamed of making the challenging east-face ascent. All three climbers had made tentative arrangements, and, after meeting and conferring with one another in Zermatt, ultimately joined forces.

Twain heard and noted all the rumors about the climb, ascent and descent, from the Zermatt villagers. His challenge was to adapt the tragic incident into a stirring adventure tale for his book—no need for him to investigate the flaws in the Whymper account. Months later in Paris, while trying to piece together his meager notes to write manuscript (he had lost but later found his Swiss notebook), Twain asked his English publisher for a copy of *Scrambles*, the better to refresh his memory: "Can't you send me *immediately* Mr. Whymper's book? It contains his ascent of the Matterhorn (about 1865) when young Lord Douglas and a guide or two lost their lives."[58] After reading Whymper's book, Twain crafted a truncated version of the Whymper story into a tale told in the Twain style. He deleted from Whymper's text passages the competition of the seven Italian climbers who had challenged the Englishmen for the summit and the immediate reaction of the survivors to the catastrophe. He tidied up the language in many of Whymper's picture-pretty descriptions. In describing the disastrous July 14th descent, however, Twain transferred, almost *verbatim*, several pages of the Whymper account of the hapless fall into *A Tramp Abroad*.[59]

Twain's ethics in lifting great chunks of the Whymper narrative could be questioned. However, undocumented appropriation of already published material to use in another author's writings was part and parcel of the popular nineteenth-century travel-book trade. Moreover, to Twain's credit, he at least acknowledged his debt to Whymper by titling the "smouched" section MR. WHYMPER'S NARRATIVE. Americans who would not recognize the Whymper name could think it was another of Twain's "Legends."

Twain's debt to Whymper, however, extended well beyond his borrowing of Whymper's words. Whymper, the son of an engraver, by profession an artist/engraver, and a partner in his father's firm Whymper and Son Engravers of London, had been commissioned by a publisher to take a 1860 Alpine trip and produce a few watercolors of the mountain landscape. "It was his artistic ability . . . that had [first] presented Whymper with an opportunity of visiting the Alps."[60] During this initial visit he fell in love with the Alps and mountain climbing.

While on the 1865 Matterhorn ascent, Whymper, as he recounted in *Scrambles*, again busied himself by "sketching" some of the mountain scenes as he happened upon them. At one point he wrote, "passed the remaining hours of daylight—some basking in the sunshine, some sketching."[61] Obviously, Whymper wanted his readers to know that he was an artist, a writer, and a climber. The "Title Page" of *Scrambles* mentions "Additional Illustrations and Material from the Author's Unpublished Diaries," and the preface declares, "I have dealt sparingly in description, and have employed illustration freely, in the hope that the pencil may perhaps succeed where the pen must inevitably have failed."[62] The history of the Matterhorn climb, Whymper's reputation as a climber-author-illustrator, and Zermatt's early tourist fame have relied on a combination of this Englishman's authoritative story and the detailed drawings of the Matterhorn affair in his book.

While reading Whymper's narrative, Twain became fascinated not only with the text but also with the sketches. He was so taken with the pictures that he decided to have some of them copied for the pages of *A Tramp Abroad*. With the publication of Twain's first edition, seven Whymper illustrations, though not all taken from *Scrambles*, still had the Whymper engraving mark prominently displayed in the corners. Twain had no reason to question the authenticity of Whymper's drawings nor, apparently, did he have qualms about having them reproduced. Twain, like most readers, mountain-climbers, and Alpine scholars of the time, assumed that "Whymper had not only engraved but drawn . . . the illustrations." A closer look at the prints, however, will confirm a much more convoluted history for these *Scrambles*, illustrations and Twain's "acquisitions."63

Not all Whymper pictures, the donkey/mountain composite print or the others, appear in the chapter entitled THE WHYMPER NARRATIVE. They are scattered throughout the book. Two engravings are used as tail pieces, without artist/engraver's marks; two other full-page engravings appear in earlier sections of the book with changed captions but with Whymper's signature. Only one full-page print and one inserted cut are found in the Whymper narrative. These two are without signatures and their captions have been changed.

Comparing the illustrations in *A Tramp Abroad* (1880) with the original pictures in *Scrambles* (1871), we can view both the similarities and the differences in each print.

|  *A Tramp Abroad* | *Scrambles Amongst the Alps* |
|---|---|
| 58. MY PICTURE OF THE MATTER-<br>HORN, p. 448 (no Whymper or<br>JM mark) | 59. THE MATTERHORN. FROM<br>NEAR THE SUMMIT OF<br>THE THEODULE PASS,<br>p. 55 (only Whymper mark) |
| 65. TAIL PIECE—ROPED TO-<br>GETHER, p. 482 (caption only<br>in List of Illustrations; no<br>Whymper or JM mark) | 66. THE RIGHT WAY TO USE<br>THE ROPE, p. 297<br>(Whymper and JM mark) |
| 67. TAIL PIECE, p. 529 (no<br>Whymper or JM mark) | 68. THE WRONG WAY TO USE<br>A ROPE ON A GLACIER, p.<br>296 (caption only in the List<br>of Illustrations; Whymper and<br>JM mark) |

69. A FEARFUL FALL, p. 415 (only Whymper mark)

70. "IN ATTEMPTING TO PASS THE CORNER I SLIPPED AND FELL," p. 108 (only Whymper mark)

71. AN OLD MORAINE, p. 463 (only Whymper mark)

72. "PINNACLES, NEAR SACHAS IN THE VALLEY OF THE DURANCE; FORMED FROM AN OLD MORAINE," p. 442 (only Whymper mark)

73. ONE VIEW OF THE MATTER-HORN, p. 475 (no Whymper or JM mark)

74. "THE MATTERHORN, FROM THE RIFFELBERG," p. 272 (only Whymper mark)

75. "ON THE SUMMIT," p. 477 (no Whymper or JM mark)

76. "CROZ! CROZ! COME HERE!," p. 378 (Whymper and JM mark)

Fig. 65. Tail Piece—Roped Together

Fig. 66. The Right Way to Use the Rope

Fig. 67.   Tail Piece

Fig. 68.   The Wrong Way to use a Rope on a Glacier

Fig. 69.
A Fearful Fall

Fig. 70.
"In Attempting
to Pass the
Corner I Slipped
and Fell"

Fig. 71.
An Old Moraine

Fig. 72.
"Pinnacles, Near Sachas in the Valley of the Durance,
formed from an Old Moraine"

Fig. 73.
One View
of the
Matterhorn

Fig. 74.
"The Matterhorn,
from the
Riffelberg"

Fig. 75.
"On the Summit"

Fig. 76.
"Croz! Croz!
Come Here!"

The only initials other than Whymper's appearing on these prints in the 1871 edition of *Scrambles* are the letters JM, the monogram of an illustrator named James Mahoney. The JM mark confirms that at least three of the prints Twain borrowed may have been engraved but were not actually drawn by Whymper; Edward Whymper had only "rough sketched" the ideas for the prints. His location sketches then were meant to be used as, what he called, "slight memoranda" for his later writings, in the same way Twain's crude journal drawings reminded him of people and places he would use later in his lectures and writings. Back in England, several other artists took the Whymper memoranda sketches and completed the final designs.

The illustrations which contributed to the fame of *Scrambles* (and Zermatt) were drawn, in fact, by several now virtually unknown artists. The most prominent and prolific of these was James Mahoney (d. 1882), who drew fifty of the final *Scrambles* prints. Little is known about Mahoney's career. The consensus seems to have been that he was a difficult man to work with, largely because of his frequent bouts of drunkenness. It is known that he had the Whymper Engraving Company do the engraving work for many of his drawings published in periodicals between the years 1864 and 1868.[64] As a draughtsman he was at his best with modern life subjects, subjects that were rough in nature. His most notable contributions were illustrations for three of Dickens novels: *Oliver Twist* in 1871, *Little Dorrit* in 1873, and *Our Mutual Friend* in 1875. In the 1871 *Scrambles* (later also found in the "Author's Preface to the Fifth Edition") Whymper included these words of praise for Mahoney: "I am much indebted to that artist for the care and fidelity with which he followed my slight memoranda, and for the spirit he put into the admirable designs. Most of his drawings will be identified by his monogram."[65]

A second major illustrator was another relatively unknown artist, and Whymper also acknowledged him, "Twenty of the remainder [i.e. remaining prints] are the work of Mr. Cyrus Johnson."[66] There is no way of distinguishing Johnson's drawings for *Scrambles* or whether any of his work was included in *A Tramp Abroad*.

The subsequent confusion in crediting Whymper with both the drawing and the engraving of the illustrations is understandable. On the title page of the 1871 edition Whymper had cited all the contributing illustrators: H. J. Boot, W. Lapworth, J. W. North, T. S. Scott, P. Skelton, W. G. Smith, and C. J. Stanland, James Mahoney and Cyrus Johnson. Regrettably, none of the other artists' signatures, except for Mahoney's, appeared on final prints. This was not, however, an unusual omission in the nineteenth-century since illustrator's work was seldom acknowledged and the rights to the prints would usually be owned by the publisher. All the prints for *Scrambles* were engraved at Whymper and Sons Engravers in London. Logically, therefore, the name Whymper appeared prominently displayed in the corners and subsequent editions bear only the Whymper mark.

With the publication of the 1871 *Scrambles*, Edward Whymper had a best seller, and was naturally less inclined to attribute any of the work, text, drawings, or engraving, to others. Moreover, when subsequent editions used the 1871 prints, the list of illustrators and Edward Whymper's credits to them moved off the title page and were found only at the very end of the "Author's Preface." In some editions the artists' names appeared in smaller font and appeared at the end of the "List of Illustrations." Consequently, as successive editions were printed, it was "presumed" that Whymper, the known artist/engraver, was author, illustrator and engraver. Even today souvenirs of the Matterhorn tragedy are identified and sold as "Whymper" prints and throughout his lifetime Whymper neglected to concede the role the other artists played in creating the illustrations for his book.

Interestingly, when the illustrated English edition of *A Tramp Abroad* was published, months after issuance of the American edition, Chatto and Windus did not include a number of the Whymper marked prints. They did use two of the tail pieces from *Scrambles*, both unsigned and without the Whymper engraving mark. This illustrated British edition also omitted several other suspect prints found in the American edition prints which Bliss had appropriated from other mountain adventure publications. There is, however, no correspondence on these matters between Chatto & Windus, Mark Twain or Frank Bliss to explain the inclusions in the American or the exclusions from the illustrated English edition.

In Paris, Mark Twain scanned the *Scrambles* pictures and realized that Whymper had omitted, or decided not to include, an illustration of the "fateful fall" of his comrades. Since Twain's version of the story focused exclusively on the accident, not on the

arrangements for the climb or the competition between the English
and Italian climbers, he deemed it imperative that a drawing of the
four men tumbling to their death be included. He had a full-page
illustration, undoubtedly worked by Walter F. Brown, which was
ultimately captioned THE CATASTROPHE ON THE MATTER-
HORN, 1865, a variant caption, ACCIDENT ON THE MATTER-
HORN (1865) appears in the "List of Illustrations" (Fig. 77). The
original concept for the illustration, however, was not Whymper's,
Brown's, or Twain's. The very first visual depiction of the tragedy
was produced by the famous French painter, Gustave Doré, a contemporary and friend of Edward Whymper. Doré, on reading of the
accident in Whymper's London *Times* letter, hastily produced two
lithographs, one entitled *AUFSTIEG* [ascent] and one *ABSTURZ*
[descent] (Figs. 78 & 79). Brown apparently used the *ABSTURZ*
lithograph as a model for his drawing, producing an accurate but
technically inferior version of the disaster.

Twain mailed Brown's picture of the fall along with a packet of manuscript to Frank Bliss in Hartford, writing, "We [Twain and
Brown] meant the Matterhorn accident for a full-pager, but had to
guess at the size."[67] The Brown illustration caused an uproar in
Hartford, not because the editors knew about his modeling after the
Doré print but because the Brown drawing was so poorly executed.
An exasperated Frank Bliss, trying to deal with Twain's manuscript,
the illustrations, and the impending production problems for the
new book, wrote back to his author:

> I've had so much to do with these pen drawings
> for the past four or five years that if I was over
> there I might give Brown some hints that he
> would be glad to get. Still he may know all the
> points himself by now.[68]

In one especially long, meticulously explicit communiqué,
Frank Bliss attempted to convince Twain of the dire consequences if
he continued with his plan to have the major portion of the illustrating work for *A Tramp* done in Europe. The letter also documents
a growing tension between the editor and author on other design
and production matters. Bliss begins his communication by patient-
ly asking Twain to relay some "fundamentals of illustration" to
Brown: Brown should work on a ruled tinted paper instead of a tint
made of fine dots (the stipple process that had produced the prob-

Fig. 77.
The Catastrophe on the Matterhorn

Fig. 78.    *Aufsteig*

lems with the Matterhorn/
donkey composite), he must
apply Chinese white to get the
best effects in large areas while
using jet black for the finely
defined lines, and he should
produce shading by a grada-
tion of lines from thin to coarse
rather than relying on a wash.
Frank also urged that Brown
be told to include more background detail to relieve the flat
character of his prints.  Bliss
also suggested that when
Brown was arranging the illustrations on the page, he should
vary the size of the cuts, use

Fig. 79.    *Austurz*

oblong and circled borders rather than only monotonous rectangles.[69]

Walter F. Brown undoubtedly needed Frank's "lessons by correspondence." Painting and illustrating are widely differing techniques and Brown had, for the last few years, treated illustration as a minor vocation while studying oil painting with his mentor, the French painter, Gerôme. By 1878, he was painting furiously, readying himself for a one-man exhibition in Paris. It must be said in his defense, however, that the beleaguered Brown was in the untenable position of having all of his work scrutinized by Twain, Frank Bliss, and even the bed-ridden Elisha Bliss. At one point a batch of Brown's drawings arrived in Hartford and Frank, determining that they were "too comical," had them looked over by his recuperating father:

> I've just been talking with Father about the drawings & looking over them again. [He] suggests that I call your attention to one point . . . : in the A. P. Co. we always try to avoid, in the illustrations, the making of a funny picture by a monstrosity. . . . Max Adeler, Billings & those writers you know get deformities for funny pictures. I like to avoid them don't you?[70]

Twain, Brown's champion and least severe critic, was probably not as inclined to object to the humor. He did, however, object to one of the Brown drawings even after the print had been sent on to Hartford. In a letter to Frank he commented, "I think I wouldn't use the picture which represents me lying on my back drinking from a bottle. It is not very well done, & there is no reference in the MS to that."[71]

Twain's response was fitting. The drawing was of poor quality, with little resemblance to the author and drinking was not referred to in the text, the narrative merely mentions "fatigue." Nevertheless, the cut was included in the first edition but was tied to Twain's words "Nothing is gained in the Alps by over-exertion" (531) and captioned, TAKE IT EASY, a caption that diverted attention from alcohol to innocent relaxation (Fig. 80). In the picture, the author appears relaxed, on a hillside, with a book by his side and a bottle raised to his lips. Twain was probably more concerned about advertising a fondness for spirits than about the quality of the print.

In these Alpine chapters Twain was not above slipping in a sexual innuendo if he thought he could get it past his censors—Olivia, Howells, and the folk at the Hartford office. To cite one example, Twain took a journal entry note and a sketch of the Jungfrau (the German word for "virgin") and combined them in a rewritten description united with a recomposed drawing. The juxtaposition reveals some surprising sexual implications.

In his notebook entry Twain had scribbled a routine reminder about the snow levels on the various mountain heights in Switzerland:

Fig. 80. Taking It Easy

> The lowest snow on the Jf seems but little above the valley level—& on the left towers a huge rampart 2 or 3000 feet high (close to us)—& it seems absurd to say that that lowest snow is higher than that (apparently) vastly higher rampart—but so it is—for the one is on the eternal snow altitude & the other isn't—as the absence of snow shows.[72]

In the published version Twain continued to extol the mountain's majesty. For his usual running art commentary, he ridiculed the overblown art crowd fashion of "Work" and "Study" while directing his remarks to his inserted line-drawing, "I took out my sketchbook and made a little picture of the Jungfrau, merely to get the shape: I do not regard this as one of my finished works, in fact I do not rank it among my Works, at all; it is only a study" (345). Preceding this pretentious pedagogy in the text, however, Twain manipulates an extended sea metaphor to describe the mountain:

> The giant form of the Jungfrau rose cold and white into the clear sky, beyond a gateway in the

> nearer highlands. It reminded me, somehow, of
> one of those colossal billows which swells sud-
> denly up besides one's ship, at sea, sometimes,
> with its crest and shoulders snowy white, and the
> rest of its noble proportions streaked downward
> with creamy foam. (345)

This anthropomorphic description, "crested snowy white shoulders
and downward creamy foam," surfaces just before a reader turns
the page to view Twain's drawing. The reader has been primed to
make the picture more than a little provocative.

When comparing Twain's journal drawing of the Jungfrau
with the published illustration one also sees how he cleverly
expanded his seductive words from journal note to print text to
match his doctored image (Figs. 81 & 82). The reworked drawing

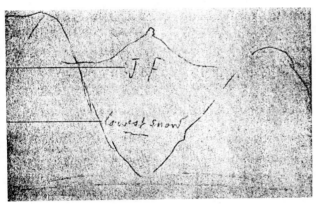

Fig. 81.
Jungfrau

Fig. 82.
Jungfrau,
Lowest Snow

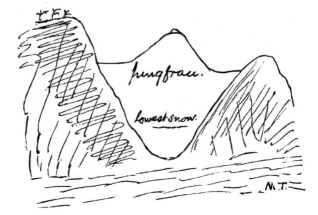

remains relatively true to the notebook sketch with an added spelling out of the Jungfrau and a M.T. penciled into the right-hand corner for identification. But the subtle, more eye-catching changes are certainly significant—some cross-hatched dark shading, a few bushes on the mountain side, a top knot on the distant mound, and the rounding out of the Jungfrau slopes.

Twain's reworked narrative, located below this suggestive image in the first edition, feminizes the image of the mountain and pushes further the tantalizing image, "Whereas the Jungfrau is not much short of 14,000 feet high and therefore **that lowest verge of snow—on her side, which seems nearly down to valley level**" (346). Twain's tailored explication works as a cunning connective between his picture and the text.[73]

A coalition of factors may have precipitated Twain's final wording of his prose and the redesign of his drawing. When laboring over his Jungfrau notes to complete manuscript, he undoubtedly called back the bewitching view of the pure white Jungfrau jutting between the two closer peaks, a view he had seen from his Interlaken hotel windows. These memories doubtless provided the impetus for his playful reconfiguration of both his text and picture.

Titillation aside, the reshaping of the narrative demonstrates Twain's skill in reworking a small journal notation, developing it into a full-blown, detailed, and engaging anecdote. Furthermore, Twain's "gendered" Jungfrau would probably remain a total enigma to a reader—especially one who knew no German and had never seen the Jungfrau—unless Twain's reworked drawing was included. It is the coupling of the visual and the verbal that allows the reader to fully grasp Twain's evocative idea, though he must be attentive and turn back to reread the text in order to recognize the full impact of the picture. The combination operates as of one of Twain's subtle revelations, a tempting gift for the alert audience.

Meanwhile, Twain's overseas control of the illustration process began to generate problems. In June letters were still circulating between author and editor about the size of prints and what engraving processes to use for best results. Twain wrote, "Perhaps you'd as well not have any of the pictures processed till you get them all, Frank. Then you could better determine which of them to make large and which to make small." Four days later he wrote, "Please 'process' that waiter with the bottle, and a few other of the pictures and send proofs for Brown to judge by. I suppose he wants to know what *sort* of a process it is, so he can draw to its best capacities. He brought some pictures last night which please me exceedingly."[74] Obviously, now most of the engraving process was being done in Hartford, though Twain was still solidly in Brown's camp when it came to major illustrations.

By late September Twain had moved on and was spending his days in Italy visiting the Palace of the Doges in Venice. While in the palace further confrontation with the "Old Masters" was unavoidable. He filled his journal with sketches and scribbled extensive notes on the Italian fine arts as reminders when later writing his manuscript. With this, his second sojourn in this canaled city, he tempered some of his earlier prejudices, prejudices such as preferring reproductions over originals that he had previously expressed so cynically in *The Innocents*. He now confessed that he was even "finding some pleasure" (561) in a few of the Masters' paintings though his rantings about the Old Masters continued. He tagged his favorite artist as Tiepolo, though he would refrain from writing about any particular Tiepolo painting in his book.

Twain's notebooks for this part of the European junket contained copious fresh material and his notes and rough sketches would serve him well as quick practical cues for anecdotes that he could call up later when writing in Paris. He had learned his lesson about careless note-taking. Embarrassed when working on manuscript for *The Innocents Abroad*, he had had to write to several *Quaker City* companions, principally Emeline Beach and Mrs. Fairbanks, to beg their help in rekindling his art experiences from the Holy Land trip.

For this journey, Twain's Italian notebook drawings captured many images, the architectural contours of the Pantheon, the Colosseum, and St. Marks (Figs. 83, 84 & 85), though these three shapes were never included in the published pages of *A Tramp Abroad*. Who made the final editorial decisions on which of the Twain drawings would be transferred into his author-illustrated book remains a mystery.[75]

While touring the Doge's Palace, Twain happened upon the Tintoretto [1518-1594] painting "Paradise," a "three acre" oil on the East Wall of the Hall of the Great Council (Fig. 86). He jotted down notes about the 10,000 people depicted in the work, concentrating most of his remarks on St. Mark's lion, "with *his* book (he always has

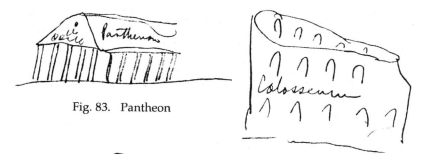

Fig. 83.   Pantheon

Fig. 84.   Colloseum

Fig. 85.   St. Mark's

a book—you never see him in stone or paint without it)."[76] In the letterpress Twain writes "The Lion of St. Mark is there with his book; St. Mark is there with his pen uplifted" (562). Twain's drawing, however, features a simple stick figure perched atop a slanting pedestal unidentifiable as a

Fig. 86.
The Great Council Hall in the Doge's Palace
from an 18th Century engraving by Brustolon and Canaletto.

lion, possibly seen as a whiskered cat. The few alterations were made from his journal sketch, some erased irregular lines, a more rounded body and less hooked tail, and a bold M. T. penned in the pedestal base. The caption, LION of ST. MARK, has an added THE when placed below the drawing in the first edition, identifying the subject (Figs. 87 & 88). Twain's accompanying sketch neglected to include the lion's book, the saint or an uplifted pen. Nevertheless, the British publishers found the sketch amusing and used Twain's skinny cat as one of the designs for the cover of the first English edition.

LION of St. MARK.

Fig. 87.
Lion of St. Mark

Fig. 88.
The Lion of St. Mark

One of Twain's Venetian fine-art commentaries was organized around a lengthy conversation with a visiting American artist.[77] In the dialogue Twain questions the figurative technique of the Master Paul Veronese [Paolo Cagliari] (1529-1588), criticizing the artist's rendering of anatomy in his giant detailed painting of "Pope Alexander III and the Doge Sebastiano Ziani meeting at the Monastero della Carita" (Fig. 89).[78] Twain's journal noted that Veronese's fisherman in a green dress had a "*port* leg, attached to the starboard side of his body"—in the final text he exchanged the seaman vernacular for standard terms to give the fellow "a right leg on the left side of his body" (559). The sub-caption, "An Old Man on his Muscle," described both the chap's knock-kneed anatomy and his pride in his musculature (Fig. 90).

Twain's next observations were about Veronese's peculiarly shaped animals. In his journal he ranted, "What *is* it people see in the old masters? . . . worst Paul Veronese dogs," while in manuscript he declared that the dogs "do not resemble dogs" while the horses "look like bladders on legs." The scripted sub-captions for the accompanying sketches of the two animals reads: "This is a cross-hatched Dog?" and "This is a Horse?" It would take a dedicated viewer to find either Twain's fisherman, his horse, or dog in Veronese's cluttered painting. One of the Hartford illustrators supplied the three figures purportedly in the Veronese work; Twain may have supplied the hand-written sub-captions and caption, "Sketches after the Old Masters" (Fig. 91).[79]

Still engaged in conversation about Veronese with the young American visitor, Twain next attacked the artist's faulty perspective in a large canvas, "where the Emperor (Barbarossa?) is pros-

Fig. 89.
"Pope Alexander III and the Doge Sebastiano Ziani meeting at the Monastero della Carita Doges, Paul Veronese"

trate before the Pope" (559). This picture, *Le Doge presente au Pape le*

Figs. 90 & 91.
An Old Man On His Muscle
&
Specimens from Old Masters

Fig. 92.
*Le Doge presente au Pape le prisonnier Othon*

*prisonnier Othon* (Fig. 92) is not by Veronese but was painted by Andre Micheli (also Vicentino), a Venetian artist working at about the same time as Veronese. Twain is right about the painter's flawed perspective when he states: "there are three men in the foreground who are over thirty feet high, if one may judge by the size of a kneeling little boy in the center of the foreground" (559). His assessment if not for the artist, at least for this work, was right on the mark.

Still wandering the halls of the Doge's Palace, Twain paused in the Chamber of the Council of Ten to gaze at a "40-foot" oil depicting "Pope Alexander III and the Doge Ziani, the Conqueror of Emperor Frederick Barbarossa."[80] Twain writes an extended, truly comical analysis of this picture painted, according to Twain's text, by Francesco Bassano (1549-15?). In his notes he attributed the work to Tintoretto with a "?" following the artist's name, then went on for pages praising the picture's "composition." In the end he focused primarily on a minuscule portion of the massive work, the "Hair Trunk," an insignificant detail at the extreme right corner of the painting (Fig. 93). These words from Twain's lengthy journal entry were the inspiration for his extended "trunk" burlesque:

But that hair trunk—
<Yes,> Now THERE! That hair trunk is the finest
thing in Italy.  *I*  think it   far better than
<Raphael's> Titian's Assumption that is so
bragged about.
   (*Note*—Compare all art with that hair trunk.)[81]

Fig. 93.
"Pope Alexander III and the Doge Ziani, the
Conqueror of
Emperor Frederick Barbarossa"

The hair trunk's
description in the jour-
nal jottings are trans-
ferred into pages in his
text in the first edition
where he compares the
arched top of this
antique piece of lug-
gage to Roman archi-
tecture and the nail
heads to those used
during the Renaissance.
He particularly empha-
sizes that the "hair" on
the trunk is "*real* hair."
His exposition explains
how Bassano cleverly
diverted a viewer's
attention from the sup-
posed central image—
the Pope and a bonnet-
less Doge—to the Hair
Trunk which is the
"supreme feature of the
picture" (564). This extravagant appreciation, of course, carries on
Twain's "sub plot," his mockery of the inflated style and reputation
of the Old Masters' and the pretentiousness of the art critics. His critique would have fallen flat, however, if the words had not been
coupled with an inserted cut of a rather battered steamer trunk—the
top of which is not a perfect half circle, the "cold-toned" leather not
well defined. With a caption of THE WORLD'S MASTERPIECE, the
combination of picture and prose allow Twain's satire to sting the
Old Masters, while taking an additional swipe at pompous reviewers (Fig. 94). Well along in his narrative, Twain's subplot is still an

Fig. 94.  The World's Masterpiece

essential part of his book's make-up.

Twain persists in his admiration of this pseudo-magnificent "Hair Trunk" into the final pages of his book. In the first paragraph of the last chapter, Twain spins out a vitriolic commentary on the "indecent license" given the visual arts, leveling his harshest words at Titian's painting of the "Venus," declaring it to be the "foulest, the vilest, the obscenest picture the world possesses" (578).[82]  He castigates Titian's corrupt "Venus of Urbino" (Fig. 95), pointing out the "attitude of her arms and hand"—delicately avoiding the exact position of her hand which rests on her pubic hair.

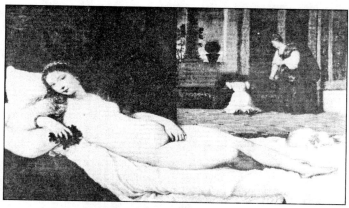

Fig. 95.  "Venus of Urbino," Titian

On the following page, however, he extols another Titian painting, the "Moses," as the having "no equal among the Old Masters," which he then semi-seriously equates with the "divine Hair Trunk of Bassano" (579). It is not difficult to assess Twain's true opinion on these matters. Obviously, "impure" nudity is corrupting and should be avoided. Yet Titian also can be rendered the greatest of all artists if he paints canvases that are uplifting. It will become apparent that Twain's objection is more that authors are restrained

Fig. 96.
Titian's Moses

while artists are given *carte blanche.*

Twain had himself created a "Moses" illustration by adding a crying, comic-strip baby to an allegedly famous painting by Titian, which became a second frontispiece (Fig. 96). If readers were confused on seeing a baby Moses as one of the earliest images in the book they would become aware of the significance of the infant's picture when they reached the final pages of Twain's narrative where he glorifies Titian's immortal "Moses":

Fig. 97.
Moses in the Ark of
Bulrushes

Titian's Venus defiles and disgraces the Tribune,
there is no softening that fact, but his 'Moses' glorifies it. . . . After wearying oneself with the acres
of stuffy, sappy, expressionless babies that popu-
late the canvases of the Old Masters in Italy, it is
refreshing to stand before this peerless child and
feel that thrill which tells you you are at last in the
presence of the real thing. This is a human child,
this is genuine. You have seen him a thousand
times—you have seen him just as he is here—and
you confess, without reserve, that Titian *was* a
Master. The doll-faces of other painted babes
may mean one thing, they may mean another, but
with the 'Moses' the case is different. The most
famous of all the art critics has said, 'There is no
room for doubt, here—plainly this child is in
trouble.'

I consider that the 'Moses' has no equal
among the works of the Old Masters, except it be
the divine Hair Trunk of Bassano. I feel sure that
if all the other Old Masters were lost and only
these two preserved, the world would be the
gainer by it.

My sole purpose in going to Florence was to
see this immortal 'Moses,' and by good fortune I
was just in time, for they were already preparing
to remove it to a more private and better protect-
ed place because a fashion of robbing the great
galleries was prevailing in Europe at the time.

I got a capable artist to copy the picture; Pannemaker, the engraver of Doré's books, engraved
it for me, and I have the pleasure of laying it
before the reader in this volume.*      (579-580)

Twain's asterisk direction to "See Frontispiece" allows his
description of Titian's "Moses"—a picture which was apparently
familiar in the Sunday-School books of the time—to alert the reader to the Moses counterfeit.

This second frontispiece had several functions. The picture
combining a fine-arts master and a comic-book paste up made a the-
matic statement in pictorial form about the contents of the book.
First a reader sees the picture, then on the first page of the book he
learns that Twain's purpose in making the journey to Europe was to
study art. The "Moses" engraving sets the tone for the rest of the

book, warning us that this will not be a scholarly treatise on the fine arts. If the reader "reads" the engraving correctly his reaction will be to smile at Twain's idea of "art." Twain's admonition to his readers is not to be too gullible and his warning against believing everything you see or read continues from this frontispiece to the final chapter.

In this final chapter we learn another reason for Twain's lengthy "art" talk. With an asterisk directing the reader to "*See Frontispiece," Twain declares he has "the pleasure of laying it [Titian's 'Moses'] before the reader in this volume." On an earlier page he had commented that: "The world says that no worded description of a moving spectacle is a hundredth part as moving as the same spectacle seen with one's own eyes" (578), confirming that Twain understood the power of "seeing," therefore, he would lay the painting before his audience. When the reader goes back to the frontispiece, however, he finds the tables are again turned. Rather than a reverent Biblical image, he is faced with Twain's comic paste-up. Twain has neatly tied up his package. First he uses the Old Master Titian's "impure" painting to argue the unfair limitations of censorship in literature; next he describes a "pure" Old Master painting to set a respectful tone, lastly he has his reader turn back to his paste-up "Moses" and his book has come full circle with a culmination of his sub-plot, the ridiculous worship of European art and the Old Masters.

In a letter to Frank Bliss in Hartford Twain explained the genesis of the picture: "It is a thing which I *manufactured* by pasting a popular comic picture into the middle of a celebrated Biblical one—shall attribute it to Titian. It needs to be engraved by a master."[83]

As it happens, this famous "Moses" which Twain would attribute to Titian was not by Titian but originally painted by Paul (properly, Hippolyte) Delaroche, 1797-1856, and engraved by Edmund Evans. It was titled MOSES IN THE ARK OF BULRUSHES (Fig. 97).[84]

Twain's frontispiece proved to be rather costly. When the author proposed to Frank Bliss that the print needed "to be engraved by a master," he suggested an expensive Parisian engraver named Pannemaker. And indeed, Pannemaker did engrave Twain's "Moses" frontispiece, his signature visible on the right-hand corner.[85]

As in so many of Twain's books, illustrations and/or their captions have become valuable bibliographical tools. It holds true again in this case. The caption, below the frontispiece of the contrived MOSES, exists as one way of verifying a first state, first edition of *A Tramp Abroad*. In the first-state, first-edition the book's frontispiece has the legend MOSES; in later states the caption was changed to TITIAN'S MOSES.[86] Presumably the editors at Hartford made the correction after reading Twain's comments about "Titian's glorious Moses" in his text. In all states the picture is recorded in the "List of Illustrations" as TITIAN'S MOSES.

About the same time Twain was producing his comic picture, he also suggested to Bliss that they try a new engraving procedure. Books during this time period were printed from electrotype plates, a process first used about 1840 to duplicate type for printing. Electrotyping involves several steps: making a mold of wax or lead, pressing the original type or design into the molding material, placing the mold in a bath of copper-sulphate dissolved in water and sulfuric acid, and passing an electric current through the solution to deposit the copper portion of the solution on the mold, thus forming a shell reproducing the type. When the disposition is complete, the mold is removed, backed with an alloy of lead, tin and antimony to strengthen it, and then readied for mounting on metal or wood. Two of the preparations for mounting are beveling of the edges of the plate and routing the "blanks," the negative areas of the plate including the margins and the areas around the illustrations. Routing was done to cut away the non-printing areas of the plate to prevent accidental inking; this was necessary since the distance between the printing surface and the non-printing body of the plate was a smaller distance than in the original type. Routing was not infrequently more a workman's job than a craftsman's job; therefore, minor damage did occur, particularly to the edges of the illustrations.[87]

At this time Twain was greatly interested in a new a "chalk plate" process called Kaolatype which he felt would "revolutionize the world of illustration."[88] Kaolatype involved coating a steel plate with a layer of "kaolin" (china clay), not wax, in which an image was cut to the metal surface. Molten metal pouring into the resulting matrix created a die for printing. At this early date Twain was trying to convince Bliss of the merits of Kaolatype, which was still in an experimental stage:

> Dan Slote [Twain's sometime cabin-mate on the *Quaker City*] has the best process in the world, but I suppose we can't use that, because in his process the pictures are not transferred, but drawn on a hard mud surface. It looks like excellent wood engraving whereas *all* these other processes are miserably weak and shammy. . . . I shall have one full page made here by a fine wood-engraver [probably Pannemaker] if he will cut it for anything under $100,—otherwise will send it over and let Dan Slote's artist try his hand on it.[89]

In the end the Kaolatype process was not used on the Moses or any of the other illustration. By 1880 Twain would buy the chalk patent, invest heavily in the invention—eventually losing about $50,000—and spend more than a year trying to develop the process.

Twain made two other tries at using the chalk process: in 1882 for *Life on the Mississippi* and again in 1883 for *The Prince and the Pauper*. Each time, however, the procedure was rejected by both the editors and the illustrators.

The famous French engraver, Pannemaker, worked on two more W. F. Brown prints drawn for Twain's book. Brown had asked Twain if he could have one full-pager, MOUTH OF THE CAVERN (Fig. 98), and another cut engraved in Paris. Pannemaker was contacted and subsequently engraved all three prints: Twain's MOSES, MOUTH OF THE CAVERN, and GENERATIONS OF BARE FEET (Fig. 99). For the illustration of "bare feet," Brown had inadvertently added shoes to the children; Twain was compelled, therefore, to add an asterisked note at the bottom of the page to explain this contradiction to his readers: "I certainly thought them barefooted, but evidently the artist has had doubts" (113).

According to Brown's ledger, the CAVERN by Pannemaker cost $44; three engravings would run approximately

Fig. 98.
Mouth of the Cavern

Fig. 99. Generations of Bare Feet

$132. The Pannemaker engravings did display superb workman-
ship and these two Brown drawings constituted some of his best
work for *A Tramp Abroad*. The cost of having Pannemaker work on
more engravings, however, would prove prohibitive.

Through the spring-summer of 1879, Frank Bliss continued
to be upset about Twain's overseas take-over of the design process.
With his author and the illustrator making important and expensive
decisions thousands of miles from the Hartford office, Frank brood-
ed he was becoming a mere bookkeeper. Moreover, he was also
worried that his Board of Directors get wind of the substantial sums
of money he kept funneling to Twain to pay for the costly illustrations. In May, Twain gave Frank his opinion on the Board's med-
dling in his business affairs:

> I received a rather impertinent letter from Mr.
> Drake [a Director of the American Publishing
> Company] a week ago, mentioning reports and
> inquiring somewhat particularly into my
> affairs,—on behalf of the Company, I suppose,—
> but I suppose he can wait for an answer as long
> as I have waited for one to the letter I wrote the
> Company on the same subject 3 years ago.

In the same rather lengthy letter, Twain included estimates for the cost of overseas processing, how various over-sized prints would increase the bulk of the subscription book, and the benefits of both additional pages and the "costs" of using his own "mighty poor" pictures:

> I remember your father telling me the artist's and engraver's work for The Innocents Abroad cost $7000. Of course we can knock down a deal of that expense, now, by using the new photo-processes.
>
> If you will send me *Eleven hundred dollars, gold,* to Paris, you shall receive, in return for it,
>
> 10 full-page plates  @  $18 . . . . . . .$180.00
> 25 half-page do       @    9 . . . . . . .225.00
> 75 quarter-page do @    4.50  . . . . .337.50
> <u>100</u> sixth-page do   @    3 . . . . . . .<u>300.00</u>
> 210 drawings           Totals . . . .$1,042.50
>
> I say $1100 instead of $1042 to cover little possible mistakes in over-sizing the plates.  I would suggest that another $50 be added to make reasonably sure of covering such mistakes.
>
> Our government will charge 25 per cent duty on the cost of the *plates,* nothing on the artist's work. (I have been consulting the law at the consulate.)  This will add $125 or $150 to the total cost (I don't know  what the freight will be on a box of plates,)—and the total cost of the 210 pictures will then be, say, $1325 or $1350, *artist's work included.*
>
> These pictures will cover a space of—
>
> 10 full-page-----------10 pages
> 25 1/2   "  ------12 1/2   "
> 75 1/4   "  ------------19   "
> 100 1/6 "  ------------17   "
>
> That is a *general* idea of the size of the pictures.  I may use only 6 or 7 full-page pictures, and split up the other 3 or 4 into smaller ones; I may use some 1/3-page ones, and fewer 1/4-page.  And so on—but the amount of space covered by pictures will remain the same and cost the same.
>
> *In addition* I propose to give several pages of space to *my own* pictures, but these will only increase the above picture-bill at the rate of $9 a

page for processing the same (and duties)—I
think I won't charge anything for artist's work,
although I've had a good deal of trouble with
these things and thrown a world of mighty poor
talent into them. . . .

If all this work is done here, the plates will be
finished by the time I finish my last chapter, and
the MS and the plates will cross the ocean in the
same ship.   But if the pictures are made in
America that will cause a delay, and the artist will
have to over-hurry his work besides.

I enclose proofs of plates, made for this book
by the processes, so that you can judge of their
merit and of Brown's drawing.[90]

Frank countered with a cost estimate of his own: "I think the
production of the plate can be done better here and at less price. It
can be done here for about 5 to 6 dollars for a full page," a saving of
over ten dollars.[91]

A month later Twain had tired of his role as editor/ supervisor and admitted to Frank Bliss: "Glad the plates are not to be
made here. . . . I have paid for the 2 or 3 plates made here—$14.60
and shall not have any more made.  I shall leave several pages for
your artist over there to fill up with after-thoughts as you suggest."[92]  By the end of July Brown's work on *A Tramp Abroad* had,
according to Twain's own records, cost $1063, and there was still a
good deal of illustration to be completed.  No figures for payments
to Brown exist beyond July 1879.  The debates between Frank Bliss
and Twain about artists and engraving processes were winding
down.

Early in the chaos of costs estimates and compromises,
however, Twain became embroiled in another scheme to have the
son of a long-time friend become one of the American Publishing
Company's illustrators. Twain, still rankling over the quality of
illustration in the subscription publishing industry, explained to his
friend Mrs. Fairbanks that it would be impossible for her son
Charles to be one of the illustrators for the travel book. He relayed
instructions to Mrs. Fairbanks as to how Charlie should submit his
work for an article, "The Great French Duel":

I wish Charlie could appear as one of the illustrators of my book; but he would be in New York &

the MS could not be there. PRIVATE: The illustrating will be done by some exceedingly cheap
artists, I suppose, who will roost in Hartford
where they can have access to the MS. But there
is that article you speak of—'The Recent French
Duel'—why shouldn't Charley illustrate that in
competition with Bliss's artist, & send the pictures to E. Bliss, Jr., American Pub. Co., 284
Asylum St., Hartford? I think Bliss would have
wit enough to use Charlie's pictures if they were
better than the other artist's.[93]

Twain had written a burlesque about a duel between two
French politicians, Leon Gambetta and Marie Francois Foutou entitled "The Recent French Duel" which was published in the
February 1879 *Atlantic Monthly*. Twain included a rewritten version
of this same encounter in *A Tramp Abroad*, though all illustrations
would eventually be drawn by Brown, not Charles Fairbanks.

In the *Tramp* rewrite, Twain placed himself in the role of
Gambetta's second. An illustration for the chapter reveals a top-hat-
ted, toy Twain in THE POST OF DANGER, "propped against M.
Gambetta's back" only to be "crushed under a mountain of flesh." In
the incident, the two duelists remained unscathed, while Twain
was "the only man who had been hurt" (82) (Fig. 100).

Twain believed in
Charley's artistic talents; he had
recommended him to Thomas
Nast and on this endorsement
the young man had spent a
brief apprenticeship with the
famous cartoonist. But far
away in Europe, touring, writing, collecting and drawing
illustrations, Twain apparently
forgot his proposal to Charlie's
mother until word of the propo-
sition reached Hartford and the
shards settled on Twain in
Paris.

Fig. 100. The Post of Danger

> By George, now I know what stirred up that hor-
> net's nest in Hartford!   It was Charley's pic-
> tures.—Privately (it must not be mentioned to
> anybody—not even to Charley or his father) I'm
> in the midst of a quarrel with the American
> Publishing Company, & Charley's sending those
> pictures there was an awful mistake.   It never
> occurred to me to remark that they should be sent
> here—to me drawn on paper, not on wood.  That
> was an important omission on my part.
> Confound it, I do get into more trouble than any
> ass that ever lived.[94]

Despite all of Charlie's trouble, making woodcuts for illustrations and submitting them directly to Hartford, he was never
hired as an American Publishing Company illustrator nor would he
ever illustrate Mark Twain's writings.

Frank Bliss could avoid commissioning Charlie since he
controlled the hiring of artists in the States.   But Charlie's sub-
missions were the last straw for Frank.   He hired several professional artists to do the massive amounts of needed illustration. He
also demanded that Twain allow these artists' drawings to be
processed in the States, thereby reducing somewhat the impact of
Brown's incompetent workmanship on the book.

Bliss first recruited True Williams, the ever-present, in-
house artist, who had worked on Twain's books since *Innocents
Abroad*. A. B. Paine, writing about the first edition, had kind words
for Williams's work while also applauding Twain's author-illustrator role.  He had harsh words, however, for Brown's designs and for
the careless workmanship in the engraving process:

> [The book's] pictures—drawn, for the most part,
> by a young art student named Brown, whom
> Clemens had met in Paris—were extra-ordinarily
> bad, while the crude engraving process by which
> they had been reproduced, tended to bring them
> still further into disrepute.  A few drawings by
> True Williams were better, and those drawn by
> Clemens himself had a value of their own.  The
> book would have profited had there been more of
> what the author calls his "works of art."[95]

The title page, with the title, author, and publishing information—with an unusual mention of Chatto & Windus, London—was relegated to a separate page after the two frontispieces and identified (if we include Twain himself) just four of the book's illustrators:

ILLUSTRATED BY W. FR. BROWN, TRUE WILLIAMS, B. DAY AND
OTHER ARTISTS—WITH ALSO THREE OR FOUR PICTURES MADE BY
THE AUTHOR OF THIS BOOK, WITHOUT OUTSIDE HELP;
IN ALL
THREE HUNDRED AND TWENTY-EIGHT ILLUSTRATIONS

True Williams supplied the majority of the Hartford produced drawings: "Thirty-six bear the name or initial of Williams," who had up-dated his logo from that used in previous Twain books; a vertical overlaid TW changed to a scripted "Williams" or "Wms." With the publication of *A Tramp Abroad*, Truman Williams (1839-1897) would provide drawings for his last Mark Twain book. In the early eighties he almost disappeared from the publishing records. Without formal academic credentials and training, he would not appear in any standard biographical reference for artists, illustrators, or engravers. He remained a shadowy figure, remembered chiefly by anecdotes about his alcoholism. Little information regarding Williams has been available to scholars until Barbara Schmidt, searching through data base files of old newspapers, was able to compile a more favorable picture of one of Twain's most influential artists.

Throughout the 1870s, Williams illustrated not only Twain books but also many works by Stephen Powers, Joaquin Miller, E. R. Miller, Matthew Hale Smith, A. D. Richardson, and Thomas Knox. His drawings for the Richardson and Knox books may account for many "borrowed" illustrations seen in the first edition of Twain's *Roughing It*.

In 1876, the same year that Williams illustrated *Tom Sawyer*, he also worked on Brete Harte's *Gabriel Conway* and Dan DeQuille's *The Big Bonanza*, writers intimately connected with Twain's western years. In 1879, Williams illustrated *The Life of the Honorable William F. Cody* for Frank Bliss's soon-to-perish publishing company. The illustrations Williams drew for the Cody book may account for the prints found duplicated in *Roughing It* and *The Adventures of Tom Sawyer*.

There are several ironies in Williams' career. After his work on *A Tramp Abroad*, the death of Elisha Bliss, and the subsequent shake-up at the American Publishing Company in 1880, Williams began working for A. D. Worthington, another Hartford publisher. Given his oft-mentioned fondness for alcohol, he would nonetheless illustrate *Platform Echoes* (1886), a reader written by the temperance orator John D. Gough. At or around 1885, Williams married and moved to Chicago, where shortly thereafter, his wife and infant son died in childbirth.

Through the 1880s until 1891, Williams was a staff artist for the Belford-Clarke Publishing Company, the firm that had pirated many of Twain's books to be sold in the Canadian market. At Belford-Clarke, Williams illustrated titles from among others, George W. Peck's "Bad Boy" series. In 1890, Belford published Williams' illustrated Frank Fairweather's *Fortunes*, a runaway boy's story of circus life and travel on the high seas and in South America. In the same year Williams released an illustrated volume of verse by his favorite authors titled *Under Open Sky*.

Belford-Clarke was destroyed by a disastrous fire in 1891 and Williams moved over to Rand McNally and Company. The 1892 edition of Glazier's *Headwaters of the Mississippi*, published by McNally, demonstrates how skillfully Williams made the transition from pen-and-ink line drawings to watercolor-like wash drawings, an illustration technique made possible for the first time by the invention of photomechanical reproduction. This radical change had swiftly made dinosaurs of many other illustrators and engravers. At the time of his death in 1897, Williams was in the process of illustrating several volumes of John L. Stoddard's educational lectures.

Williams' participation in all of Twain's subscription books through *A Tramp Abroad* positions him as Twain's most meaningful illustrator. In addition to forging some of the first images of Huckleberry Finn, Tom Sawyer, and an innumerable assortment of Twain's most popular characters, Williams continued in the creation of Twain's image as he drew the many caricatures of the author that appear in *A Tramp Aboard* (one of the first pictures seen in the book is Williams caricature of Twain as he writes his "Memories" of the European trip) (Fig. 101). His scribbly engravings greatly added to the puckishly satirical tone of all of Twain's subscription books and were a major component in the development of Twain's popular

Fig. 101.   The Author's Memories

persona.  Ultimately Williams' participatory role in many of the books upon which Twain reputation was established attests to the illustrator's lasting influence on Twain's career as a writer and personality.[96]

Paine's estimation of both True Williams and Walter Brown's work in his review was clearly on target.  Williams' work was professional, while Brown's cartoon-like characters were often amateurish with most of the small outline-drawings devoid of detail.  Only a few illustrations—the Pannemaker prints of MOUTH OF THE CAVERN and GENERATIONS OF BARE FEET—are worthy of mention.  Brown's artistry pales in comparison to the technical skills of the workhorse Williams.

Fig. 102.   A River Bath

Stamped into *A Tramp Abroad*'s black cloth cover—a few were bound in brown or 3/4 morocco—was a variation of a Brown tail piece, A RIVER BATH. The artist, probably not Brown, deleted the river-drenched threesome accompanying Twain (Twichell one of the group), and embellished Twain's climbing costume with a patch to his pants, a feather to his slouch hat, and an interesting curlicued ribbon to form the "A" of the gold embossed title on the top of Twain's umbrella. The book's spine featured a similarly costumed, cigar-smoking Twain with his fancy umbrella unfurled and, at the bottom edge, a gold shield with the American Publishing Company logo (Figs. 102, 103 & 104). The back cover carried no illustration but was embossed and stamped with the logo "APC" of the Hartford company.

A secondary but very significant artist listed on the title page was Benjamin Henry Day (1838-1916). Day contributed at least twenty-two signed illustrations for the *Tramp*. The son of a well-known journalist of the same name, Day had learned his trade as an apprentice in his father's publishing house and made his mark as a staff artist for *Vanity Fair*. Day's cuts for *A Tramp Abroad* are representative of his *Vanity Fair* style: delicate, fashionable, detailed, and full of appealing charm.[97] Unfortunately, *A Tramp Abroad* would be the only Twain book this artist would be commissioned to help illustrate.

Three of the "Other Artists" listed on the title page were either hired by Frank Bliss or he appropriated their prints from other sources. Alfred R. Waud (1828-1891) was an Englishman who had traveled with the Union Army during the Civil War as an artist for *Harper's Weekly*. He was blue-eyed, bearded, and a remarkable

Fig. 103.  Cover and Spine, *A Tramp Abroad*

quick-sketch artist.  After the war he traveled to New Orleans and made many memorable sketches of the Crescent City in the trou-

Fig. 104.  Various Bindings for *A Tramp Abroad*

blesome days of the Reconstruction.  By 1871 Waud was still in the South and had teamed with a journalist, Ralph Keeler, to produce a series entitled "On The Mississippi" for a Boston journal called *Every Saturday*.  In 1872 he did an impressive job on prints for *Beyond the Mississippi* and Bryant's *Picturesque America*.  His reputation was built on his "reportorial style but [he was] capable of doing work of real merit."[98]  Waud's initialed signature appears on two full-page prints, DEATH OF A COUNTESS (Fig. 105), and BATHERS AT LEUKE (Fig. 106), though he undoubtedly completed many more of the unsigned illustrations.[99]

William Wallace Denslow (1856-1915) contributed six illustrations to Chapter XLVII, three of them signed W. W. D.  One half-page print, captioned HAVING HER FULL RIGHTS, depicts

Fig. 105. Death of a Countess

both a mustached Twain and a bespectacled Twichell (Fig. 107). Denslow would later come into his own with his work for L. Frank Baum, first illustrating *Father Goose* in the late nineties and later creating the characters for *The Wizard of Oz*.[100]

One print appearing in the chapter on mountain climbing, and a few pages before the Twain-Whymper "doctored donkey," was "borrowed" from the pages of *Harper's Weekly*. The original, captioned A GOOD LOOK-OUT, was from a series titled ALPINE TOURISTS and had been drawn by Louis Braun— his initials lettered into

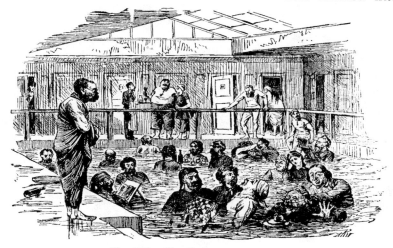

Fig. 106. The Bathers at Leuke

Fig. 107.　Having Her Full Rights

the rock formation at the bottom right of the print. This Braun original—reduced and recaptioned SUMMIT OF THE GORNER GRAT and still bearing Braun's initials—somehow found its way into this late chapter of Twain's book. Unfortunately, the illustration contradicts the text; Twain having described his mountain climbers as wearing formal attire while in the Braun work there is not a top-hat or tailcoat visible. This smouched Braun drawing, covering a full-page with a blank verso in *A Tramp Abroad*, was probably appropriated by Frank Bliss in Hartford as a last-minute addition (Figs. 108 & 109).

Fig. 108.
"A Good Look Out"

Fig. 109.
Summit of the Gorner Grat

Another Bliss appropriation comes from the American Publishing Company's personal stock of electros. ASCENDING MT. BLANC had appeared in Junius Henry Browne's *Sights and Sensation in Europe* which had been published by American in 1872 (Fig. 110).

Fig. 110.   Ascending Mt. Blanc

There are several unusual markings on a number of other prints unidentifiable at this time: two signed C. H. J. B.; one signed Morison; one with the marking Alex de Bar; one captioned "self portrait," though the person portrayed is unknown;[101] one signed P. Sheldon; and one S. R. (perhaps Roswell Shurtleff, who had illustrated scenes for both *Innocents Abroad* and *Roughing It*). There are also two legible engraving-company markings: Photo Eng. Co., and O. F. and Co. Since neither of these

Fig. 111.   European Carving

engraving companies is known to have been used by Bliss, these cuts can also be presumed to be "borrowed" (Figs. 111-117).[102]

Fig. 112.   Tail Piece

Fig. 114.
Occasionally Met With

Fig. 113.   The Mer De Glace (Mont Blanc)

Fig. 115.
The Village of
Chamonix

Fig. 116.
The Sunrise

One tail piece signed "Beard" (Fig. 118) (195) may be the work of either J. C. Beard or his brother Thomas Francis Beard, one of the brothers having drawn an illustration for *Roughing It* many years before.[103] Because the Beard print in *Roughing It* was suspect, suspicions also arise as to how this tail piece came to appear in *A Tramp Abroad*.

Two other tail pieces were purloined from Twain's previous works: A YOUNG BEAUTY (Fig. 119) (89) from *The Adventures of Tom Sawyer* and PRETTY CREATURE! (Fig. 120) (566) from *Roughing It*. In at least five tail pieces in the Alpine chapters the characters drawn have features and styles that indicate they may have been borrowed from a mountain book of the time (Figs. 121 & 122). There are also many "stock" tail pieces which were available to all publishing houses. Some, like the picture of a knight and his lady, presented superior illustrating talent (Fig. 123). Most of the tail pieces were uncaptioned in the American edition but were captioned in the English edition. This gave the British reader an added advantage in providing linkage between print and pictures.

Frank Bliss had his team of artists draw many of the illustrations for the book while also larding the edition with unsigned, full-page "travel prints" whose sources are unidentifiable to this date. For example, VIEW IN VALLEY OF ZERMATT, a full-page print though the page is unnumbered, is listed as SCENE IN VAL-

Fig. 117.
Jersey Indians

Fig. 118.   Tail Piece

Fig. 119.
A Young
Beauty

Fig. 120.
Pretty Creature!

Fig. 121.    Tail    Fig. 122.
Pieces

Fig. 123.   Tail Piece

LEY OF ZERMATT (406) in the "List of Illustrations" (Fig. 124).

Illustration was considered such an important factor in Twain's travel books that in *Innocents, Roughing It,* and *A Tramp Abroad,* the "List of Illustrations" page precedes the "Contents" page. As usual Bliss's "List of Illustrations" did not prove flawless, though there were no major errors—a few neglected quotation marks, a few abbreviated or minor changes in captions, two tail pieces obviously added at the last minute to fill an almost empty page and not included in the "List of Illustrations"—a stock addition (283) and the

Fig. 124.   View in Valley of Zermatt

last tail piece in the book (631). Adding these two prints (Figs. 125 & 126) swells the total number of illustrations to 330 rather than the 328 listed on the title page and in the "List of Illustrations' of the first edition.[104]

Mark Twain's personal artistic contributions were not singled out, the only hint that he was the illustrator, his initials for one illustration, THE JUNGFRAU BY M. T. in the "List of Illustrations." A reader is left to ponder which are Twain's "crude and rude" drawings until he stumbles on them and see his initials in the corner. The only reference to him as illustrator is on the title page,

Fig. 125.   Tail Piece

Fig. 126.   Tail Piece

"WITH ALSO THREE OF FOUR PICTURES MADE BY THE AUTHOR OF THIS BOOK, WITHOUT OUTSIDE HELP." Twain drew fifteen illustrations, eight unsigned and seven signed, usually with a simple M. T.

Of the three hundred and thirty illustrations in *A Tramp Abroad*, over one hundred and twenty can be

Fig. 127. Mark Twain

attributed to Walter F. Brown. With the addition of prints from Bliss's Hartford illustrating team—notice most of the "other artists" cuts are in the last pages of the book—Frank Bliss was able to meet the publishing deadline.

One last minute problem, probably generated by Twain, caused a slight delay. Someone decided as the final pages were being put together to include a steel engraving of the author as a full-page insert facing the "Moses" frontispiece. The "POR-TRAIT OF THE AUTHOR [STEEL ENGRAVING]" was engraved by J. A. J. Wilcox of Boston and probably depicts

Detail of frontispiece, State A, showing vertical underlying line

Twain in his 37th year. The "original plate of the engraving showed 'spots' during the course of print-ing and it became neces-sary to re-engrave it" (Figs. 127 & 128).[105] The second processing took only a few days and Twain signed the plate with his distinctive signature. This second frontispiece meant that the "title page" was actually the fourth page in the

Fig. 128.
Detail of Frontispiece

Detail of State B showing the slanted underlying engraving

book facing the blank verso of the "Moses" print. The edition was officially launched with the original issuing date unchanged.[106]

A *Tramp Abroad* was produced in three different pressrooms making the priority of states difficult to prove. Blind-stamped borders on the covers are found with both a filigree decorated gilt rule at the top and bottom and with a substituted, saw-tooth decorated gilt rule. This travel work was also the last of his subscription books published in the familiar bulky black cloth. Customers could, however, order the book with gilt edges, in full sheep, in three-quarter leather, or in full morocco. The earliest editions were printed on heavier paper that bulk the copies 1-5/8 inches; later editions measure 1-3/8 or 1-1/2.[107]

The advertisements and the sales agents' Prospectus carried the unspotted portrait engraving of Twain, touting the picture as "a superb steel engraving of the Author, being the only one in existence."[108] Also inserted were copies of advance reviews which played up the fact that Twain had created a number of the drawings himself.

Frank Bliss had proved himself a patient and more than capable editor. One writer, after praising the illustrations for their "quaint humor," even predicted that the illustrations alone, quite apart from the text, would "secure the sale of the book."[109] Mark Twain, not quick with compliments for his editors, was pleased with the book but worried about "left-handed" newspaper notices and lagging sales figures. He wrote his sentiments to Elisha Bliss, not to Frank, as would have been more appropriate, since Frank had done all the work while Elisha lay abed recuperating:

> I like the book exceedingly well; it is handsomely gotten up, (barring the old type) and I believe it is going to take. *Roughing It* and *Gilded Age* sold nearly double as many copies, in this length of time, so I imagine the Canadians have been working us heavy harm. I am glad no newspaper has had a chance to give it a black eye with a left-handed notice.[110]

And indeed, the Canadian pirates had managed "to get advance-sheets from the several steam-press establishments"[111] and were able to issue almost as soon as the American edition was printed. Harm from the Canadians, however, was slight. A *Tramp Abroad* had 48,000 advance orders before Frank Bliss started the presses for the first printing and by September had sold 55,000 copies.[112] The agreement between Twain and the American Publishing Company to stick closely to the subscription formula in size (639 pages), illustration (330 with 34 full-pagers), and content (a humorous travel book) proved effective. With the addition of Twain's own drawings and a steel engraving of the author, all subscription market bases had been covered. *A Tramp Abroad* became the "best seller" Twain wanted and needed.

Producing the English edition, however, was anything but a straightforward task. Some of the same confusion that had surfaced with *Tom Sawyer*—the late shipment of electros and a delay in obtaining a secure copyright—fueled lengthy and unfriendly letters between Twain and Moncure Conway (his British agent) and a similar exchange of correspondence between Twain and Chatto (his English publisher). Much of the blame was on Twain's shoulders since he had early decided to supervise the production of the illustrations from Europe. Four illustrations reached Chatto from Paris allowing the British publisher to believe that the English and American illustrated edition would be synchronized. However, no more "electros" arrived. A frustrated Andrew Chatto wrote directly to Twain demanding "a complete set of the electros of the illustrations." Twain, who chaffed at being the middle man, wrote to Chatto blaming Bliss: "Bliss promised to be sure & attend to everything right along—proofs, electros & all." Twain then responded to Chatto's demand through Conway:

> Jesus Christ, how mad I am! This man is *forever* ignoring Bliss and writing *me* about electros and matters strictly within Bliss's province. . . . I tried to act so, once, in the matter of the Tom Sawyer electros, and the result was trouble and unpleasantness. . . . There is nothing for it, then, but for *me* to order Chatto's electros for him and sign a paper making myself and the estate responsible for the $450 if Chatto dies or defaults. This is simply a hell of a way to do business.[113]

Next, Twain wrote directly to Chatto:

> I have nothing to do with publishing my books; and I *won't* have anything to do with it, either

here or in England. With Mr. Conway right at
your elbow, you keep writing to *me*. When you
want electros, you write me—I have no electros,
and never have *had* any electros. Why do you not
write Bliss who *has* electros?[114]

In a letter to Twain a few weeks later Chatto was doubly
furious because, "Mr. Bliss by issuing the American edition without
giving us sufficient notice, has contrived to very seriously to emper-
il your English copyright."[115]  Bliss may have considered he had
secured some protection for the English edition's copyright by an
unusual feature added to the American edition, "Chatto & Windus,
London" printed below American Publishing Company on the title
page.

Moncure Conway, who had been hired to attend to these
details, shuffled the blame back to the American Publishing
Company, accusing Frank Bliss of a faulty chain of communication.
There was plenty of guilt to go around: the electroplates and over a
hundred pages of text were still not in Chatto's hands a full two
months after the American edition was issued. When the last of the
text pages finally reached England, "Chatto and Windus quickly
printed an unillustrated two-volume 'Library Edition.'" Later, when
electroplates with the illustrations arrived, they followed up with a
more expensive illustrated edition.[116]

The illustrated English edition was printed with a smaller
format and typeset. Therefore, the pictures did not always correspond to the related letterpress as they had in the American edition.
The plain red-cloth cover was stamped in black and gold and carried not an alpine-attired Mark Twain but images of his OLD BLUE
CHINA cat, his THE LION OF ST. MARK, the cut-out "donkey"
(without Whymper's Matterhorn background), plus a silhouette by
Brown of four wounded Alpine climbers (Fig. 129). Chatto obviously wanted to capitalize on the fact that Twain had done some of
the drawings. The spine featured a black-stamped, version of
Brown's anonymous mountain climber FITTED OUT (Fig. 130) with
"ILLUSTRATED" and the title, author's name, and publishing company's name stamped in gold.

There was no PORTRAIT OF THE AUTHOR, only a full-
page copy of Twain's comic Moses captioned TITIAN'S MOSES, as
the single frontispiece. In the Chatto edition, the "List of Illustrations" appears after the "Contents" page. Of the three hundred

Fig. 129.
Cover, *A Tramp Abroad*

and thirty prints inserted in the American edition, only three hundred and fourteen were included in the English edition. The various deletions were: CLIMBING THE MOUNTAIN, SNOW CREVASSES, A FEARFUL FALL, A TERMINAL MORAINE, FRONT OF A GLACIER, AN OLD MORAINE, GLACIER OF ZERMATT WITH LATERAL MORAINE, VILLAGE OF CHAMONIX, ONE VIEW OF THE MATTERHORN, ON THE SUMMIT, Brown's reproduction of THE CATASTROPHE ON THE MATTERHORN, AIGUILLE SU DRU AND AIGUILLE VERTE, IN THE MONT BLANC CHAIN, tail piece, and ASCENDING MT. BLANC.

Of particular interest are a few of the tail pieces, captioned in the English but usually uncaptioned in the American edition. In some instances the captions add interest to the illustration. For example, a touch of humor is created for the tail pieces captioned PERCHED ALOFT

Fig. 130.
Fitted Out

(Fig. 131), or A REST (Fig. 132); irony is found in the captioned PRETTY CREATURE (see Fig. 116)—an illustration which had also appeared in Twain's own *Roughing It*. There is no apparent reason for A YOUNG BEAU-TY (see Fig. 115), the last illustration in both *Tom Sawyer* and *A Tramp Abroad*. The tail piece is irrelevant to this added appendix in which Twain expounds on make-up of German journals, retelling the murder of a young boy and explaining that the German illustrations are "finely drawn." Twain cites a "dilapi-dated tramp" and a "commer-cial traveler," as his examples of German pictures with no men-tion of an adolescent young girl. The tail piece is uncap-tioned in the Bliss edition but

Fig. 131.   Perched Aloft

captioned in the English. Many of the full-page American prints were scaled down and inserted as half- or quarter-page cuts. For example, the full-page OLD BLUE CHINA was introduced as a small cut with Twain's "scripted" text in regular typeset.

Unfortunately, *A Tramp Abroad* would contain no strong, simple narrative line, it was not the careful-ly knit chronicle *The Innocents* had been. It often unraveled and became a meandering nar-rative that would never adhere. Despite this the book was a success in all markets: "According to the

Fig. 132.   A Rest

first annual report of sales . . . the book sold 62,000 copies" in the United States.[117] Brisk sales in both Canada and England, even with the trouble from Canadian pirates and the delay in publishing the "illustrated" British edition, healed some of the wounds between Chatto and Twain. Relations between Frank Bliss and Twain, however, were a different matter. Twain, always inclined to be suspicious about how publishers could be cheating him, investigated every entry in the company's ledger books, often hindering the production process that the competent younger Bliss had in place to assure getting the book through the press and into the hands of readers. To his credit, Bliss put up with Twain's interference and his astute business sense was vindicated in the final balance sheets. *A Tramp Abroad* generated a handsome profit of $32,000 the first year of sales.

Mark Twain owed much of his fortune and reputation as a writer to the Bliss family, father and son. Their publishing house had sold 337,902 of Twain's books between 20 July 1869 and 31 December 1879.[118] Still suspicion and ill will festered in Twain's mind. He was impatient with the policies of the American Publishing Company and longed to put an end to the business connections between himself and the firm. His desires were soon answered; after the publication of *A Tramp Abroad* everything changed. Elisha Bliss died on 28 September 1880; Twain was finally free of all Bliss family contractual restraints. It would be another fourteen years before a Mark Twain book would bear the American Publishing Company imprint on its title page.

### Notes

[1] Samuel Clemens, *A Tramp Abroad* (Hartford: American Publishing Company, 1880), Title Page. Henceforth all references will be to this edition and the page numbers will be inserted into the text.

[2] MTLP, p. 108, n. 1. Copy of the Frank Bliss contract in Documents 1878, MTP.

[3] MTLP, p. 72, n. 2.

[4] Documents, 1879, MTP.

[5] Elisha Bliss to SLC, 13 February 1878, MTP.

[6] Frank Bliss to SLC. 26 March 1879, MTP. Partially quoted in MTLP, p. 113, n. 5.

[7] SLC to Frank Bliss, 15 April 1879. MTLP, p. 112 without ampersands.

[8] MT&EB, p. 128. Since True Williams did the illustrations for Frank Bliss's "Cody" book, it is possible that Williams himself duplicated some of

his former designs from Twain's books. See Nathan M. Wood, "True Williams' Pen Drew Literary Giant of Old," Watertown [New York] *Daily Times*, August 30, 1938, p. 11.

[9] Documents 1879, Elisha Bliss, 1 November 1879, MTP. See also MTLP, p. 119, n. 1 and MT&EB, p. 143.

[10] SLC to Frank Bliss, 8 September 1879, MTLP, p. 119, n. 1. As early as 1872 Twain had suggested appointing the lawyer, Charles E. Perkins, to handle all contracts. See MTLP, p. 71.

[11] MTLP, p. 35.

[12] SLC to Joe Twichell, 23 January [1879]. See MTLP, pp. 110-111. Also in MTMF: "I am making part of the illustrations for it [*A Tramp Abroad*] myself." SLC to Mrs. Fairbanks, 6 March 1879. In 1876 Twain contributed two deliberately rough illustrations for *Tom Sawyer*: Tom's oath (95)—not strictly an illustration—and Tom's dismal caricature of a house, captioned TOM AS AN ARTIST (70).

[13] "Some Valid Reasons Why He Doesn't Write a Funny Book About England," New York *World*, 11 May 1879, p. 1, col. 2-3. Twain later also alerted Frank Bliss to his scheme, writing from Paris, "I propose to give several pages of space to *my own* pictures. . . . I think I won't charge you anything for the artist's work" MTLP, p. 115.

[14] SLC to Frank Bliss, 10 May 1879. MTLP, p. 114. Brown was born in Providence, Rhode Island and began his studies at Brown University. In one of his early efforts he drew illustrations for Charles Miller's "Roger Williams." After his Ecole des Beaux Arts years he adopted Venice, Italy as his home and specialized in paintings of the Italian landscape. He died in Venice in 1929.

[15] SLC to Frank Bliss, 10 May 1879. MTLP, pp. 114-115. George P. Bissell & Company were Hartford bankers and brokers with whom Clemens had an account. (See note 10). In 1882, Bissell sent Clemens a prospectus describing the American Bank Note Company of New York, a consolidation of all the leading Engraving Companies which would virtually make a monopoly of the business of engraving and printing for banks, railroads, insurance companies, and world governments. Perhaps Twain was considering using this company as engravers for *Huckleberry Finn* or *Life of the Mississippi*.

[16] MTLP, p. 108.

[17] *Heidelberger Zeitung*, 6 Mai 1878. Today the Schloss Hotel, shorn of its bird cages after World War I, remains perched on the hill above the town. Since 1960, the building has functioned as an International Student Center.

[18] *Album von Heidelberg*, Heidelberg: L. Meder, 20 August 1844. For information on T. Verhas, *Allgemeines Lexikon Der Bilden Kunstler* (Leipzig: Verhas Von E. A. Seeman, 1940), p. 248. For information on Bachlier, *Allgemeines Lexikon Der Bilden Kunstler*, Vol. 2 (Leipzig: Verlag von Wilhelm Englemann, 1908), 311-312.

[19] This, and many other full-page prints in the first edition, have a blank page on verso.

[20] "All the 'legends of the Neckar' which I invented for the unstoried region, are here," SLC to Twichell, 16 March 1880, Albert E. Stone, Jr., "The Twichell Papers and Mark Twain's *A Tramp Abroad*," *Yale University Press Gazette*, April 1955, p. 152. Hereafter cited as Stone, *Yale*.

[21] On a manuscript page Twain wrote: "Put in the Music on the Lorelei." MTP. See also N&J II, 125, "Furnish the music to 'Ich weiss nicht was soll es <beteud> bedeutend.'" The sheet music appears on pages 144-145 of the first edition.

[22] Original drawing with this penciled note is in the MTP, Docs. 1879, #793. Goodspeed's Book Sale Catalogue 169 documents "The pen-and-ink sketch is by Clemens on heavy cardboard and signed, 'Die Lorelei,' S. L. Clements, Artist, 1879."

[23] MTP, Docs. 1879, #793.

[24] In the English illustrated edition the tail piece has an added feature, a snake swimming in the waters below the prostrate maidens.

[25] Appendix A, titled THE PORTIER, includes an illustration by Williams captioned A TWENTY-FOUR HOUR FIGHT, p. 585; Appendix B, titled HEIDELBERG CASTLE, includes the illustration by B. Day captioned GREAT HEIDELBERG TUN; Appendix C is titled THE COLLEGE PRISON and includes not only the "Bismarck" print but also a Tail Piece with the signature Morison; Appendix D, titled THE AWFUL GERMAN LANGUAGE, includes a Brown illustration captioned A COMPLETE WORD in German which stretches over a fanciful countryside; Appendix E, titled LEGENDS OF THE CASTLES, has no illustrations; Appendix F, titled GERMAN JOURNALS, has a tail piece unsigned and unrelated to the content of the section.

[26] SLC to Frank Bliss, 13 July 1878, MTLP, p. 108 (italics mine). See also N&J II, 105, n. 118.

[27] N&J II, 107.

[28] There is a possibility that Bismarck's son Herbert did inhabit the *Karzer* on these dates—he would have been twenty-five years old. No documented proof is available. The cut of the alleged Bismarck appears on page 597 of the first edition. In an odd turn of events, an article by Maria von Krebs cites that A. C. Doyle of Sherlock Holmes fame, borrowed the Rache idea from Twain for his book *A Study in Scarlet*. "'Rache' is the German for 'Revenge.'" *Baker Street Journal*, X, n.s. (January), 12-14.

[29] N&J II. 76.

[30] Twain's visit to the dueling inn was on 17 May 1878. The picture of the dueling room in the Hirschgasse Inn dates from 1850 when Vandalia was pitted against Borussia.

[31] According to Twain's journal, the sword drawn by Twain belong to a Mr. Pfaff. N&J II, 82.

[32] In his notebook Twain wrote: "Drawing a tooth in the army—with a brigade of yellers for audience. The patient doesn't wince, then." N&J II,

136. Also, Stone, *Yale*, 155.

[33] The Brown illustrations of Harris appear on the following pages of the first edition: HARRIS ATTENDING THE OPERA, p. 99; AN UNKNOWN COSTUME, p. 104; "A DEEP AND TRANQUIL ECSTASY," p. 129; EXPERIMENTING THROUGH HARRIS, p. 167; THE RIVER BATH [Tail Piece], p. 183; HARRIS ASTONISHED, p. 255; LION OF LUCERNE, p. 259; HE LIKED CLOCKS, p. 262; THE CONSTANT SEARCHER, p. 281; A SUMMIT SUNRISE, p. 297; EXCEEDINGLY COMFORTABLE, p. 302; RATHER MIXED UP, p. 399; "WE ALL RAISED A TREMENDOUS SHOUT," p. 519. The Day illustrations of Harris appear as follows: WE MISSED THE SCENERY, p. 338; EVERYBODY HAD AN EXCUSE, p. 453; SPRUNG A LEAK, p. 455; A SCIENTIFIC QUESTION, p. 458; A WILD RIDE, p. 497; THE INDIGNANT TOURIST, p. 505; STOCK IN TRADE, p. 556. Pictures of Harris signed by W. W. Denslow appear as follows: HAVING HER FULL RIGHTS, p. 547; HOW SHE FOOLED US, p. 549; "YOU'LL TAKE THAT OR NONE," p. 552, and unsigned, A LIVELY STREET. Two other unsigned prints, NO APOLOGY and NONE ASKED are undoubtedly also by Denslow.

[34] Frank Bliss to SLC, 30 May 1879, MTP.

[35] There are three illustrations signed by Harris in the first edition: OUT START (BY HARRIS) (103), UNKNOWN KNIGHT (151), and OUR ADVANCE ON DILSBERG (172).

[36] MTHL I, 249. In an "unused" preface to *A Tramp Abroad*, Twain stated his desire to reconnect with the fine arts: "I had a couple of minor purposes, also, to acquire the German language, and to perfect myself in Art" (MTLP, p. 110, n. 1). Perhaps this preface was not used because it was more a true than an ironical statement of his intentions.

[37] In his journal Twain had written: "Tower (tall & square & old) of Ehrenberg on left bank an hour below Wimpfen—100 ft. above river in middle of steep bank. . . . An ancient roofless vine-clad ruin adjoins the tower." N&J II, 132. Twain's information on Wimpfen and its tower came from *A Handbook for Travellers in Southern Germany* (London: John Murray, 1871), p. 104.

[38] The legend is in Mark Twain's handwriting and the cut is signed MT.

[39] "Smith [American consul in Germany] took me to 3 antiquarian shops—my pet detestation—& examined 3 brass beer mugs. . . . I wouldn't have such rubbish in the house. I do hate this antiquarian rot, sham, humbug; cannot keep my temper in such a place & *never* voluntarily enter one." N&J II, 256. Twain's "tear jug" is now housed in the Mark Twain Papers with a list describing the relics he brought back from his 1867 *Quaker City* trip. See N&J II, 110, n. 126.

[40] In the English edition, p. 162, OLD BLUE CHINA is not a full-page print and Mark Twain's "scripted" text is in regular typeface.

[41] This Neckar "rafting sequence" is another of Twain's adaptions of the Dollinger tale he used in *Roughing It* which was apparently inspired by

Coldridge's "Rime of the Ancient Mariner."

[42] Twain wrote in his journal: "Slender naked girl snatched a leafy bow of a bush across her front & then stood satisfied gazing out upon us as we floated by—a very pretty picture." N&J II, 134.

[43] MTHL I, 249-250.

[44] MTHL I, 249. See also N&J II, 118, n. 11 and N&J II, 132, n. 40.

[45] Twain's 1873 edition of Baedeker relates a "prison story" about Dilsberg Castle which apparently was not interesting enough for Twain to use as his Dilsberg legend. Also during this Neckar cruise, Twain collected material for a tale of the "fabled women of Weibertreu"—incorrectly spelled as Weinberg in his journal. The source for this tale, which appears on pages 110-111 of the first edition, was John Murray's *A Handbook for Travellers in Southern Germany* (London: John Murray, 1877), p. 13. See N&J II, 74.

[46] N&J II, 102, n. 113 & 123.

[47] "The Legend of the Spectacular Ruin" appears on pp. 150-153. W. F. Brown also used Twichell as a model for other of his illustrations.

[48] N&J II, 140. The "Yale" student also appears in one of Livy's letters: "We met again the American boy that asked so many questions. . . . We hoped he would not discover us but there was no such good luck for us." 2 September 1878, MTMF. Also in N&J II, 168.

[49] MTB II, 666. See also Albert E. Stone, Jr., "The Twichell Papers and Mark Twain's *A Tramp Abroad*," *Yale University Library Gazette*, XXIX (April 1955), 152.

[50] Reference to Von Berlichingen appear on pages 107-108 with shorter mention on p. 106, pp. 110, 122 and 132 of the first edition.

[51] Frank Bliss to SLC, 30 May 1879, MTP. See also MTLP, p. 117, n. 1.

[52] SLC to Frank Bliss, 10 June 1879, MTLP, p. 117. There are several other "stipple processed" illustrations in *A Tramp Abroad* that demonstrate both Bliss's and Twain's correct evaluation of the results.

[53] Frank Bliss to SLC, 27 June 1879, MTP.

[54] N&J II, 163, n. 11. Later Twichell read to Twain from the Baedecker about, "the catastrophe on Matterhorn in '65." N&J II, 163.

[55] The Cervin was the first hotel built in Zermatt (Cervin being the French name for the Matterhorn). Coincidentally, it was constructed by Anton Clemenz (no relation to Samuel Clemens). Clemenz was also the *Conseiller d'Etat* and the official who had presided over the court investigation of the 1865 Matterhorn accident.

[56] N&J II, 164. Also see note 14 on the same page.

[57] "Note: in *Scrambles* he [Whymper] describes the jumping of a crevasse between rocks and the glacier with dramatic detail and emphasis wholly absent from the bald account in his diary." F. S. Smythe, *Edward Whymper* (London: Hodder and Stroughton Limited, 1968), p. 84. Hereafter cited as F. S. Smythe.

[58] MTMF, pp. 230-231, n. 2.

[59] The text of the incident appears in Edward Wymper's *Scrambles*

*Amongst the Alps* (London: John Murray, 1937), p. 321; in *A Tramp Abroad* on pages 478-481. Hereafter cited as *Scrambles*, 1937. While in Paris Twain was anxious to get Whymper's book and wrote to his London publisher, Chatto & Windus requesting a copy. N&J II, 164. Twain also wrote to Mrs. Fairbanks, "I mustn't get into a mournful mood, it isn't suited to the chapter I've mapped out. . . . I can't burlesque Mr. Whymper & the other fantastic Alp-climbers with a solemn underpinning to my thought—it would be a failure. MTMF, p. 230, n. 2.

60 F. S. Smythe, p. 74.

61 *Scrambles*, p. 310.

62 *Scrambles*, 1937, Preface, x-xi.

63 Louis Baume, "Notes on the 1974 Facsimile Edition," Edward Whymper, *The Valley of Zermatt and the Matterhorn* (Reading, England: Gaston's Alpine Books, 1974), p. 10. There is one suspicious print from another Whymper book, inserted into the pages of *A Tramp Abroad*, THE LAKE AND THE MOUNTAIN (MONT PILATUS), signed Whymper, which appears on page 273. Other suspicious unsigned prints include: CLIMBING THE MOUNTAIN, p. 375; SNOW CREVASSES, p. 376; A TERMINAL MORAINE, p. 461; FRONT OF GLACIER, p. 462; AIGUILLE DU DRU AND AIGUILLE VERT, IN THE MONT BLANC CHAIN, p. 495; ASCENDING MONT BLANC, p. 517. All appear in the American edition.

64 *Victorian Illustration: The Pre-Raphaelites, and the Idyllic School and the High Victorians*, Aldershot, Vermont: Scholar Press, 1996, pp. 292-294. The following are Whymper engravings of Mahoney magazine illustrations: *The Argosy*, "Autumn Tourists," August 1866, facing page 217; *The Cottager and Artisan*, "The Old Cobbler and His Pupils," p. 69, 2 September 1867; *The Leisure Hour*, "Adventures Ashore and Afloat," 6 May 1865, pp. 273-385, eight illustrations and "Finding the Body of William Rufus," facing p. 743, 24 November 1866; *London Society*, "Gossip from Egypt," pp. 481, 509, "Holiday Hearts," p. 57, "Mr. Dawbarn," facing p. 48 and on p. 51, "Sir Stephen's Question," facing p. 112; *The People's Magazine*, "The Governor's Daughter," pp. 657-801, 5 October to 28 December 1867, eleven illustrations; *The Sunday at Home*, "The Miller and His Daughter," p. 769, 3 December 1864, "The Forty Acres," pp. 1-49, 7 January to 28 January, four illustrations "Fisher Bill," pp. 65-113, 4 February to 25 February, three illustrations, "The Two Voyages," pp. 417-513, 8 July and 19 August 1865.

65 *Scrambles*, 1937, Preface, xi.

66 *Scrambles* (1871) "Author's Preface," xi.

67 MTLP, p. 115.

68 Frank Bliss to SLC, 30 May 1879, MTP.

69 Frank Bliss to SLC, 30 May 1989, MTP.

70 MT&EB, pp. 141-142.

71 SLC to Frank Bliss, 17 June 1879, MTP.

72 N&J II, 141. The Jungfrau illustration appears on this same page.

73 Many of the subsequent editions of *A Tramp Abroad* contain a

toned-down version of this drawing in Chapter XXXII. Rasmussen, *Mark Twain A to Z*, p. 266.

[74] MTLP, p. 118.

[75] Mark Twain's drawings of the Colosseum, the Pantheon, St. Marks, and Lion of St. Mark which did not make it into *A Tramp Abroad* are reproduced in N&J II, 257-258.

[76] N&J II, 200. Tintoretto's "Paradiso," painted with the help of his son Dominique, measures 72 by 23 feet and covers the end wall of the Great council Chamber in the Doge's Great Council Hall. There are several works containing images of St. Mark's lion in the palace; it is pure conjecture whether the famed lion appears in this massive painting by Tintoretto.

[77] Twain's artist friend was "William Graham, an American painter of Venetian scenes long resident in Venice and Rome." N&J II, 201, n. 78.

[78] There is a work in the Doge's palace by pupils of Paul Veronese: "Pope Alexandre III *reconnu par le doge Ziani sur la place de la Charite*." Max Ongaro, *Venise: La Palais Ducal* (Milan: Alfieri & Lacroix, 1913), p. 61.

[79] For Twain notes on Veronese see N&J II, 200, n. 75. Twain's scripted sub-caption reads "Sketches after the Old Masters" while the printed caption reads SPECIMENS FROM OLD MASTERS.

[80] A work by Francois Bassano (Fr. da Ponte) (1480-1530) titled hangs in the Doge's Palace "*Le pope remet au doge l'epee epndant qu'il est en train de s'embarquer contre Barberousse.*" It is the only work of this papal series done by Bassano/da Ponte. However, Twain may be referring to the same Micheli painting where he writes of faulty perspective. It is only speculation whether the painting contains a "hair trunk." Max Ongaro, *Venise: La Palais Ducal* (Milan: Alfieri & Lacroix, 1913), p. 61.

[81] N&J II, 202. The inserted illustration has the marking C.H.J.B. in the bottom left-hand corner. Presumably the initials of a to this date unidentifiable illustrator. Jacobo Bellini was the first painter to decorate the halls of the Great Council; and his son, Gentile later restored frescoes by Pisanello and Gentile da Fabriano. It is not know if Bassano did any of the work in the Great Council Hall.

[82] Twain's hyperbole here suggests he is protesting too much. Though Twain adopted most of society's prohibitions against sexual references in literature—probably at Olivia's urging—in *Tramp* he complained about the contrasting standards between literature and other art forms: "Art is allowed as much indecent license today as in earlier times—but the privileges of literature in this respect have been sharply curtailed within the past eighty or ninety years" (577).

[83] MTLP, pp. 116-117.

[84] *Mark Twain Journal*, Vol. 27, No. 1 (Spring 1989), back cover. The identity of this image was originally published by Hiroshi Okubo, "Supplement to 'On the Image of Moses by Mark Twain' (1) Titian's Moses in *A Tramp Broad*" (Tokyo, *Japan Bulletin of the Faculty of Liberal Arts, Hosei University*), No. 73 (February 1990), 205-215 (in Japanese).

⁸⁵ The two pictures and the derivations are featured on the back panel of the *Mark Twain Journal*, Vol. 27, Spring 1989.

⁸⁶ BAL II, p. 193. See also BMT, p. 34. The illustrated English first edition has TITIAN'S MOSES as the caption for the frontispiece and it is listed as TITIAN'S MOSES in the "List of Illustrations."

⁸⁷ *Mark Twain: A Bibliography of the Collections of the Mark Twain Memorial and the Stowe-Day Foundation* (Hartford: McBride/Publishers, 1987), pp. 99-100.

⁸⁸ MTB II: 727.

⁸⁹ SLC to Frank Bliss, 10 June 1879. See also MTLP, pp. 116-117, n. 3. See also Rasmussen, *Mark Twain A to Z*, 268.

⁹⁰ SLC to Frank Bliss, 10 May 1879, MTLP, pp. 113-115.

⁹¹ Frank Bliss to SLC, 30 May 1879, MTLP, p. 117, n. 2. The final count of full-page prints in the first edition was 36.

⁹² SLC to Frank Bliss, 10 June 1879, MTLP, p. 117.

⁹³ SLC to Mrs. Fairbanks, 6 March 1879, MTMF, pp. 226-227.

⁹⁴ SLC to Mrs. Fairbanks, 15 May 1879, MTMF, p. 231.

⁹⁵ MTB II, 665.

⁹⁶ Nathan M. Wood, "True Williams, Pen Drew Literary Giant of Old," Watertown (New York) *Daily Times*, August 30, 1938, p. 11. Details from this article are presented in greater depth in a series by Barbara Schmidt, "Reading Illustrations in *The Adventures of Tom Sawyer*," *The Oxford Mark Twain*, New York: Oxford University Press, 1996. Williams drew 36 prints which appear on pages 17, 33, 81, 105, 130, 160 (2), 164, 169, 174, 176, 178, 180, 188, 189 (full), 213, 216, 223, 228, 229, 234, 249, 259, 262, 293, 325, 330, 334, 342, 352, 360, 362, 366, 382, 386 and 585 of the first edition. See also Sinclair Hamilton, *Nineteenth Century American Book Illustrations*, I (Princeton: Princeton University Press, 1968), p. 224. Hereafter cited as Hamilton I.

⁹⁷ Hamilton I, p. 116. Ben Day's prints appear on pages 35, 337, 388, 393, 399, 406, 421, 422, 424, 453, 455, 458, 469, 488, 497, 505, 510, 526, 539, 542, 556 (2) and 592 of the first edition.

⁹⁸ Hamilton I, 217.

⁹⁹ Waud's full-page print is facing page 389 but actually has no page number though it is listed in the "List of Illustrations" as DEATH OF COUNTESS HELINCOURT appearing facing page 388 which is a text page. This Waud print, therefore, was probably a late addition. A tail piece on page 400, related to the section on mismatched clothing (captioned SLOVENLY in the illustrated English edition), though unsigned is probably also by Waud. Twain's text of both the Bathers at Leuke and Countess Helincourt's death are taken from Baedeker's *Switzerland* (1877), pp. 153-154. These two Waud prints may have been appropriated by Frank Bliss since Waud's cuts from *Beyond the Mississippi* had been used by the American Publishing Company in *Roughing It*. Waud died the year after *A Tramp Abroad* was published.

¹⁰⁰ Location of Denslow's other cuts: NO APOLOGY & NONE ASKED, p. 544; A LIVELY STREET (not signed but in Denslow's style), p. 546;

HOW SHE FOOLED US, p. 549; I'LL TAKE THAT OR NONE, p. 552. See *Myth, Magic, and Mystery: One Hundred Years of American Children's Book Illustration* (Boulder, Colorado: Robert Rinehart Publishers, 1996); see also "Denslow, William Wallace" entry in Rasmussen, *Mark Twain A to Z*, pp. 109-110. In his later career Denslow would specialize in children's books and stage extravaganzas. With many of his later prints he adopted a "sea horse" as his illustrating mark.

101 Twain wrote about his "American Grandee" and Brown drew a full-figured illustration of him on page 441. A few pages later Twain states, "I have made honest portraits of them, not caricatures" and perhaps Bliss thought another portrait was needed—though this cut does not seem in Brown's style nor is it signed.

102 The C.H.J.B. print captioned THE WORLD'S MASTERPIECE (the Hair Trunk print) appears on page 565; EUROPEAN CARVING appears on page 573; the Morison print appears on page 600; Alex de Bar captioned THE MER DE GLACE (MONT BLANC) appears on page 533; "self portrait" captioned OCCASIONALLY MET WITH appears on page 444; P. Sheldon print captioned THE VILLAGE OF CHAMONIX appears on page 472; S. R. Captioned THE SUNRISE appears on page 303; A VIEW FROM THE STATION is in a similar style on page 291. The Photo Engraving Company print appears on page 203; the O. F. Company print (illustrator S. R.) appears on page 303.

103 Hamilton I, p. 224. In *Roughing It*, the Beard print was "borrowed" from Albert Richardson's *Beyond the Mississippi* and appeared on page 147 of Twain's book and page 495 of Richardson's work. Another brother, Daniel Carter Beard, would later become the principal illustrator for Twain's *A Connecticut Yankee*.

104 There are a number of interesting deviations in captions and the "List of Illustrations": A GERMAN SABBATH is changed to KEEPING SUNDAY (232); 228, SOCIAL BATHERS is changed to A STRANGE SITUATION (388).

105 BMT, pp. 34-35. The engraving has the marking "J. A. J. Wilson Sc. Boston and is signed with the familiar" Yrs truly Mark Twain signature.

106 The English illustrated edition did not carry the signed Mark Twain engraving as a frontispiece.

107 Kevin MacDonnell, "The Primary First Editions of Mark Twain," *Firsts: The Book Collector's Magazine*, July/August 1998, pp. 42-43.

108 "Circular," 1880, MTP.

109 MTCH, p. 4.

110 SLC to Elisha Bliss, 20 March 1880, MTLP, p. 121.

111 SLC to Chatto and Windus, 1 December 1880, MTLP, p. 127.

112 SLC to Chatto and Windus, 1 December 1880, MTLP, p. 127, n. 2.

113 SLC to Moncure Conway, 20 April [1880], MTLP, pp. 122-124. See also Welland, pp. 99-100. Chatto would ask the author to intercede with Bliss

to cut the costs of the electros. Bliss remained firm and Chatto finally paid the full price.

[114] MTLP, p, 124, n. 1.

[115] Chatto to SLC, 3 May 1880, MTLP, p. 124, n. 2.

[116] *The Prince and the Pauper*, ed. Victor Fischer and Lin Salamo (California: University of California Press, 1979), p. 402.

[117] Hamlin Hill, "Mark Twain's Quarrels with Elisha Bliss," *American Literature*, XXXIII, No. 4 (January 1962), p. 454.

[118] Hamlin Hill, "Quarrels," p. 454.

## List of Illustrations

All citations for the illustrations are from *The Oxford Mark Twain: A Tramp Abroad*, 1996, unless otherwise specified.
All postcards reproduced are from the author's personal collection.

# Chapter III

## *The Prince and the Pauper*

"Merrill probably thinks he *originated* his exquisite boys himself, but I was ahead of him there."[1]

Though Frank Bliss had proved himself an able editor with
the successful publication of *A Tramp Abroad,* Twain expressed concern about his ability to manage single-handedly a large subscription house after the death of his father. In a letter to his brother
Orion he concluded: "I shall probably go to a new publisher . . . for
I am afraid that Frank, with his poor health, will lack push and
drive."[2] Frank Bliss's physical condition and lack of initiative had
little to do with Twain's decision. The author had long wanted to
end what seemed to him a somewhat restrictive relationship with
the American Publishing Company.

Twain had in mind as his new editor and business partner,
James Osgood. Twain and Osgood had talked of working together
for years: coming very near signing a contract for *Sketches, New and
Old* in 1870; nearer still with *The Adventures of Tom Sawyer* in 1872;
and actually publishing an insignificant trade book, *A True Story and
the Recent Carnival of Crime,* in 1877.[3]

Any of Twain's plans for collaborations with other publishers had always been subverted by Elisha Bliss. Now Bliss was
dead and Osgood had broken his alliance with Henry Houghton of
Houghton, Osgood and Company and formed his own inde-
pendent house. Twain and Osgood had a verbal contract by
November 1880, though an official contract was not signed until
9 February the next year. In the written contract Osgood agreed to
a rather unusual arrangement, one that reversed the roles of pub-

lisher and author. With the American Publishing Company Twain usually had had a royalty contract under which Elisha Bliss paid all production costs while Twain received a percentage of the advertised price for every copy sold. With the James Osgood and Company contract Osgood would receive a 7.5 per cent royalty while Twain would be responsible and pay for the design and production process. Two sections of the contract read:

> 3rd.    Upon receipt of said manuscript said Osgood & Co. shall proceed to have suitable illustrations drawn and engraved therefor, subject to said Twain's approval, and to have said work and the illustrations therefor electrotyped in a style to be mutually agreed upon, and shall cause to be manufactured such edition or editions as may be deemed expedient by said Twain. And in such preparation and manufacture said Osgood & Co. shall use their knowledge, experience, and facilities to procure the best results at the most reasonable prices. All bills for said work shall be rendered by said Osgood & Co. to said Twain, accompanied with proper vouchers when desired, and shall be paid by said Twain within one month after being so rendered.

> 4th.    Said Twain shall own all illustration plates and stock belonging to said work.[4]

Mark Twain had always believed that the profits in publishing were on the production not the writing side of the business. Also, he was a touch paranoid about how manufacturing costs were often manipulated by an editor to the disadvantage of an author. Since Moncure Conway's suggestion that he publish *The Adventures of Tom Sawyer* as a commission book, Twain had been anxious to try this arrangement. Another most important benefit for Twain with a commission contract was that he would own his own plates. He could then reproduce editions of his own work and reap the profits from reprints—a policy that the Bliss organization had been following to their advantage and Twain's disadvantage for years. Royalty monies from American Publishing for *A Tramp Abroad* and other books still on the market gave Twain a steady cash flow at this point in his career. With the availability of an experienced efficient publishing house, owned and operated by a reputable editor like James Osgood, Twain's dream of controlling production costs with a commission contract was possible and he was anxious for this alliance with Osgood.

Unfortunately, Osgood and his partners in the company, the Ticknor brothers Benjamin and Thomas, had spent their whole lives in trade, never in subscription publication. Twain, however, realized that the big money (though not the credibility) lay in subscription sales. Therefore he persuaded Osgood have his firm try this unfamiliar publishing territory. Since Osgood knew nothing about the mechanics of subscription publication and since the contract stipulated that Twain controlled the money for production, the publisher had to rely heavily on Twain's advice and instructions. Twain had been in the business for over a decade and believed himself sufficiently competent to make the essential decisions. Luckily, Osgood could also rely upon Ben Ticknor (who would be the intermediary for many of the negotiations between Osgood and Twain), and A. V. S. Anthony, who would supervise production. A major problem with respect to selling the subscription book surfaced immediately: the company had no general agents in the field; Osgood had always sold directly to bookstores. Osgood decided, however, that he or Twain could overcome this hurdle by going to Frank Bliss and asking for his advice on agents and subscription practices. He wrote his idea to Twain:

> This letter suggests the question whether you could obtain from Bliss and furnish to us the names of the principal agents, the territory they cover, the terms on which they buy, and any other particulars for the good of the book. If he would give me access to these facts I would come down there and take memoranda. Do you think he would? If *not*, could *you* get them either as a personal matter, or in your functional relation as director of the Co.? Of course we can pick up all these points, but it would save trouble to get them this way.[5]

Twain was able to secure from the American Publishing Company production figures for *A Tramp Abroad*, which he and Osgood then used to project costs on *The Prince and the Pauper*. They were hopeful of reducing manufacturing costs considerably below the subscription company's figures—from sixty-seven cents to about fifty cents a book."[6]

Naively, Osgood also believed that Frank Bliss would share his confidential sales secrets with his new competitor.

By April Frank Bliss agreed to talk to Osgood. He even invited him to Hartford and encouraged him to take notes about business practices. When Osgood arrived the publisher engaged him in friendly conversation while at the same time divulging only the names of his poorest agents and letting slip false information about the agent's sales percentages. In this way Frank Bliss could continue to control his more profitable general agents, flood the market with cheap reprints of Twain's previous works, and not worry about his competition.

Osgood returned to Boston feeling confident he had solved the marketing problem; Twain and his gullible publisher went forward with their new publishing venture. In high spirits "Osgood would come down to Hartford and spend days discussing plans and playing billiards, which to Twain's mind was a proper way to conduct business."[7] This leisurely pace coupled with Bliss's false canvassing information ultimately damaged sales for Twain's new book. It also contributed to Osgood's financial ruin. Eventually Osgood would go to work for *Harper's* in New York.

Coincident with the official signing of the contract, Twain received correspondence from Anthony, the man who would be responsible for design decisions, asking when to have artists submit illustration samples for *The Prince*. In the letter Anthony also questioned the ultimate dimensions of the book. Twain replied to both questions:

> Very well  then, I do say 'go ahead' to the artist who is ready to make a  couple of drawings on approbation.
>
> I don't know what the size of the new work will be. I suggest that it be the size & shape of "Sketches, New & Old"—I think Osgood approves. In fact I had the idea (vaguely, but still I had the idea) that Osgood & I settled it, here, once, that the book was to be the size & shape of "Sketches." I guess we'll let it stand at that.[8]

With the size and shape set, deliberations on other format matters continued. Twain (and, according to the author, Olivia) decided that *The Prince and the Pauper* was to come out in an elegant edition:

> Livy says . . . [*The Prince*] is going to be elegantly gotten up, even if the elegance of it eats up the publisher's profits and mine too. I anticipate that publisher's melancholy surprise when he calls here Tuesday. However, let him suffer; it is his own fault. People who fix up agreements with me without first finding out what Livy's plans are take fate into their own hands.[9]

Whether it was Livy or Twain himself who made the final decision for ornate ornamentation for the first edition, the fact remains that the book was going to depart significantly from the normal subscription layout. Twain was caught up in the idea of becoming a cultured rather than a comic writer and he felt that if this book was historically accurate, with well researched illustrations, it would establish him as more than a just a humorist. Moreover, the elaborate and factual illustrations could act as tutors and appeal to the literary tastes of his sought-after readers.

Twain had written that he created his historical saga simply for the love of it. Planning to publish the book with luxurious designs for sentimental reasons was foolish; mixing emotion and business seldom produced profits. Moreover, lavish illustration put an immediate strain on the production budget. That Twain was well aware of the risks involved in opulent pictures is obvious in a letter he wrote to his sister Pamela, "High-priced artists & engravers are already at work on my new book (which I am going to issue at my sole & heavy expense & take all the profit myself—if any)."[10]

Twain and Livy weren't the only participants involved with the "elegant" ideas. Osgood, inexperienced in subscription book standards, questioned Twain's determination to have extravagant design and illustration. He wrote to his author questioning the need for so many drawings and expressed uneasiness about the costs for such an extravagant product. Twain responded to his query with: "Yes, must have nice pictures, & a generous sufficiency of them, too. Make the limit the figure you suggest—$2,800."[11]

The man who would manage the "high-priced" artists, to

whom Twain had referred to was Andrew Varick Stout Anthony (Fig. 1). Anthony, though his role here was strictly supervisory, had been an illustrator and engraver himself with a well-earned reputation as a master craftsman. During his career he had worked in a number of publishing houses. In 1866 he took a job as superintendent of illustration for books issued by Ticknor and Fields; he then moved with Osgood to Fields, Osgood and Company; and finally he settled at the new firm James R. Osgood and Company.[12] Like Osgood and Ben Ticknor, Anthony had spent his entire career in trade publication. Nevertheless, he would continue in his usual supervisory position for the subscription publication of *The Prince and the Pauper*: arranging for artists, selecting subjects for illustration, writing captions, designing page layout, final proofreading, and controlling costs.

Fig. 1.  Andrew Varick Stout Anthony

By March Osgood and Anthony had commissioned three artists for Twain's book: Frank Merrill, John J. Harley and L. S. Ipsen. At first they had difficulty in finding just the right illustrators for Twain's "nice pictures." When Frank Merrill (1848-?) submitted some drawings and they were sent to Twain, he heartily approved. It was decided that Merrill would be the principal illustrator, though he actually would draw fewer prints than Harley. At this time he was only moderately established in his illustrating career. He had spent his entire life in Boston, studied at both the Lowell Institute and the Boston Museum of Fine Arts, and held membership in the prestigious Boston Etching Club. He had worked on studies for

*Punchinello,* a comic newspaper-magazine, yet his book illustration commissions were few, the most important being for Louisa May Alcott's *Moods* (1870), the first of the illustrated editions of this work. He was just thirty-two when commissioned to work on *The Prince,* and had yet to strike his stride. As Sinclair Hamilton points out, "the bulk of his work as an illustrator, and his most important work, belongs to the period after 1880."[13] His style was flamboyant. He signed his prints with his "F. T. Merrill," or "F. T. M." signature, these marks appearing on sixty-one of *The Prince* prints.

Information on Harley's life is scarce. He was born in St. John, New Brunswick, Canada in 1840 and became a naturalized United States citizen in Boston Massachusetts in 1888. He had been one of the many engravers for the monumental *Picturesque America* in 1872-1874, a book that many critics proclaimed the best American landscape print portfolio produced on this continent. In 1872 he was a staff artist on Fenimore Cooper's *The Prairie* for Appleton while also working part-time on small cuts for Osgood's Company on Harriet Beecher Stowe's *Oldtime Fireside Stories.*[14] *The Prince and the Pauper* was, as far as is known now, his first work as a major illustrator. Later he would be the principal artist for Twain's *Life on the Mississippi,* and later still create the cover for *The Stolen White Elephant.* Eighty-five of his drawings for *The Prince* were signed, most of them bearing a lone "H," with a few having the full surname, "Harley." It is impossible to ascertain how many of the unsigned drawings in the book are Harley's, however, a considerable number of them are in his style. He died in 1918.

A third artist commissioned by Osgood for *The Prince* was L. S. Ipsen. He created thirty-five unique chapter headings which were listed as "half titles" in the List of Illustrations. Of Twain's former books, only *The Gilded Age* and *The Adventures of Tom Sawyer* contained ornamental illustration with intricate initial letters in the chapter headings. For *The Gilded Age* the often criticized mottoes were accompanied by vignettes and initial letters. Fanciful vignettes with related inserts and extended initials also appeared in *Tom Sawyer*—possibly as necessary padding for the small novel. Ipsen's designs for *The Prince,* however, were deliberately more decorative and designed to historically "set the stage" for each chapter—though there is no denying that they were also page fillers for what would be another rather slender subscription publication.

In theory, an artist's chapter heading should open the door

to the author's text. Ipsen's designs certainly opened wide the door and much more. His designs were not only true to the text but exquisitely imaginative, and scrupulously accurate. Each of Ipsen's half-titles featured glorious calligraphic initial letters emblazoned across a detailed vignette directly related to the action in the chapter. Since his chapter headings were seen before the reader turned to read the text, his pictures visually introduced and helped interpret the ideas that followed. When the scene takes place around the peasants the accouterments were simple and ordinary with earthenware jugs and wooden staves; when the scene takes place in the palace or with royalty the accouterments were regal crowns and ornamented shields.

Mark Twain had written "at the top of his manuscript on which Chapter II begins, . . . 'View of London?'—possibly a suggestion to the illustrator."[15] Ipsen and/or Anthony undoubtedly read Twain's recommendation but decided the London view would be appropriate for Chapter I, not II, with a half-title reading THE BIRTH OF THE PRINCE and the PAUPER.

Ipsen's split image has a circle rule frame flanked with pennant flags, a base with a Prince of Wales crown resting on an ermine-trimmed cloak, and the top half with a view of an authentic jumble of rooftops in the "ancient city of London" (Fig. 2). This intricate design was printed in the middle of a blank page with a blank verso. A reader turning to Ipsen's chapter heading on a very first page finds the illustrator has cleverly established the background for both the Prince and the Pauper.

Ipsen, undoubtedly with Anthony's approval, would continue a disregard for empty white space—a major departure from usual subscription book standards—in each of the thirty-four

Fig. 2.  The Birth of The Prince and the Pauper

headings. Even in the "Notes" section—a scholarly appendage that also deviated from usual subscription publications—the chapter heading has its own full page with blank verso.

Ipsen's half-titles, however, served as more than just interpretive tools and decorative volume stuffers. He had probably been cautioned that historical accuracy was an essential element in his designs and had done research with the help of books on sixteenth-century regalia sent to him by Anthony and Osgood.

After the suggestion from Twain about the London view, Ipsen set about his task armed with information about England and the days of Edward III. For Chapter III, since it takes place in the palace, Ipsen created a design featuring imperial accessories: a ruled frame draped with a cloth of gold embroidered with fleurs-de-lis (Italian gold hangings were amongst the King's most expensive possessions), the royal ermine-attired greyhounds (which were often used as supporters for the royal arms), and a shield on which the bearer's arms (symbols of the Prince of Wales) are displayed. A now-knowledgeable Ipsen quartered the shield with lions passant guardant in the dexter chief and sinister base, while he placed Tudor Roses at the dexter base and in the sinister chief. Edward's shield carried the rose, symbol of the Tudor dynasty, his not yet having attained the right to use the king's royal charges of lions with fleurs-de-lis (Fig. 3).

Ipsen continues with his Tudor Rose charges for Chapter IV where the shield is crested with a St. Edward's crown, the state crown of England. The crown is complete with fleurs-de-lis, quadruple arches, and a minor cross at the base of the central arch.[16] In a nice touch when depicting the "trouble" in

Fig. 3. Tom's Meeting With the Prince

the wording of the half-title, THE PRINCE'S TROUBLES BEGIN, Ipsen skewered the shield with a brambled branch (Fig. 4).

By Chapter V the royal heraldic symbols continue as before, Ipsen now changing from his usual shield. A rondel, or circular shield, holds a lion crested with a closed crown while the lion's paw rests on the royal orb surmounted with a cross—the globe a symbol of the dominion and the cross symbol of the faith of

Fig. 4.   The Prince's Troubles Begin

the king.   The background has a pattern of fleurs-de-lis (Fig. 5).

Fig. 5.   Tom as a Patrician

Though most frequently associated with France, by the twelfth-century the fleurs-de-lis had become a full-fledged heraldic ornament common to English aristocracy.

In Chapter IX, when the text has "several great English nobles, with their attendants" arrive to pay honor to "Lord Edward, Prince of Wales," Ipsen's chapter heading incorporates a crown-crested shield ornamented with lion charges, another with ordinaries of the bend and chevron and still others with charges of roses and fleurs-de-lis. All this regal paraphernalia semi-circles around two state barges festooned with pennants, and elaborately carved prows. The half-title on a ribbon at the base reads THE RIVER PAGEANT (Fig. 6). Placed in the middle of a blank page, it invites the reader to turn the page and experience with Tom Canty one of the river-front ceremonials when commoner and courtier alike get their first glimpse of Tom as the Prince.

When Henry VIII dies in Twain's story, Ipsen's half-title is lettered in French, *LE ROI EST MORT* and below *VIVE LE ROI.*

Fig. 6. The River Pageant

This roundel-backed chapter heading features a bordered shield draped with a funeral scarf, flanked by leafy fronds and crested with a large royal crown—two Tudor roses appearing at the base. Ipsen's visual message corresponds to the text; with the death of Henry the Tudor Rose charges will now be linked with the royal crown (Fig. 7). In the later chapters Ipsen continues using the Tudor Rose charge, even though in Chapter XXXI the royal crest reads "E VI." In Chapter XXXIII the half-title EDWARD AS

Fig. 7. *Le Roi Est Mort—Vive Le Roi*

KING is inscribed over a shield crested with a helmet adorned with the three feathers of the Prince of Wales (Figs. 8 & 9).[17]

Ipsen astutely used all the regalia possible to correspond to the themes in Twain's story. The pomp and ceremony of the royal symbols contrast with the commonplace utensils of Cheapside life. Ipsen's pictures led the reader into the many worlds of England's past. Ipsen was not alone in demonstrating his allegiance to the historical accuracy of Twain's tale. The two other illustrators spent a prodigious amount of time researching each of their respective assignments.

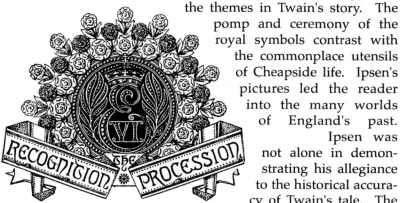

Fig. 8. The Recognition Procession

Reviewers of the time—and even scholars today—criticize Twain's book as "providing no sense of being present at the events it describes . . . having dialogue that is a labored attempt at Elizabethan English."[18] Twain's three illustrators took up the cudgel and "presented the events." What Twain's verbal ability lacked the artists' drawings supplied. All the pageantry, and poverty of sixteenth-century England is visualized for the reader. They are led down the alleys of Offal Court, and tour Westminster Abbey; personages from Henry VIII to the schoolboys of Christ's Hospital can be identified. What easier way to travel, be taught history and be entertained, all at the same time.

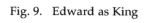

Fig. 9. Edward as King

By mid August, Twain received his first batch of proofs that contained an illustration for Chapter I. Ticknor, when sending on the proof, explained to Twain that the "illustration had been made too large and would need to be redone." Reducing the illustration to fit as an appropriately sized insert also required resetting the type for the whole first chapter. Twain wrote back in a "damned the expense" tone: "Yes, that is the correct idea—do the cut over again; process it down to the required reduction."[19]

The picture under discussion was captioned "SPLENDID PAGEANTS AND GREAT BONFIRES." In final printing it was reduced and let in along the margin of the first page of text, though this was actually the twenty-third page of the edition. The minutely detailed, unsigned drawing gives visual expression to the holiday spirit felt by Londoners with the birth of the new baby, Edward Tudor, and royal figures riding through the streets while the townsfolk celebrate with great bonfires at every corner (Fig. 10). This illustration, without the overlapping bonfire insert, was used as part of the cover design for the English first edition.

Drawings related to the text were divided between Frank Merrill and John Harley: Merrill concentrating on the royal figures of the palace; Harley doing the low life of Offal Court and Cheapside. Since more of the story takes place in the streets than in the royal household, Harley drew the greater share of the designs. Because the figure work was divided between Harley and Merrill, the age and appearance in illustrations of the two major characters had significant discrepancies. Early on even Twain had difficulty in deciding the ages of his

Fig. 10.
"Splendid
Pageants and
Great Bon-Fires"

young heroes. In his working notes he had jotted: "Call one Tom, aged 6 & tother The Prince of Wales, aged 6."[20] By the time he had completed the manuscript, however, Twain wrote to Anthony revising his ideas on age and how the illustrators should depict the youthful lads:

> I knew I was making them too wise & knowing for their real age . . . so I studiously avoided mentioning any dates which would remind the reader that they were under 10 years old. Perhaps I mention the date of Henry VIII's death, but I don't mention the date of Prince Edward's birth. . . . [Have] the artist always picture the Prince & Tom Canty as lads of 13 or 14 years old.[21]

Fig. 11. Offal Court

Days later, when a batch of pictures arrived for Chapter II— undoubtedly drawn by Harley, his signature appearing in one illustration—Anthony looked them over and sent them on to Twain, commenting:

> I sent you two drawings, 'Offal Court,' and 'Canty and the Priest.' Tom is a little younger, perhaps, in the drawing, but I take it that when he was learning his Latin and getting his head full of the possible splendors of life, he might have been, say, 10 or 11 years of age (Figs. 11 & 12).[22]

Anthony's guess at Tom's age appears fitting; the lad is depicted as a curly-headed, ten-year-old studying Latin with the priest. However, in the next chapter, when the scene shifts from Offal Court to the Palace,

Fig. 12.
"He Often Read the Priest's Books"

young Tom's age, as well as his clothes, change. When Frank Merrill draws Tom in "DOFF THY RAGS, AND DON THESE SPLENDORS," he is transformed from a sturdy, rag-shirted, barefoot boy into a slender, long-legged adolescent clad in a puffed-sleeve doublet and soft slippers in (Fig. 13). Returning to the streets in the next chapter, when "A DRUNKEN RUFFIAN COLLARED HIM," the Prince, now in Tom's rags and drawn by Harley, recovers both his former immaturity and tattered attire (Fig. 14).[23]

This curious alternating style for Twain's adolescents continues through the pages. When Harley is at work drawing Tom in Offal Court or the palace, the youngster emerges thickset, round-faced and dark-haired; when Merrill takes over with Tom either as street kid or masquerading as the Prince, he is oval-faced, blonde and lanky. Moreover, this depiction conflicts with Twain's description of the Prince who in the text is termed "tanned and brown" (38).

Yet Merrill's illustrations correspond closely to the real

Fig. 13.
"Doff Thy Rags, and Don These Splendors"

Fig. 14.
"A Drunken Ruffian Collared
Him"

Prince Edward in feature and dress. Merrill's Prince, later King, favors the many portraits of the sickly royal child, with the high-bridged Tudor nose, wan pallor and lean stature of the Prince who would eventually die of tuberculosis. Merrill deviated only slightly from Twain's text as he replicated the Prince's feathered hats (Twain had the "plumes drooping"), beribbon-sleeved tunics embroidered with three ostrich feathers—the badge of the former Black Prince and an emblem which all future Princes of Wales have used (Fig. 15).[24]

This shifting visual incongruity between Harley and Merrill's versions of the boys taxes the reader's imagination. Obviously each artist worked on their renditions independently. The differing youngsters could never have exchanged roles; the urchin Tom would never be mistaken for

Fig. 15.   Edward VI

the "blue-blood prince." In the illustrations there is no mystery in the identity of the two. Since this is a major theme in Twain's book, his illustrators failed in this aspect of their task.

This discrepancy with which the two artists portrayed the boys seems even more troublesome when coupled with Twain's insistence on identical depictions for the boys. In Twain's working notes he had specified, "Make portraits from the same photograph, & let artist dress one in rags 'tother *en prince*."[25] Anthony, who was to edit and supervise the illustrations, appears to have been more concerned with the quality of the art work than with a consistency of character. Furthermore, by Chapter XV in the drawing of Tom as King, the young boy has aged considerably. The reader now views a teenager though the action of the story calls for a lapse of only a few weeks (Fig. 16).

While researching for *The Prince and the Pauper*, Twain's "studied" Hippolyte Taine's *The Ancient Regime*. Taine's book advised Twain on how to assist a reader's imagination by providing "particularized" accounts of architecture and costumes, the utensils of the hermit's hut, the grounds of the nobleman's estate, and myriad other specifics. This advice also served as an imaginative spark for the reader when the artist's pictures provided the same detailed "particulars" in their illustrations.

The artists carefully carried out this particularization to detail in many of their prints. Harley, his "H" visible in the "SET UPON BY DOGS" drawing, adhered meticulously to Twain's costuming for the Christ Church ruffians. In Chapter IV, Twain directs his readers to "*See Note 1, at the end of the volume." This asterisked note comes just after the disguised prince

Fig. 16.
Tom Had Wandered to a Window

is dragged away by a "delighted and noisy swarm of human ver-
min" (53), and refers to a passage describing the sufficiently ugly
costume of the schoolboys that Twain had copied from Timbs'
*Curiosities of London*:

> Each had on the crown of his head a flat black cap
> about the size of a saucer, which was not useful as
> a covering, it being of such scanty dimensions,
> neither was it ornamental; from beneath it the
> hair fell, unparted, to the middle of the forehead,
> and was cropped straight around; a clerical band
> at the neck; a blue gown that fitted closely and
> hung as low as the knees or lower; full sleeves; a
> broad red belt; bright yellow stockings, gartered
> above the knees; low shoes with large metal
> buckles. It was a sufficiently ugly costume.[26]

If the reader turns as directed to the "Notes" section at the back of
the book, Twain fills him in on the complete description of the
Christ's Hospital uniform directly from Timb's *Curiosities*.

Unable to produce the various blue, red, and yellow color
designations, Harley nevertheless authentically drafted the Christ

Fig. 17.
"Set Upon by Dogs"

Church costume with its long coat, clerical collar and buckled shoes (Fig. 17). Hats, however, proved a small problem for the artists. In this print it is the prince who wears a hat that approximates the "flat black cap about the size of a saucer." It should be the schoolboys, not the disguised prince, wearing this hat. And in the previous chapter when Tom first meets the prince and they change clothes, Tom's hat was not flat. Hats would change, appear and disappear with regularity throughout the illustrations. More importantly, despite Twain's desire for historical correctness, this unique school uniform had not been adopted until "soon after Edward VI founded Christ's Hospital in 1552, five years after the period of Mark Twain's story."[27]

Twain, like Anthony, seemed almost obsessed with the historical requirements and paid little attention to the accuracy of characterization in the drawings. He reported his pleasure with Merrill's work to the Boston office:

> Merrill probably thinks he *originated* his exquisite boys himself, but I was ahead of him there!—in these pictures they look and dress exactly as I used to see them in my mind two years ago. It is a vast pleasure to see them cast in the flesh, so to speak—they were of but perishable dream-stuff, before.[28]

Authenticity in sixteenth-century detail became an imperative with Twain for this book. In the same letter where Twain commented on the "exquisite" boys he also directed Ticknor not to "forget to glorify the illustrations; also that you call attention to the historical accuracy of the costumes."[29]

Though Harley and Merrill may have disagreed on the appearances of their young charges, they were inventive in the way they presented the two boys to the reader. In the illustration where the Tom is first introduced to the Prince, Merrill eliminates Twain's "golden bars" (38) so there is nothing to come between the young boys. He then builds a compositional hierarchy to make the Prince the dominant figure. In this picture captioned "LET HIM IN," the halberdier at present arms splits the vertical plane of Merrill's drawing, forcing the Prince and the Pauper into a space of their own. The Prince is seen as taller than Tom and is framed by the halberd and the back view of the Pauper which pushes him to the cen-

ter of the illustration. Against the two dark
figures the Prince, looking directly at Tom
and dressed in white with an embroidered doublet and "dainty buskins"
(39), stands out.   Merrill's picture
makes the reader con-
centrate on the Prince
and increases the dra-
matic interest in this
royal figure at a critical
juncture in the narrative.
Both Merrill and Harley
cleverly    orchestrated
their costuming: which
ever boy dominates a
chapter, he is the one
attired in white while the
secondary    character
appears   in    darker
shades (Fig. 18).

     When    Twain
has Tom as the Prince
don "several pieces of a
suit of shining steel
armor" (93), his working
notes reveal that he took
his description from the

Fig. 18.   "Let Him In!"

Abbotsford edition of Scott's *Quentin Durward*.[30]  Merrill's illustration, "TOM PUT ON THE GREAVES," finds Canty fastening the leg
armour while a mailed gauntlet lay on the floor at his feet (Fig. 19).
Careful attention to detail can be seen in the visored helmet with its
three Edward Tudor ostrich plumes in the background while Tom is
seated in a replica of an authentic Winchester chair.

     Merrill's ailing, gouty Henry VIII in Chapters V and VIII
was faithful to the image nineteenth-century readers would expect
of the much-married, reprobate King.  Twain's text softened the
character of the King.  In one scene he has the Prince remembering
a long succession of loving passages between his father and himself.
Merrill's vision of the royal monarch—who by just before his death
was bald with eyes lost in folds of fat—also tempered the reality of

Fig. 19
"Tom Put on the
Greaves"

the invalid, obese king, drawing him as stout rather than fat and adding vestiges of the younger and handsomer Henry of the Holbein reproductions (Figs. 20, 21 & 22). Henry, in text and picture, became a more kindly father than most readers would naturally assume.

The Ladies of the Court were faithfully costumed down to the whimpled headdress and the squared bodice (Figs. 23, 24, 25, 26 & 27).[31] However, of the three pictured royals—Lady Elizabeth, fourteen-year old half-sister and eventually to become Queen;[32] Lady Jane Grey, thirteen-year old cousin (known as the nine-day Queen, a mere hiccough in history); and Lady Mary, half-sister to Edward often described as having a "gloomy mien"—unfortunately all are drawn as interchangeable portraits, a simple exchange of purse or necklace, added embroidery on the front skirt panel or hem the only defining differences. In real-life Jane Grey was just "comely," while the smaller Lady Mary was rather flabby with no eyebrows. As with Henry, more romanticized than accurate, the illustrator's renditions of these noble ladies was mellowed. Remember, this is Twain's melodramatic history not Timbs *Curiosities* and the stuff his reader's expected.

Yet the artists' pictures represented the texture of the times. The halberdiers (usually clad in Tudor decorated livery with colors in "habits of red"—reduced in number from the 600 strong in 1520 to 80 at the end of Henry's reign) carried true sixteenth-century shafted weapons with axe-like cutting blades. The pages were appropriately garbed in laced ruff and close-fitting doublets without sleeves (Figs. 28, 29, 30 & 31). The trappings on the royal steeds

Fig. 20.   "He Dropped Upon His Knees"

Fig. 22.
Henry VIII in Old Age

Fig. 21.
Henry VIII

Fig. 23.
Hertford and the Princesses

Fig. 24.
"The Boy Was on His Knees"

Fig. 25.
Lady Jane Grey

Fig. 26.
The Princess Mary

Fig. 27. "Commanded Her To Go To Her Closet"

Fig. 28.
"Arrested as a
Suspicious
Character"

Fig. 29.
Yeoman of the Guard at
the Time of Henry VIII

Fig. 30.
"Welcome, O King!"

Fig. 31.
Page Boy,
Time of Edward VI

were marvelously ornamented as they would have been in Edward Tudor's day (Fig. 32).

To anyone thumbing through the illustrations it is obvious the illustrators had access to the many historical texts, many of which Twain had referred to in his manuscript. In one of Harley's early drawings appearing in Chapter III, "AT TEMPLE BAR," he recreated the old "wooden" structure down to

Fig. 32.
"A Largesse! A Largesse!"

the print-houses adjoining the gate—a new Temple Bar had been rebuilt by Wren in 1670 and the whole structure removed in 1877

Fig. 33.
"At Temple Bar"

(Figs. 33 & 34). Harley's drawing positions Tom Canty with his back to the reader, as if he were viewing the wonder of the worlds that lay beyond this gate. If the illustration is read carefully, it reinforces the passage when Twain writes that Tom "passed on out-side the walls of London" (37). Through print and picture the reader, with Tom, will go forth in to the royal world beyond Offal Court.

A celebrated drawing of the "Burning of Anne Askew and Others" was also

Fig. 34.
Old Temple Bar in the
Time of James I

Fig. 35.   The order and manner of the burning of *Anne Askew* and others.

obviously available for one of Harley's drawings in Chapter II. For his "SAW POOR ANNE ASKEW BURNED" he duplicated the architectural details of the rooftop buildings and the tower in the town of Smithfield where the incident took place.  He also reduced the crowd, replaced the royal viewing stand with billowing smoke, removed the preaching ex-bishop from his lectern positioning him nearer the stake, and foregrounded a barefoot, apprehensive Tom Canty, with his head down and too stressed to look directly at the burning pyre (Figs. 35 & 36).[33]  In this way Harley softened the reader's reaction to this horrible spectacle and took the sting out of Twain's cynical line just below the illustration, "Tom's life was

Fig. 36.
"Saw Poor
Anne
Askew
Burned"

varied and pleasant enough, on the whole" (31).

Merrill was meticulous too in his copying of sixteenth-century furniture. He drew various royal chairs, the most important of these the seats of authority, thrones, which were designed to elevate the sitter but would only be considered "royal" when in an ensemble with a canopy, dais, footstool, cushion, and rug. Merrill drew several of these royal ensemble pieces in his illustrations. The chair and canopy in the Great Hall in Chapter XIV when "A SECRETARY OF STATE PRESENTED AN ORDER," are drawn with the celer (the drapery) decorated with the royal coat of arms, the tester (the framework), a tasseled cushion, and a royal "cloth of state" pulled back from the entrance (Fig. 37).[34] The Coronation Chair of

Fig. 37. "A Secretary of State Presented an Order"

Westminster Abbey in Chapter XXXII (Figs. 38 & 39) is also accurate with its post and boarded seat, elevated steps (elevated only at a coronation otherwise there are usually two stairs not three), with support legs of four lions and fleurs-de-lis embroidered curtains. This is the same chair Mary refused to use on her coronation day because it had been polluted by the seating of Edward VI, a Protestant.[35]

Fig. 38.
"And Fell on His Knees Before Him"

Fig. 39.  The Coronation Chair

Merrill's replications extended to another aristocratic seat, the so-called Winchester chair, a famous X-framed chair that was used by many persons of authority. Henry VIII's Winchester chair was "timber, covered in a yellow cloth of gold, fringed with Venice gold and with four balls of silver and gilt,"[36] not unlike the fringed seat in

Merrill's illustration "TOM ROSE AND KISSED THE KING'S HAND" (Figs. 40 & 41).

Fig. 40. The Winchester Chair

Authentic details were not confined to costuming, persons, and royal paraphernalia. Deviating again from normal subscription practices, the frontispiece provided for the book was not the usual portrait or caricature of the author. Instead, the frontispiece page was blank and on the verso was printed a manuscript facsimile of a letter from Hugh Latimer to Lord Cromwell, the facing recto containing a translation of a printed version of the same manuscript. The letterhead would verify its authenticity: "FROM THE NATIONAL MANUSCRIPTS PRESERVED BY THE BRITISH GOVERNMENT" (Figs. 42 & 43). Hugh Latimer, a Protestant Bishop of Worcester, had been in favor at the time of Prince Edward's birth and Latimer had been a lecturer/teacher of the young Prince. With the ascension

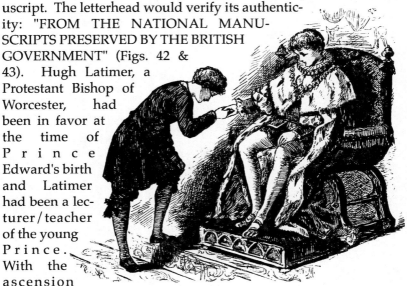

Fig. 41. "Tom Rose and Kissed the King's Hand"

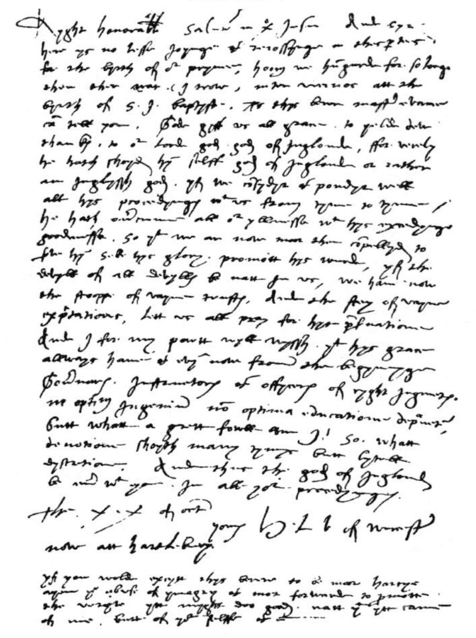

Fig. 42.
Hugh Latimer, Bishop of Worcester, to Lord Cromwell, on the birth of the Prince of Wales

to the throne of Mary Tudor in 1553 and the return of the Holy Church of Rome, Latimer was out of favor. He was charged with heresy and burned at Oxford on 31 December 1555. This document may have been a last-minute addition by Twain since it is not listed in the "List of Illustrations" and there is no mention of Latimer in Twain's story.

Anthony had the

artists copy directly from a print    of the government record taken from a volume in Twain's personal library.    Twain even supplied the book, writing to Ben Ticknor, "hand that book to Osgood. . . . If it is too bulky, I guess we'll tear out that particular facsimile & let him take that."[37] This duplication of original documents is reminiscent of Twain's use of a mock

Fig. 43.
Hugh Latimer, Bishop of Worcester, to Lord Cromwell, on the birth of the Prince of Wales

Ryght honorable, *Salutem in Christo Jesu,* and Syr here ys no lesse joynge and rejossynge in thes partees for the byrth of our prynce, hoom we hungurde for so longe, then ther was (I trow), *inter vicinos* att the byrth of S. I. Baptyste, as thys berer, Master Erance, can telle you. Gode gyffe us alle grace, to yelde dew thankes to our Lorde Gode, Gode of' Inglonde, for verely He hathe shoyd Hym selff Gode of Inglonde, or rather an Inglyssh Gode, yf we consydyr and pondyr welle alle Hys procedynges with us from tyme to tyme. He hath overcumme alle our yllnesse with Hys excedynge goodnesse, so that we ar now moor then compellyd to serve Hym, seke Hys glory, promott Hys wurde, yf the Devylle of alle Devylles be natt in us. We have now the stooppe of vayne trustes ande the stey of vayne expectations; lett us alle pray for hys preservatione. Ande I for my partt wylle wyssh that hys Grace allways have, and evyn now from the begynynge, Governares, Instructores and offyceres of ryght jugmente, *ne optimum ingenium non optimâ educatione depravetur.*

Butt whatt a grett fowlle am I! So, whatt devotione shoyth many tymys butt lytelle dyscretione! Ande thus the Gode of Inglonde be ever with you in alle your procedynges.

The 19 of October.

Youres, H. L. B. of Wurcestere, now att Hartlebury.

Yf you wolde excytt thys berere to be moore hartye ayen the abuse of ymagry or mor forwarde to promotte the veryte, ytt myght doo goode. Natt that ytt came of me, butt of your selffe, &c.

*(Addressed)* To the Ryght Honorable Loorde P. Sealle hys synguler gode Lorde.

facsimile of the Horace Greeley letter in the first edition of *Roughing It*. In the western book the aim was humor; in this writing of royals the goal was historic credibility. This type of frontispiece would not appeal to the mid-western backwoodsman, but that was not the audience Twain was seeking. He was aiming at a more cultured market and for them the letter would be appropriate.

In the same Ticknor letter that praised Merrill's renditions of the switched boys, Twain expressed concern about another reproduction, the Great Seal, central to the action of his novel. He was uneasy about including this illustration and he chided Ticknor: "The Great Seal wasn't to be engraved—ole Brer Osgood forgot that, I reckon. I'm afraid to put it in."[38] Some scholars have determined that Twain was concerned because he felt a picture of the seal "would blunt impact of the coronation scene."[39] This uncaptioned replica facing the title page, accurate in every aspect to the original—the "HONI SOIT QUI MAL Y PENSE," motto of the Garter, visible circling the edge—is many pages previous to the coronation chapter though some smaller, almost unidentifiable versions of the seal, appear in Ipsen's half-titles earlier in the story. Whatever the reason for the worry, the Seal did appear in both the American and the English editions and is cataloged in the "List of Illustrations" as the frontispiece (Figs. 44, 45 & 46).

Fig. 44.   Great Seal

Below the reproduction of the Great Seal is a signature unidentified in the "List of Illustrations." Uncaptioned, and there-

Fig. 45.
Great Seal worn by Henry VIII

fore possibly unrecognized by most of Twain's American readers, it is a duplication of the signature of Henry VIII and it replicated the royal habit of "Henry's genuine H . . . made without lifting the pen (Fig. 47)."[40] Though the Great Seal is listed in the "List of Illustra-tions" as the "frontispiece," there is no mention of Henry's signature.

Why all this fuss with precision, this insistence on meticulous detail and historical exactness? Livy, of

Fig. 46.
Caption not listed in "List of Illustrations"

Fig. 47. Series of Autographs of English Kings and Queens

course, had requested that the book be "elegantly gotten up" and Twain had himself demanded "historical accuracy of the costumes"—his NOTES describing not only costumes but also loving cups and salads. James Osgood, and his partners Anthony and Ticknor, were no less interested in the elegance and precision of design. In the decade preceding they had had a rough patch of it in the publishing market—few successful books in their former ventures, a devastating fire that destroyed Osgood's place of business and the dissolution of the once fruitful Osgood-Houghton partnership. When Twain and Osgood contracted for a "deluxe edition" and the author agreed to pay for "elegant design" no matter the expense, the limits were boundless.

Moreover, Twain, not Osgood, understood the subscription market. Even though he was moving into a new, more cultured style, he recognized that his readers would want prolific illustration, pictures that would satisfy their hunger for history, travel, royal people, and palaces. They had visited the Holy Land with Twain in *Innocents Abroad* and tramped all over Europe with him in *A Tramp Abroad*. These were the books his readers had made into best sellers. With *The Prince and the Pauper* Mark Twain would appeal to the more learned by touring them down the alleys of Offal Court and visiting the palace of one of the most famous of the English Kings, Henry VIII. In the same painstaking way that Twain tried to present sixteenth-century language and customs in print, his illustrators presented the sixteenth-century in pictures. The pictures would render the verbal story of the two boys of London's past into a visual world of poverty and palaces.

Typesetting of the first edition began in April but was delayed until the company had prepared, and Mark Twain had approved, a sizable number of illustrations. By July Twain asked the company to send him "proofs of the pictures that are thus far completed for my book" and reminded them that "Osgood promised, but Osgood forgot."[41] By the thirty-first of the month Twain reported that, "Proofs of a hundred and fifty of the engravings for my new book came yesterday, & I like them far better that any that have ever been made for me before."[42] On seeing the engravings Twain suggested they have a "special printing" of some of these illustrations to be neatly bound in boards for several friends. Writing his idea to Ticknor he proposed:

> As to the pictures, they clear surpass my highest expectations. They are as dainty and rich as etchings. I would like to have you print twelve or fifteen full sets of them for me, each picture in the centre of a sheet of fine India paper about double the size of this I am writing on (I mean the sort of paper they print etchings on—or any other paper that will best bring out their excellencies), and bind each set simply and neatly in boards. Can this be done at a reasonable expense? I want to give them to a few especial and particular friends.[43]

Two weeks later he was more hesitant and wrote again to Ticknor:

> 'If it is going to be too extravagantly costly to make 20 books of them on India paper—a large item of the expense is the mounting, doubtless—maybe we can print them on a heavy *tinted* paper and survive the outlay. . . . But I don't know but I shall have to borrow enough money to get *one* set printed on India paper, anyway.'[44]

He finally decided to print a small private edition of the entire book.[45]

By August, with the completion of so many pictures, Twain instructed Ben Ticknor to "Put titles under the pictures yourself" then added, "I'll alter them in proof if any alteration shall seem necessary."[46] Since, in Twain's own words, he "hadn't put any fun in [*The Prince*],"[47] he probably felt words directly from the text would suffice as picture captions, there would be no need for his usual by-play with double entendre humor that he had often added in captions for *The Innocents, Roughing It,* and *A Tramp Abroad.* Osgood's staff supplied the captions quoted directly from the text.

Osgood also made sure that accuracy in illustration had a prominent space in the publisher's announcement which was included in the canvassing prospectus for the book: "No pains have been spared to make the representation of the characters, costumes, buildings, and scenery historically accurate, as well as artistically correct and attractive."[48]

Anthony's job as supervisor of illustration, however, was again complicated by a Twain suggestion about the engraving process. The author had earlier tried to persuade Frank Bliss to use the Kaolatype process on illustrations for *A Tramp Abroad,* to no avail. This time he would make the same suggestion to Osgood for illustrations for *The Prince.*

Twain had set up the Kaolatype Engraving Company with offices in New York, himself as President, Slote as treasurer, and his Hartford lawyer Perkins as secretary. While working on *The Prince,* he had pushed to gain complete control of the company. Dissatisfied with Slote's management, he brought in his nephew Charles Webster to straighten out the firm. This was a first venture with his uncle for Webster, a civil engineer from Fredonia, New

York. Twain made him Vice-President and gave him $100 worth of stock.

Webster wrestled with the Kaolatype process, spurred on by his relative and boss. Twain wanted to expand the business a hundred-fold by applying the process to printing wallpaper and "the moulding of bookbinders' brass stamps, in place of engraving them, [and] trying to find a somebody who could invent a flux that would enable a body to mould hard brass with sharp-cut lines & perfect surfaces."[49]

Webster's immediate job was to experiment with alloys to perfect the process. He tried every metal: steel, copper, and brass, with minimal success. Finally, in March, Webster produced a first set of plates. Twain happily wrote back, "Those impressions came just in the nick of time." However, a line in the last paragraph of the letter warned of future trouble: "Old Kaolatype is a bit expensive."[50]

Undaunted, Twain directed Webster to experiment with the cover design for *The Prince and the Pauper.*

> Trot that [cover] design through; and when you have it cast in spelter, ship the cast to Providence and ask them to cast it in brass with their utmost nicety—cast it and re-cast it till they get a perfect plate. Then let them ship it to Osgood to be finished up by a first-class finisher.[51]

It was already September. Webster was working against time. He had concurrently assumed a role as a general agent for Osgood's firm. Twain wrote to his nephew pressuring him about priorities: "It is of vast importance that no time be lost—for it might delay the issue of my canvassers' copies, & cost me several thousand dollars. Consequently, I would a good deal rather hurt your K business a hundred dollars or so by your absence."[52]

A few days later Twain had to apologize to the home office in Boston for the delays caused by Kaolatype's cover:

> I got the cover-design last Sunday—mailed it to New York that evening; expected it to be in our artist's hands by 9 A.M. Monday; expected it to be *out* of his hands (in the form of type-metal facsimile), some time during Wednesday; I hoped it would reach Chelsea that night, be cast in brass

and finished-up on Thursday and be in your hands and ready for the press on Friday.

But everything went wrong, of course. The design did not reach our artist until sometime on *Tuesday*; the Thanksgiving or Prayer holiday [day of prayer for the recovery of the wounded President Garfield] stopped the work on it yesterday, no doubt; and now comes a telegram to say it won't be ready for the brass founder till *Monday*.

So I am instructing my nephew to take the spelter-cast to Boston Monday night, and get it cast in brass, in Chelsea, Tuesday.

I am not foreseeing any difficulty about it; but if our work *should* be inferior and unsatisfactory to you, you can fire away and have the plate *cut*, by the die sinkers. Webster will bring you the original design.[53]

By late October Twain finally had to admit the Kaolatype cover was not working out as well as he had predicted:

I had to order new Prince & Pauper stamps from the die-sinkers. The fault was not in the *casting*, but in the crudeness of the original pattern; the lines are not in shape, the lettering was not shapely. The cutting in Kaolatype was too hurriedly done.[54]

The advent of the "heated" machine press around 1830 made it possible to stamp binding in gold leaf before they were bound to text. Splendidly ornamental, the books then mimicked the look of gold-tooled leather, thereby carrying the association of cultivation and privilege. This was the style Twain wanted for the cover of *The Prince*.

The intricate cover design was created by Ipsen and incorporated the same elaborate spirit as his half-titles. An all-over black stamped design of "suns," a base band of black with fleurs-de-lis in green, crested shields with various charges and ordinaries, all items were enclosed in a triple-ruled border. The title and Twain's name were spelled out in ornately seriffed gilt letters. Displayed in a gilt frame were many of the accouterments of an English sovereign: a golden shield (with Tudor Roses and lion passant charges), the royal scepter, bludgeon, and orb. Cresting the frame is a gilded enclosed crown (Fig. 48).

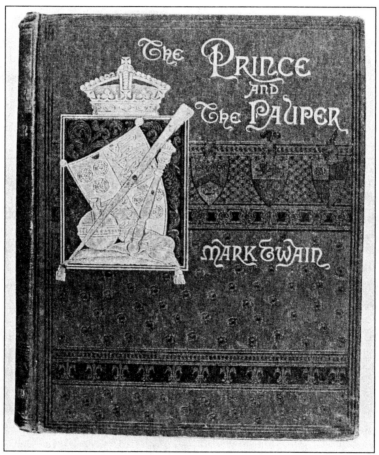

Fig. 48. *The Prince and the Pauper*

"The spine is gold stamped with the first four lines described on cover color [usually green] on gold field, [with] other lettering in gold . . . there are also black stamped decorations. Back cover is totally undecorated."[55]

The stamping on the spine varies. Unquestionably two separate and almost identical sets of brasses were used in the stamping. "The most readily apparent variation (and the one most easily described) is in the position of the uppermost, central <sic>, rosette on the spine [a scant 1/16" below] in relation to the horizontal fillet above it" (Fig. 49).[56]

Fig. 49.
*The Prince and the Pauper,*
Spine

Two different presses printed the final editions, the Franklin Press and the John Wilson University Press, each placing its own imprint on the copyright page, the Franklin being the first printing. Franklin Press electroplated the illustrations and, later, the book itself.

The prospectus for *The Prince* was finally ready for shipment to sales agents. "On October 19, Twain expressed to Osgood his pleasure with the appearance of the canvassing book and added that he believed that the illustrations also could have been engraved to perfection in Kaolatype . . . and about as cheaply and quickly, and a dern sight deeper and stronger. That is, I *think* I could have done them to perfection—it won't do to swear to anything, these days."[57]

The saga of the Kaolatype continued into the publishing of *Life on the Mississippi* when Anthony, in a lengthy letter to Twain, explained the reasons for refusing to use the Kaolatype process in illustrating the Mississippi book (see chapter on *Life on the Mississippi*). Twain's Kaolatype Company had an ignominious end. Other engravers began infringing on the engraving process and there were a series of lawsuits. The only "enduring monument to Kaolatype is the binding of the first American edition of *The Prince and the Pauper* on which Twain persuaded Osgood to use the engraving process."[58] The upshot of all this Kaolatype business was confusion and no real authentication for first editions or issues.

The "deluxe" edition was printed by Franklin Press and dis-
tributed as gifts to family and friends.  It was printed on India
paper, a paper  thinner than in regular editions, and placed on an
oversized leaf, which was bound in "white linen, stamped in gold,
inner hinges of blue linen, [with] white end papers grained in imitation of wood, [and] top edges of gilt."[59]  The cover, however, did
not have the Ipsen design featured on the first editions.

With the sub-title of *A Tale For Young People of All Ages* and
the dedication to his daughters Susy and Clara, Twain gave two of
his deluxe copies to Edward House's adopted daughter Koto and
W. D. Howells' daughter Winifred.  In a thank-you note to Twain,
Winifred Howells spoke of her enchantment with the book but also
her dissatisfaction at the placement of a particular illustration (Fig.
50):

> I have not finished it [*The Prince*] yet, but I think
> the loveliest place I have read is where the Prince
> finds the calf in the barn and  is so glad to cuddle
> up to something warm and alive. After his hor-
> ror at first feeling something beside him it was
> such a relief to find what it really was that I was
> almost angry with the picture for letting me
> know a little too soon.[60]

The little girl's
remarks demonstrate
how easily an im-
prudently inserted pic-
ture can change the
way a sensitive reader
responds to a passage.
One picture of the
prince bracing to reach
out for "WHAT
SEEMED TO BE A
WARM ROPE," was
placed just before the
line, "this petrified
him, nearly, with

Fig. 50.
"Cuddled Up to the
Calf"

fright. . . .  He thought he would rather die than touch it again"
(232).  In this illustration the "warm rope" is barely visible in the

background. Unfortunately, on the facing page is the picture "CUDDLED UP TO THE CALF." Seeing the image of the prince "cuddled" with the calf before reading of the identity of the Prince's fright, Winifred lost a sense of the Prince's fear and the mystery surrounding why he "would rather die than touch it again."

There were a few other problems that carried over from text into the illustrations. In Chapter XI of first state of the American, Canadian and English edition, the text read "canopy of **estate**." A correction had to be made for the second state, probably to correct the discrepancy between the uncorrected text reading and the caption of the illustration [CANOPY OF STATE] on the same page. In the second printing both text and caption read "state."61

Fig. 51.   "God Made Every Creature But You!"

In another instance the first American edition, first state caption read "GOD MADE EVERY CREATURE BUT YOU!" and was taken "from a passage in the manuscript where Miles Hendon curses the mule." Howells had suggested the "cursing" section be deleted and it was omitted. The illustration with the caption was included but made little sense since this quote by Hendon was not in the text. The editors for the first English edition noticed the discrepancy and recaptioned the illustration "THEN FOLLOWED A CONFUSION OF KICKS AND PLUNGINGS" (Figs. 51 & 52).62 For the second state of the American edition and thereafter, the caption was

Fig. 52.   "Then Followed a Confusion of Kicks and Plungings"

changed but appeared two pages after the picture since there was already an illustration of the "fettered little king" on the page with the quote.

Also for the first edition Harley designed an illustration "THE CHILDREN'S MOTHER RECEIVED THE KING KINDLY," with an irregular rule border, "intending that the printer fill the notch with type" as he had with so many irregularly shaped inserted cuts. "The printer, however, simply centered the illustration, making a strangely unbalanced page" (Fig. 53).[63]

Both Merrill and Harley were well schooled when it came to the use of ruled borders for their illustrations. The simple "L" shape had been a product of German design and changed the elements of the archaic page layout — usually squares or rectangles—which ran out to the margins.

Fig. 53.
"The Children's Mother Received the King Kindly"

The "L" design breaks the monotony and there is room on one side for a quadrant of text. With a release from the static straight border, both illustrators then became inventive with their framing techniques. Often the they would create two or three notches to be filled with short pieces of text; sometimes they would eliminate rule borders altogether and have the design run off into the text—as in the picture of Tom putting on is greaves (see Fig. 19). Yet even with this design the artists carefully controlled the composition so there was no "unbalanced feel" to the picture.

The most interesting variety of framing devices was their use of Gothic arches to border the illustrations: a simple rounded arch when Tom is learning Latin with the priest, a "blunt" arch when the boys "doff" their clothing, a 4-centered or Tudor arch when Tom eats with his fingers (91). These arches set a mood and were usually and appropriately employed when the subject was religious or royal, not in peasant scenes.

An incorrect historical fact appeared with the royal "ceremonies of the bedchamber"—a ritual demanding the passage of clothing through the hands of fourteen servants before a royal personage was allowed to dress (Fig. 54). This was a formality more likely to have been observed by the household of the French King, Louis XIV, than by that of Henry VIII.[64] Nevertheless, a drawing by

Fig. 54. "The First Lord of the Bedchamber Received the Hose"

Merrill included all the participants in this tedious routine, from the Archbishop of Canterbury in his appropriate robes along a line of fourteen variously garbed attendants.

Mark Twain's subtle mind can be read in this passage about a pair of the Prince's hose. The text reads:

> The First Lord of the Bedchamber received the hose and was about to incase Tom's legs in them, when a sudden flush invaded his face and he hurriedly hustled the things back into the hands of the Archbishop of Canterbury with an astounded look and whispered, "See, my lord!"— pointing to something connected with the hose. The Admiral passed the hose to the Hereditary Grand Diaperer, and had hardly breathe enough in his body to **ejaculate**, "See my lord!" [emphasis mine]. (164-165)

A most interesting verb to be used in this paragraph.

With most of the pictures finished (to Twain's delight) the author was on to other issues, his Canadian and English editions. Both Twain and Osgood were anxious about Canadian pirates who had done so much damage to the sales of *Tom Sawyer*. Osgood was issued copyright on 13 October and filed 12 December 1881. In an attempt to forestall pirating, Twain went to Montreal in November where he met with Dawson of Dawson and Brothers, whom Osgood had dubbed a "thoroughly honorable man." Twain then worked out a deal to have the book set and plated in Boston by Rand, Avery, and Company. The plates were then shipped to the Dawson firm to print an unillustrated 275-page "paper-wrapped" edition to protect copyright—the Canadian edition lacks the facsimile Latimer letter (Fig. 55).

Twain's "temporary" residence in Canada did not satisfy the right to copyright, the law stipulated that he be "domiciled." As he and Osgood had feared two pirated copies of *The Prince* were printed. The devious Rose-Bedford Publishing Company and John Ross Robertson again outwitted Twain and Osgood by circumventing the "imperial" law and having pirated editions printed in the United States and then shipped into Canada. The Rose "red cloth stamped in gold" covered edition did not publish until April 1882 and

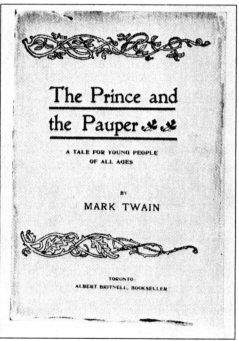

Fig. 55. *The Prince and the Pauper*

Robertson's edition later that same year. With these late issues there was little damage to American sales.

Fig. 56.  "Longing for the Pork-Pies"

Another copyright quandary surrounded the Chatto English edition. Remembering the difficulties for the English edition of *Tom Sawyer*, Osgood and Twain determined that electros for both pictures and text should arrive in Chatto's office in time for the American and the English edition to be issued on the same day. A skeptical Chatto had a fall-back position. If the shipment was delayed he would publish an "unillustrated" two-volume edition. Thanks to Osgood's efficient team in his Boston office, the shipment of electros was on target and Chatto printed and issued the illustrated English edition on 1 December, two days before Osgood's publication.

The Chatto edition changed the design for their cover, using instead a red overall cloth cover with the author's name black-stamped and the title in bold gilt letters. Running diagonally across the cover was a reproduction of Tom Canty "LONGING FOR THE PORK-PIES" (Figs. 56 & 57), from Chapter II

Fig. 57.
*The Prince and the Pauper*

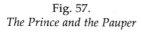

overlapping a circle-ruled design of "SPLENDID PAGEANTS AND GREAT BON-FIRES"—without the original small overlapping cut of the bonfires of Harley's illustration in Chapter I.

Despite the fact that Chatto had chosen different designs for his cover, he announced that he was delighted with the illustrations and cabled Twain: "We found the illustrations so important that we concluded it would be better to start at once with the single volume illustrated edition at 7/6." Chatto also slipped in a comment on the quality of the American edition, "The paper & print are beautiful, but I believe our engravings come out a little clearer and better than yours do."[65]

The American reviews were mixed. Howells set the tone for critical reaction in the New York *Daily Tribune* as early as October by citing evidence of Twain's change in style. He inferred that he had found "growth in a man who ought still to have his best work before him."[66] Another early review, in the December 1881 *Atlantic Monthly*, praised the book and agreed with Howells that Twain had made a successful radical new departure in his writings. The review in *Harper's* was also admiring, calling Twain a: "veracious chronicler" and saying the book was "rich in historical facts and teachings."[67] One reviewer commented that the illustrations were drawn in the "spirited, florid old style, adding that they would 'amuse the children.'"[68] *Century* strongly disagreed stating, we "do not think his [Twain's] 'new departure' is a conspicuous success."

Twain was undisturbed by the *Century* but delighted with the *Atlantic* critic's assessment. He wrote to the reviewer, H. H. Boysen:

> I went for the bulk of the profits, and so published the volume at my own expense, opening with an edition of 25,000 copies, for the manufacture of which I paid $17,500. . . . I find myself a fine success, as a publisher and literally the new departure is a great deal better received than I had any right to hope for.[69]

Twain was surprised that the English reviews were "profoundly complimentary" with only a few dissenters and a remonstrance from the critic Purcell in the *Academy* who pointed out the "incongruities in the king's levee"—the bedchamber ritual business.[70]

Twain kept an eye on sales and at first believed he had been successful. "By May 1882, Chatto was able to report a sale of 8,880 copies and the send L 1509.0 s.l.d in royalties."[71] Twain had opted for royalties rather than a commission contract with Chatto. But the bloom of good sales would soon fade. Twain was disappointed and blamed Osgood "for doing not great things with [the sale of] *The Prince and the Pauper*."[72] He wrote to Osgood in mid February faulting the "too brief a pre-canvass, and the subsequent performances of the Bliss gang of general agents. . . . There is just one thing *sure*— we'll have a very different genl agent system, hereafter, and not any Bliss's in it."[73]

Because sales were still slow by summer, Twain considered "dumping" the book into the trade market bookstores. However, Osgood, who felt that sales would pick up later in the year, persuaded him to abandon the plan.

Osgood and Twain agreed to revamp their sales organization and work on a better campaign for the next book, *Life on the Mississippi*. As part of the reorganization, Webster would take over as head of the general agents. Twain breathed a fervent hope: "We will see if we can improve on the Prince & Pauper's luck."

## Notes

[1] MTLP, p. 140.

[2] SCL to Orion Clemens, 24 October 1880, MTLP, p. 126. Mark Twain had completed manuscript for *The Prince and the Pauper* on 14 September 1880. Elisha Bliss died on 28 September 1880. In this same letter Twain said that he would stay with Frank Bliss to get all the money he felt owed him if Elisha Bliss were still alive.

[3] Osgood's publication was an illustrated, ninety-six page volume containing four illustrations. The book included "A True Story" (Osgood's version did not contain the sub-title "Just as I Heard It") and "Facts Concerning the Recent Carnival of Crime." Both stories were also printed in *Sketches, New and Old* and illustrated by True Williams. "A True Story" had previously been printed in the *Atlantic Monthly* (1876) without illustration.

[4] "The new contract was on commission. Clemens retained copyright, paid the cost of printing, binding and advertising; stood the loss if the book did not pay for itself; reaped the profit if it did; paid Osgood a commission—usually a percentage of production costs. Clemens had verbal agreements as early as 27 November 1880, but a written contract was not until 9 February 1881. Frederick Anderson and Hamlin Hill, "How Samuel

Clemens Became Mark Twain's Publisher: A Study of the James R. Osgood's Contracts," *Proof*, 2 (1972), pp. 121-122.

⁵ Osgood to SLC, 2 April 1881. SLC to Osgood, 31 December 1881, MTLP, p. 149.

⁶ SLC to Osgood, 7 March 1881. *The Prince and the Pauper*, ed. Victor Fischer and Lin Salamo (Berkeley: University of California, 1979), p. 10, n. 34. The manufacturing costs on the initial 25,000 volumes of *The Prince and the Pauper*, amounted to $17,500—an average of seventy cents for each book. Clemens to H. H. Boysen, 11 January 1882, MTLP, p. 152, n.1.

⁷ Carl J. Weber, *The Rise and Fall of James Ripley Osgood* (Waterville: Colby College Press, 1959), p. 181. Hereafter cited as Weber, *Rise*.

⁸ SLC to A. V. S. Anthony, 3 March 1881. The first line is in MTLP, pp. 189-190. The remainder is in photocopy in the MTP.

⁹ Weber, *Rise*, p. 181.

¹⁰ Clemens to Pamela Moffett, 16 March 1881, *Businessman*, p. 151.

¹¹ SLC to Osgood, 30 March 1881, MTLP, p. 135.

¹² "A. V. S. Anthony," *Our American Artist*, ed. S. G. W. Benjamin, Vol. II (Boston: D. Lothrop and Company, Publishers, 1965), 58-63. In 1883 Anthony would draw, engrave, and supervise the design of Sir Walter Scott's *Lady of the Lake* in a deluxe edition published by James R. Osgood and Company with F. T. Merrill, E. H. Garrett and L. S. Ipsen as part of the illustrating team.

¹³ Hamilton I, p. 119. He had worked on many lesser known Boston-published books: *The Deerings of Medbury, Eighty Years Ashore and Afloat*, and was part of a team of artists for the 1876 *The Great Bonanza* where he worked and signed the frontispiece.

¹⁴ Hamilton, I, 119

¹⁵ P&P, Iowa, p. 424. n. 49.1. Ipsen would design similar half-titles for Sir Walter Scott's *The Lady of the Lake* published by Osgood in 1883.

¹⁶ St. Edward's crown was a ubiquitous piece of iconography in both England and America and would make a familiar symbol for Twain's Victorian readers. A fully detailed St. Edward's crown was drawn to surmount Ipsen's chapter heading for Chapter XXXII. Ipsen would draw the crowd worn by a "baron" to crest his chapter heading HENDON HALL, probably creating the design before Twain realized that "baronets" did not exist in the time of Henry VIII.

¹⁷ Ipsen would continue to work the Tudor Rose arms design into the insignia in all his half-titles. All Merrill's designs would feature the royal lions and fleur-de-lis.

¹⁸ Everett Emerson, "Afterward," P&P, Oxford, p. 8.

¹⁹ P&P, Iowa, p. 391.

²⁰ Previous to this note directing the artists Twain wrote "Make portraits from the same photograph." The photo referred to is unknown. P&P, Iowa, p. 375, n. 1. In Twain's whipping boy's story, "A Boy's Adventure," the author had written: "The time of this scene is early in the year 1548, conse-

quently Edward VI is about ten years of age; the other lad is fourteen or fifteen." P&P, Iowa, p. 377.

[21] SLC to Anthony, 9 March 1881, P&P, Iowa, p. 8 and p. 11.

[22] Anthony to SLC, 12 March 1881, MTP. The cuts in the first edition are unsigned. The captions read OFFAL COURT and "HE OFTEN READ THE PRIEST'S BOOKS."

[23] In Twain's working note he specified, "Prince dress—p. 31 Ken." P&P, Iowa, p. 359. This abbreviation referred to the Abottsford's edition of Sir Walter Scott's *Kenilworth*, a handsome set owned by Twain.

[24] In Chapter VII Tom is seen "donning a costly suit of armour he finds in the Prince's apartments." For details of the costume Mark Twain referred to an illustration in Chapter V of the Abbotsford edition of Scott's *Quentin Durward*." In later working notes Twain wrote "(Dress of arms about p. 54, Q. Durward)." P&P, Iowa, p. 360 and p. 363.

[25] P&P, Iowa, p. 375.

[26] Samuel Clemens, *The Prince and the Pauper* (Boston: James R. Osgood and Company, 1882), p. 50. Hereafter cited as Prince, 1882.

[27] P&P, Iowa, p. 383, n. 68.7-16. "At the following Easter [1553], the boys and 'mayden children' were in 'plonket,' or blue; hence Christ's Hospital also became called the Blue Coat School. It has been imagined that the coat was the mantle and the *yellow*, as it is technically termed, the sleeveless tunic of the monastery; the leathern girdle also corresponding with the hempen cord of the friar. . . . It is most reasonable to regard the dress as copied from the costume of the citizens of London at this period [1552], when long blue coats were common habit of the apprentices and serving men, and yellow stockings were generally worn [the School is vulgarly called 'the Yellow Stocking School']." John Timbs, *Curiosities of London*, rev. ed. (Detroit: Singing Tree Press, 1968), p. 96. Hereafter cited as Timbs.

[28] SCL to Ben Ticknor, 14 August 1881, MTLP, pp. 139-140.

[29] MTLP, pp. 139-140. See also P&P, Iowa, p. 359, where in Twain's working notes he recorded, Prince dress—p. 31 Ken, presumably meaning Kenilworth.

[30] P&P, Iowa, pp. 364-365. Twain would refer to an illustration in Chapter V of the Abbotsford edition and to descriptions on pages 54 and 88 of the Scott novel in his working notes.

[31] In Twain's working notes he would refer to Scott's *Kenilworth* for descriptions of "lady's dress." P&P, Iowa, p. 357.

[32] In Mark Twain's working notes he stipulated "Elizabeth dressed with exceeding simplicity in Edward's time—60 Court of Q.E." The page citation refers to Lucy Aiken's *Memoirs of the Court of Queen Elizabeth* published in 1818. In notes earlier Twain wrote: "The ball & mask after banquet—see Hunt [presumably Leigh Hunt] for costumes." P&P, Iowa, p. 367.

[33] In Twain's working notes he had written, "Anne Askew & 3 others burnt as Sacramentarians July 16, '46." P&P, Iowa, p. 347.

[34] In Chapter XI of first state of the American and English edition,

the text read "canopy of estate." A correction had to be made for the second state, probably to correct the discrepancy between the uncorrected text reading and the caption of the illustration [CANOPY OF STATE] on the same page. P&P, Iowa, p. 428, n. 124.

[35] Not seen is the oblong rough stone called Jacob's Pillow, brought from Scone in Perthshire, which is usually placed beneath the chair.

[36] Simon Thurley, *The Royal Palaces of Tudor England* (New Haven & London: Yale University Press, 1993), p. 238.

[37] SCL to A. V. S. Anthony, 28 April 1881. Years later when another editor discovered that the transcription was "*wrong* in many places," Frank Bliss assured everyone that "Clemens wrote December 31, 1900 to let it stand & not make corrections. 'They are not important.'" P&P, Iowa, p. 422, n. 29, 6-32.

[38] SLC to Ticknor, 14 April 1881, MTLP, p. 140. The seal appears rather inconspicuously in two other Ipsen drawings of half-titles in the first edition: TOM RECEIVES INSTRUCTIONS (p. 71), and THE QUESTION OF THE SEAL (p. 95).

[39] P&P, Iowa, p. 11, n. 37. The inscription around the edge of the seal, "Honi Soit Qui Mal Y Pense," was later used by Dan Beard as a ribbon decoration for his illustration in Twain's *A Connecticut Yankee*, with the caption DECORATION OF SIXTH CENTURY ARISTOCRACY.

[40] Charles Knight, *Popular History of England*, VI (London and New York: Frederick Warne and Co., n.d.), 270.

[41] Clemens to the Osgood Company, 2 July 1881, Yale. P&P, Iowa, p. 390.

[42] SLC to Mr. and Mrs. Karl Gerhardt, 31 July 1881 and SLC to Benjamin Ticknor, 15 August 1881, P&P, Iowa, p. 391.

[43] SLC to Ben Ticknor, 1 August [1881], MTLP, pp. 138-139.

[44] SLC to Ticknor, 14 August [1881], MTLP, pp. 139-140.

[45] P&P, Iowa, p. 11, n. 39.

[46] MTLP, p. 139.

[47] Letter of January 31, 1881, published in *Mark Twain the Letter Writer*, ed. Cyril Clemens (Boston: Meador 1932), p. 37.

[48] P&P, Iowa, p. 11.

[49] *Businessman*, p. 148. Also in N&J II, 352.

[50] *Businessman*, p. 151.

[51] SLC to Charles Webster, 7 September 1881, MTLP, p. 141, n. 1.

[52] *Businessman*, p. 169.

[53] SLC to Ticknor, 9 September 1881, MTLP, p. 141.

[54] *Businessman*, p. 172.

[55] MTB, p. 40.

[56] BAL II, p. 196. "The most readily apparent variation (and the one most easily described) is in the position of the uppermost, central <sic>, rosette on the spine in relation to the horizontal fillet above it."

[57] MTLP, p. 141, n. 3. The prospectus was stamped from yet a third

set of brasses which, while almost identical with the two first edition covers lacks the delicate detail of both. Hamilton I, p. 196.

58 MTLP, p. 129. Twain tried to sell his shares in the company by 1887 and eventually lost $50,000 in Kaolatype.

59 BAL II, p. 197. Ticknor proclaimed there were fourteen copies printed by Franklin Press, himself and Anthony being recipients of copies. BMT, page 40. The only existing copy is housed in the Berg collection of the New York Public Library.

60 MTHL I, 383.

61 P&P, Iowa, p. 428, n. 124 and p. 401, n. 33.

62 P&P, Iowa, p. 432, n. 236.

63 P&P, Iowa, pp. 431-432, n. 218.

64 An English reviewer pointed out the incongruities in "the young king's levee." E. Purcell's review, *The Prince and the Pauper*, *Academy* (London) 20 (December 24, 1881): 469. Hereafter cited as Purcell.

65 Welland, p. 108.

66 New York *Daily Tribune*, 25 October 1881, p. 6.

67 *Harper's* 64 (March 1882): 635.

68 MTCH, p. 91.

69 MTLP, p. 152, n. 1.

70 Purcell, 20: 469.

71 Welland, p. 108.

72 Weber, *Rise*, p. 181.

73 MTLP, p. 152.

### List of Illustrations

All illustrations for *The Prince and the Pauper* from The Oxford Mark Twain, *The Prince and the Pauper*, 1996.

**Fig. #**

# Chapter IV

## *Life on the Mississippi*

"I will not interest myself in anything connected
with this wretched God-damned book."[1]

Mark Twain's deviation from subscription format for *The
Prince and the Pauper* had won him critical acclaim but did little to
fill his purse. Poor canvassing practices, high production costs, and
Twain's attempt to write historical fiction—a genre his audience did
not associate with the name of Twain—had proved unsuccessful.
For his next major publication, the author determined to return to
the principles of the subscription book and produce a text modeled
on his former travel works. "He even considered, then rejected,
titles that would relate this new book to *The Innocents Abroad*"—[2]
titles like *Abroad on the Great River* and *Abroad on the Mississippi*,
appropriate since the book would be an informative travel-narra-
tive documenting the Mississippi River.

For years Twain also had resolved to fashion a "historical
history" of the Great River, a history which was fast becoming
unknown. In a letter to his mother as early as 1866, he wrote that "a
history" was a "pet notion of mine," and in 1871 he advised Olivia,
"When I come to write the Mississippi book, *then* look out!"[3]  His
idea was to select early newspaper and journal writings about the
river—the towns and folk of his youth—then add current observations of steamboating. The book would not be fiction or autobiography but a history of past events that he could couple with observations made while on a projected contemporary field trip—a "standard" work, in the nineteenth-century meaning of the term. The
subject of the Mississippi was a "virgin field" in his eyes and Twain

considered himself the only privileged and authoritative historian capable of the task.

But Twain also knew that no matter his subject, his readers would expect a book similar to his former subscription works. If a subscription book was to sell, it had to entertain as well as inform; humor was as important as statistics. And it must be a bulky tome, filled with personal yarns and anecdotes; a massive text crammed with illustration. Twain understood that he'd need to combine his genius in writing with the expertise of skilled illustrators. Only then could a book be fashioned that would meet subscription best-seller requirements. The scenes, past and present, should be histor-ically correct; caricatures of himself as a bumbling tourist should be realistic; and the humor in the illustrations should parallel the wit in his tall tales. Twain was assured that Osgood's firm again would hire a team of artists with the highest qualifications.

Twain and Osgood signed another commission contract, much the same as their arrangement for *The Prince and the Pauper*; Twain as publisher and Osgood as agent and distributor. The con-tract provided a sliding scale of commissions: "Clemens to pay all costs of producing the book and receive all the receipts while Osgood & Co., as ostensible publishers . . . be paid a commission of 7 1/2 % on the first 50,000 and 5% afterwards."[4] A standard format for a subscription book was agreed upon—Twain did not insist that *Life on the Mississippi* have the "deluxe" packaging, elaborate initial letters and expensive paper as he had with *The Prince*. Ben Ticknor and A. V. S. Anthony would again supervise the manufacturing process, a task they had performed most competently for the former book. There would, however, be several other personnel shifts. Twain pressured Osgood to move Charles Webster from his management of the Kaolatype process and he was put in "full charge of the matter of running the book."[5] Webster's letterhead bore the title "Publisher." The American Publishing Company agents Osgood had used in distributing *The Prince* (the incompetent sales people Frank Bliss had suggested) were replaced. Webster immediately began to recruit new general agents.

*Life on the Mississippi* should have been a simple second ven-ture for both author and publisher. In 1874, Twain had written to Howells about traveling to New Orleans "to see the old Mississippi days of slumbering glory & grandeur as seen from the pilot house."[6] He next suggested the topic to Osgood on 12 February 1875, while he was working on several pieces about the Mississippi. The following year Twain published seven serialized articles titled "Old Times on the Mississippi" in the *Atlantic Monthly*. But after publication, the river project stalled and he shifted his attention to plans for a book of boyhood adventures, ideas that eventually would become *The Adventures of Tom Sawyer* and the *Adventures of Huckleberry Finn*. It would be six years before the *Atlantic* articles surfaced again as Chapters IV through XVII in the publication of *Life on the Mississippi*.[7]

By April 1882, Twain had put in place arrangements for a cruise to "pump the river pilots" for anecdotes to include in a Mississippi book. Osgood agreed to accompany Twain part of the way and the journey was to be made less burdensome for the author by hiring a stenographer to take and transcribe impressions. For the secretarial position, Osgood first contacted Edward Dickenson who declined, pleading other engagements. Next Twain contacted Roswell Phelps, a stenographer for the Continental Life Insurance Company. After an interview "Phelps and MT signed a contract whereby MT paid the secretary $100 a month, all traveling expenses, and a dollar per thousand words of transcription."[8] Unfortunately, what should have been a relaxing river excursion became a complex journey of contradictory emotions. In notes to Olivia, Twain at one time wrote of having a "powerful good time," yet a few letters later he described the passage as "this hideous trip."[9] There is little doubt that resuscitating the memories of his Southern past clashed with the harsh realities of the South's present.

Twain's plan had been to run up to Hannibal and take the narrow packet boats down the river, stopping at certain villages on the way. Unfortunately, these plans immediately went awry. The smaller ships were no longer plentiful. Being forced to take the larger steamboats, which could only steer the main course, the sight-seers bypassed most of the small towns. Nevertheless, it was during this trip that Twain discovered the unfortunate destinies of his former "starchy-boy" friends. He saw the destructive shifts of the river's course, and viewed the slow decay of once familiar towns. These dispiriting images nurtured his building prejudice about his beloved South where, he determined, religion and railroading had taken over the land.

The Hannibal of his youth was gone; the town now little more than a place for melancholy reflection. He did, of course, visit the site, staying for three days. He even stopped at "the house which was my home when I was a boy" (537). The book's pages contain three pictures of Twain as a mature man talking to residents and reminiscing about old friends. A number of prints are included of Twain as a boy when he lived in Hannibal: one of his dream vision of Jimmy Finn, the town drunk, who was burned to death in jail; one of a group of lads—Twain not identified—skinny-dipping in a muddy creek before a friend, Dutchy, is drowned. Even though a chapter is titled MY BOYHOOD'S HOME, there is be no illustration of Twain's house, the town, or any other Hannibal landmark except a "shuttering" Bear Creek, a spot famous for breeding "chills and fever in its day" (546). There is a significant tail piece (Fig. 1) showing all the townsfolk deserting Hannibal for St. Louis (529). The book contains artists' renditions of scenes from many other southern towns—New Orleans, Memphis, Napoleon and others. But Twain's sadness at seeing the decline of a town that had held happy memories of his youth may explain why he did not have his illustrators provide a setting that would reflect Hannibal in 1882.

Fig. 1.  Tail Piece

The river trip covered eight hundred miles, from St. Louis south to New Orleans, then back north to St. Paul. By the time he returned home, Twain's mood had mellowed. He had four months to "set [sic] down with Phelps's notes and write pages and pages for Osgood to use in the projected book."[10]  His plan was to compose the necessary mountain of manuscript at Quarry Farm where he could write without distraction.  Unfortunately, the Quarry summer through to fall was consumed with family illnesses: Jean and Susy came down with scarlet fever, Twain himself battled lumbago and possibly malaria.

Osgood, returning from a summer spent in Europe, was energized and immediately began the production process, signing artist's contracts and making arrangements for the book's design. He hired two illustrators who straightway began working from the unillustrated, already published articles from the *Atlantic Monthly*. John J. Harley [1840-1919], who had shared work on character sketches with Frank Merrill for *The Prince and the Pauper*, was hired on as principal illustrator and became a permanent staff artist for the Osgood firm.[11]  His assignment was to draw amusing sketches of the river folk and renditions of Twain as a cub pilot.  Edmund Henry Garrett [1853-1927] was given the job of doing Mississippi landscape and shoreline scenes.

Harley's credentials had been established with his work on *The Prince*.  Background information on the illustrator Edmund Henry Garrett [1853-1929], however, is very sketchy.  He was, at the time he worked on *Life on the Mississippi*, a thirty-year-old illustrator-painter who had "studied at Academie Julien, Paris; a pupil of Jean Paul Laurens."[12]  After returning to the States, he designed bookplates for institutions and posters for the Boston *Sunday Herald*. He continued with his painting career exhibiting in shows at the Boston Etching Club with his friend Frank Merrill.  Garrett's friendship with Merrill undoubtedly played an important role in his being hired by Osgood.

Meanwhile, at Quarry Farm, Twain decided to begin the book by chronicling the river's history using Francis Parkman's description of the LaSalle expedition.  To give authenticity to his river documentary, he added extracts from Schoolcraft's Indian legends and appended the memoirs of early travelers like Harriet Martineau.  For local color, he cribbed articles from southern newspapers and long citations from various regional history and travel books.

By September Twain, back in Hartford, plodded along.  He wrote sometimes as little as two hundred words in five hours. Discouraged with his inspirational drought, Twain asked Osgood to "set a cheap expert to work to collect local histories of Mississippi towns and a lot of other books relating to the river for me."[13] Osgood dutifully attended to the request.  As Hamlin Hill writes, "On 22 July, W. Rowlands replied for JRO that they were mailing

*Emerson's Magazine* with J. A. Dallas's 'Up the Mississippi,' and a lot of books relating to travel in the U. S. by English people in the first half of this century; twenty-five volumes in all."[14] When this fresh batch of material was sent on to Twain, he labored on.

By late October he wrote to Howell's: "I went to work at nine o'clock yesterday morning, and went to bed an hour after midnight. Result of the day (mainly stolen from books, tho' credit given), 9500 words. So I reduce my burden by one third in one day. . . . I have nothing more to borrow or steal; the rest must all be writing."[15] Twain subsequently acknowledged his debt to sixteen works (ten copied *verbatim*), while scholars have cataloged several more.[16]

In November Twain wrote dejectedly to Howells, "The printers must wait, the artists, canvassers, and all the rest. I have got everything at a dead stand-still, and that is where it ought to be."[17] With his creative imagination at low ebb, Twain decided to slip in some of his already completed work to fatten the manuscript to the bulk dictated by the subscription market. Into Chapter III he incorporated the "Raftsmen's Passage," written in 1876 and intended for Chapter XVI of *Huckleberry Finn,* and elsewhere he worked in several leftover parts from *A Tramp Abroad.* It was mid-January 1883 before the manuscript was near completion. A grumbling Twain remarked to Howells, "I never had such a fight over a book in my life before."[18]

As early as June complications on the production end arose and Twain suggested to Osgood that they try the Kaolatype process for the book's cover and some illustration. At Twain's insistence, Charles Webster had continued to work in his spare time on the "chalk-type" process, despite the disappointing results exhibited for *The Prince and the Pauper.* To convince Osgood of the merits of the Kaolatype procedure, Twain had Osgood ship some brass stamp patterns to Webster. Webster was to use them to demonstrate the superiority of the Kaolatype approach. Osgood wrote back to Twain that he had put into the capable hands of design director Anthony, the evaluation of the chalk process:

> Anthony is going to make a parcel of the drawings and Kaolatype reproductions which I will send forward to you today by express. He will also write a letter giving the artist's view of the objectionable features in the reproductions.[19]

The returned package contained both Anthony's "lessons in illustration" and principal illustrator Harley's reaction to the Kaolatype reproductions. Anthony pointed out the failures in technique. He explained how illustration should interpret character and compared various methods of turning original drawings into final prints. He also gave a brief definition of style. All the samples in the packet had come from illustrations drawn for Chapter VI of *Life on the Mississippi*:

> (Identification of the page numbers and captions for first-edition prints appear in brackets.)
>
> No. 1
> Please note the difference in the character and expressions of the heads, the loss of color and drawing in the figures, and the folds of the drapery, the rankness and thickening of the delicate lines and the general stiffness of the "handling" ["OUR PERMANENT AMBITION" on p. 63 of the first edition] (Fig. 4).
>
> No. 6
> All of the above applies to this picture also [Tail piece on p. 69 of the first edition] (Fig. 3).
>
> No. 2
> Will pass, but there is a radical change in the face, in the snouts of the pigs, and a general thickness of line over all—["WATER-STREET CLERKS" on p. 62 of the first edition] (Fig. 2).
>
> No. 4
> Will pass although the face is much changed, and the whole thing comes heavy and rank ["THE TOWN DRUNKARD ASLEEP ONCE MORE," p. 66 of the first edition] (Fig. 5).
>
> No. 3
> Note the change in the heads of the two negro drivers, the stiffness of the lines throughout, the entire loss of character in the mules' heads, the very cheap lines on their necks, the omission of the blacks on the loss of the foreground shaft-mules which makes them blend with, and stick to, the steamboat, and the general change of

"manner" ["ALL GO HURRYING TO THE WHARF," p. 64 of the first edition] (Fig. 6).

No. 5
The change in the heads, and the lining on the figures, etc. ["A SHINING HERO," p. 68 of the first edition] (Fig. 7).[20]

Fig. 2.
"Water-Street Clerks"

Fig. 3.
Tail Piece

Fig. 4.   "Our Permanent Ambition"

Fig. 5.   "The Town Drunkard Asleep Once More"

Fig. 6.
"All Go Hurrying to
the Wharf"

Fig. 7.
"A Shining Hero"

In his long letter Anthony also compared the estimated plate costs, artist's fees, and differences in procedure between the Moss engraving Company process and the Kaolatype process:

> These plates will cost by the Moss process[21] about $2.00 each—price being regulated by size. By the Kaolatype process Mr. Webster tells me they think cost about $5.00 each—
>
> Looking at the results of the two methods for this peculiar kind of work, Mr. Harley thinks, and I agree with him, that it is almost impossible to reproduce his 'landing' by any other than a photographic method, when no *redrawing* is required as it is in the Kaolatype. That his freedom will be much cramped and lost by redrawing. That he does not want his name on them unless they are reproduced by the Moss or some kindred process. And that his interest would be lost unless his drawings were reproduced absolutely. I have got estimates from other artists for similar work and their prices are as follows:
>
> | E. B. Bensell | about | $12.00 | | each |
> |---|---|---|---|---|
> | W. P. Snyder | " | $15.00 to $25.00 | | " |
> | A. W. Rogers | " | $15.00 to $24.00 | | " |
> | A. Brennan | " | $20.00 to $40.00 | | " |
>
> Mr. Harley's price is $8.00 to furnish all needed material. No matter by what process the pictures are reproduced I must still go over the plates with a graver in order that the best printed results may be obtained.
>
> To sum up the whole thing the Kaolatype misses the original about the same as would the recital of the 'Jumping Frog' by a Baptist minister from memory—. The bald facts might possibly be preserved but the *style*, the *go*, the *handling*, would undoubtedly be lost.
>
> Will not the general result be helped by saving these three things?[22]

Webster's attempts to make satisfactory cover patterns and illustrations ended in failure. In a letter to Webster, Twain related Anthony's assessment of the process, pointing out in particular the increased costs.

> When I got to Boston the pictures had been sent to
> Hartford, so I did not see them until I got back. I
> listened to what they had to say, and examined the
> pictures when I got home. To my mind yours were
> better than the Moss, but as the artist did not feel
> so, I gave orders to have the rest done by the Moss
> Company. An additional reason for this was, that
> they said you charged double what Moss
> charged.[23]

This exchange of letters essentially spelled the end of Twain's attempts to use the Kaolatype process to illustrate his own work. Webster was finally allowed to give up his part-time Kaolatype duties. Yet even with this latest failure of the chalk process, Twain still argued that Osgood should invest in the company. He didn't dispose of his own stock until August 1886.

Meanwhile, Osgood sailed back to England to arrange with Chatto and Windus for the publication of the English edition of *Life*. On his return to Boston he encouraged Twain to press on with his work on the Mississippi book. By September 1882, sounding remarkably like Elisha Bliss during the trying times of *Roughing It*, Osgood was pleading with Twain for more manuscript.

> Now we must go to work at once on the prospec-
> tus-books. For this purpose we need the title and
> a selection of pages including type and cuts. Also
> your preface, or such introductory or explanatory
> matter as you choose to prefix. We particularly
> need the title at once, that we may have the cover-
> stamp prepared. Anthony tells me that there are
> about 100 cuts ready, or nearly so, (about one-
> third of the whole number proposed) and that he
> will soon be needing more copy to go on with.
> Let me hear from you as soon as possible on these
> points, as we can make no progress until they are
> settled.[24]

When new manuscript began trickling in, Osgood put the illustrators to work on the prospectus. Drawing for Chapters I, II and parts of III, as well as a few illustrations for Chapter XXXIII, Harley busied himself with the contemporary figures while E. H. Garrett worked on the historic persons, costumes, and landscapes. By December the prospectus was printed featuring several full-page

Fig. 8.   Spines of various editions,
*Life on the Mississippi*

illustrations—though there were no pictures from after Chapter XXXIII in the sales agent's book.

Harley worked the spine and the cover—essential elements for the prospectus. His design for the spine was stamped in gold and featured a youthful steamboat cub pilot at the wheel, purposefully scrutinizing the contours of the river—presumably an inexperienced Sam Clemens learning his trade (Fig. 8).[25]  A re-working of this vignette (because of size limitations) appeared on the narrow spine of the prospectus. Harley's cover, also stamped in gold, depicted a stoop-shouldered roustabout—his posture attesting to his years of physical labor—wistfully smoking his pipe atop a cotton bale, oblivious to the steamboat in the background that is bypassing his landing (Fig 9).  While the spine suggests a young cub's experience with life on the river in its former commercial glory, the cover faithfully portrays the idleness of a dock worker watching his present-day world float by.  The illustrator's images, Twain's cub days juxtaposed with the decline of the steamboat trade, capture and highlight the central drama of Mark Twain's story.

For his semi-fictional books Twain frequently used illustration as a supplement to his verbal characterizations. Illustrations regarding an individual's appearance were sometimes a necessity since often he or she was not described in physical terms.  In

Fig. 9.  Cover, *Life on the Mississippi*

Harley's characterization of Twain as the young cub both for the inserted prints and the spine, he religiously followed the author's text, depicting Twain as a "gawky small-town boy."  The reader

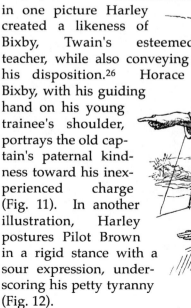

Fig. 10.
"All Well—But Me"

would not see or read of
Twain as the mature twenty-
one-year-old that he actually was during his cub days.
Moreover, Harley's young
cub bears no real resem-
blance to the lad who
would become Mark Twain
(Fig. 10).

Yet the illustrators
often went beyond the routine task of being faithful to
the text.  In many instances they also
caught the personality of Twain's characters.  For example, Captain Bixby and Pilot
Brown are not described in their size and
shape by Twain, however, clearly they are
characterized through their actions.  Therefore,
in one picture Harley
created a likeness of
Bixby, Twain's esteemed
teacher, while also conveying
his disposition.[26]     Horace
Bixby, with his guiding
hand on his young
trainee's shoulder,
portrays the old cap-
tain's paternal kind-
ness toward his inex-
perienced        charge
(Fig. 11).  In another
illustration, Harley
postures Pilot Brown
in a rigid stance with a
sour expression, under-
scoring his petty tyranny
(Fig. 12).

Fig. 11.  "That's a Reef"

Harley also supplied abbreviated views of the last steamboat on which Mark Twain served as a cub with Horace Bixby, the *Aleck Scott*. The *Aleck Scott* was an old side-wheeler that made "regular weekly packet runs between New Orleans and Vicksburg" (Figs. 13 & 14).

Garrett, too, was able to supply elements not clearly defined by Twain's text. He added authenticity and attitude to the explorers DeSoto and LaSalle. Twain had placed the men in history but did not describe them or their uniforms. Garret supplied Hernando DeSoto with his sixteenth-century ruffed collar and plumed Spanish helmet as he points to his discovery of the mighty river (Figs. 15 & 16). The artist also carefully documented the tragedy of DeSoto's death, 21 May 1542, with an accurate but dark and somber scene as the explorer's body was consigned to the waters of the Mississippi near Ferriday, Louisiana (Figs.

Fig. 12.
Pilot Brown

17 & 18). For LaSalle, Garrett creates a military costume, without buckled shoes, now accurate for the French in the seventeenth-century. The artist also adds an interesting perspective to the French explorer, posing him in an uncompromising pompous manner while "consecrating the robbery" (Fig. 19) of the "simple children of the forest" (37).

Fig. 13.
"Burst into a Fury"

When Twain characterized Joliet

Fig. 14.  Alex Scott, 1843

Fig. 15.   DeSoto Sees It

Fig. 16.   DeSoto Sees It First

Fig. 17.
Burial of DeSoto
*Harper's*

Fig. 18.   Burial of DeSoto

↔ Fig. 19.
Consecrating the Robbery

and Father Marquette by their professions, Garrett supplied their attire—though he had both men more appropriately garbed in clerical than merchant clothing—as they greeted the Indian Chief who had "taken off his last rag in order to appear at his level best" (34). Discreetly Garrett drew a back-view near silhouette of the "naked" chief with the amusing caption HOSPITABLY RECEIVED (Fig. 20).

Some of Harley's inspired and detailed efforts are seen in his renditions of the New Orleans Mardi-Gras festivities. In the New

Fig. 20.
"Hospitably Received"

Orleans chapters Twain admits that he was too late to sample the Mardi-Gras, his recollections only harking back to a spectacle "twenty-four years ago." Harley presented his own grotesquerie, a raucous rendition of a Mardi-Gras crowd of costumed revelers with a head-dressed Indian dancing with a bear in the foreground and a procession of spear-carrying Roman charioteers trooping across the mid-line. The backdrop for this carousing is authentic, depicting the buildings at one of New Orleans' busiest and most famous intersections, Canal and Royal Streets, called "Monkey Wrench Corner" by the locals (Figs. 21 & 22). Though Twain's account generalized about "giants, dwarfs, monstrosities, and other diverting grotesquerie" (465),

Fig. 21.  Mardi-Gras

Harley's interpretation embellished the "girly-girly romance" described in Twain's narrative.

Harley's next illustration adheres more closely to Twain's report, where the author blames Sir Walter Scott for everything from the Civil War to the decline of Southern literature. Taking a slender cue from Twain's description of Scott's "sham chivalries of a brainless and worthless long-vanished society" (467), Harley portrays a

Fig. 22.  Monkey Wrench Corner, New Orleans

lance-carrying medieval knight at a joust, ostrich-plumed, fully armored and mounted on a reeling charger with the caption reading CHIVALRY. While Harley's image of the New Orleans pageant runs counter to Twain's idea of the "romantic mysteries" of the New Orleans jubilee—and his chivalrous knight never even appears in Twain's narrative—both MARDI-GRAS and CHIVALRY complement the author's satirizing of a return to "the Walter Scott Middle-Age sham civilization" (Fig. 23).

Interestingly, CHIVALRY presages the superb frontispiece drawn by Dan Beard in 1889 for *Connecticut Yankee*, still six years away. There is a close resemblance between the design and the smile on the knight's helmet, suggesting that Beard may have referred to Harley's illustration (Fig. 24).[27]

Fig. 23.
Chivalry

Yet despite Harley's often perfect visual complements to Twain's prose, several of his characters in the first half of the book lack individual identity and appear as paste-board figures with similar

Fig. 24. "I Saw He Meant Business"

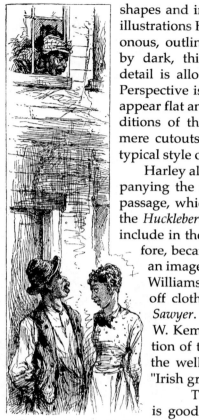

shapes and interchangeable faces. In his early illustrations Harley too often slips into a monotonous, outline-style. His images are centered by dark, thick strokes, and the background detail is allowed to fade into broken dashes. Perspective is lost (or ignored), and his figures appear flat and lifeless. Moreover, Harley's renditions of the Blacks of the South appear as mere cutouts and mimic the shameful stereotypical style of the cartoons of the time (Fig. 25).

Harley also worked the illustrations accompanying the now famous "Child of Calamity" passage, which Twain had written as a part of the *Huckleberry Finn* manuscript but "lifted" to include in the Mississippi book. Harley, therefore, became the second illustrator to create an image of Huck Finn, the first being True Williams when he drew Huck in "the cast-off clothes of a full-grown man" for *Tom Sawyer*. The third, of course, would be E. W. Kemble, who created for the first edition of the *Adventures of Huckleberry Finn*, the well-known image of Huck with his "Irish grin" (Figs. 26, 27 & 28).

There is good

Fig. 25. "No Foolin!" reason to suppose that Harley also provided the illustration's original description from Clarence Chatham Cook's *The House Beautiful: Essays on Beds and Tables, Stools and Candlesticks*

Fig. 26.
Huck Finn by Harley

Fig. 27.
Huck Finn by True Williams

Fig. 28.
Huck Finn
by
E. W. Kemble

(1877). Twain rewrote Cook's version to more accurately define the Grangerford house for the *Huck Finn* book. When he decided to use this same living room in *Life*, he "refurnished" the parlor, divesting it of all "the details expressive of Grangerford's character, in the interest of making the symbolism more universal."[28]  The illustrator's rendition of the room's interior corresponded to Twain's revised text.  The parlor (Fig. 29) is meticulously accurate to the

Fig. 29.  An Interior

book's description, including the centre table and the books piled with cast-iron exactness; the "polished air-tight stove, with pipe passing through a board which closes up the discarded good old fireplace"; and the sentimental family portrait with the two young children "simpering up at mama, who simpers back" (404). The artist gave life to the parlor of Twain's "wealthiest and most conspicuous citizen." The full-page illustration is unsigned, though the style suggests it was reproduced by Harley.

In this book Twain was eager to have his "history" document both prosperity and poverty. He wanted special attention drawn to the rise and fall of a real labor union, the Western Boatman's Benevolent Association.

He devoted two chapters to the organization and in these chapters, two illustrations of the buildings bear the signs "The Pilot's Benevolent Association" (not Western Boatman's), both illustrations sketched by Harley. The first cut is captioned "RESURRECTED PILOTS" and it pictures the dregs of the pilot's society arriving "on crutches, on drays" to collect their twenty-five dollar allotment, just as Twain had described them in his story (Fig. 30). A second illustration portrays a confused member of the association, papers in hand, who had just been "added to the fold" (Fig. 31). The pictures may stimulate the reader as he wades through Twain's detailing of the laws, dues, and new resources of the pilot's association. In this section the author seems to have forgotten that he should entertain as well as inform.

Fig. 30.
"Resurrected Pilots"

Many of the illustrations in *Life* represent architecturally interesting structures, well-known geographical shorelines, and his-

Fig. 31. "Added to the Fold"

torically accurate city-scenes. From the first page of Twain's "chronicle," Garrett as illustrator proved his competence. Garrett's frontispiece, with the carefully delineated balconies on the steamboat *Baton Rouge*, immediately establishes for the reader the grandiose style of the river boats (Figs. 32 & 33). For this, a most important first glimpse of Twain's world of the Mississippi, Garrett employed a variety of techniques: graded tonal values in the ruled-line background and the dark shapes of the bales and barrels in the foreground allow the steamship itself to dominate the drawing. The strong, dark horizontal lines bring out the ornamental detail of the *Baton Rouge*, and Garrett controlled the sight lines with two black smokestacks and the cupola of the pilot house to center the illustration. Curiously, this print has a mirror-image of Garrett's signature in the corner, indicating that he may also have been the engraver, incising in his name which, when reproduced, shows the signature in reverse. The original photograph of the *Baton Rouge*, still in existence in the McKinney Collection at Vassar College, authenticates the precise detailing of Garrett's work.

Garrett's meticulous accuracy is reflected also in his faithfulness to the text. When Twain described the Mississippi as "the crookedest river in the world" (21), Garrett produced a meandering shoreline in an irregularly stepped frame (Fig. 34). From his Mississippi River Valley landscapes of Spanish-moss-draped trees in Vicksburg (Fig. 35) to the bustling frontage of St. Paul (Fig. 36),

Fig. 32.   The "Baton Rouge"

Fig. 33.   *City of Baton Rouge*

Fig. 34.
View on the River

Fig. 35.
Early Navigation

Fig. 36.
St. Paul.

Garrett's sketches evoke the geography and natural backdrop against which Twain's social drama unfolds.

Some of Garrett's best work, like Harley's, is apparent in the New Orleans chapter, with his distinctive balconied architecture, cobblestone streets, and long rows of horse-drawn streetcars and carriages (Fig. 37). Garrett's style is immediately recognizable and his signature appears on forty prints in *Life on the Mississippi*, though his talents are evident in many others.

Canvassing for the book began in January. With time growing short and publishing deadlines near, panic set in. Osgood deemed it impossible to complete the design process with only two working illustrators. He "employed a third artist, one A. B. Shute, to draw various landscapes, portraits, and wharf scenes."[29]

Fig. 37.   Canal Street

If little is known about Garrett, present information about A. B. Shute is sketchier still. He was a staff artist for Osgood's firm but dropped out of sight after working on *Life*. Shute exhibits more variety in his designs than Harley but less than Garrett. Yet he was a very competent illustrator and his humor seems to have blended well with that of his author. This commission required him to draw a wide spectrum of subjects: caricatures, figures, landscapes, and city scenes. His caricatures are filled with personality and he drew many of Mark Twain. One cut of a rattled, wide-eyed Twain aboard the *Baton Rouge* when seeking shelter from a thunderstorm below decks, undermines the text in which Twain states that he alone tarried in the pilothouse to watch the raging storm before going nonchalantly down into the hold "to see what time it was" (502). Shute's caricature of Twain makes the author look the frightened fool (Fig. 38). The caption, I AM ANXIOUS ABOUT THE TIME, draws attention to Twain's lame excuse and amplifies both the humorous human elements of the situation and the real terror of a storm on the river. It is possible that when Twain saw the illustration, he suggested the caption since he knew his readers would expect the professed fearlessness in his words to be a fraud.

In *Life*, however, Twain was not portrayed as the fool as often as he had been in *Innocents* and *Roughing It*. The author as bumbling, naive tourist is seen infrequently in this, Twain's more serious effort at "historical history."

In the *Baton Rouge* chapter Shute

Fig. 38.
I Am Anxious About the Time

entered again into the spirit of a Twain anecdote.[30] Twain tells of meeting a boyhood friend—a former blacksmith cub who had become irrecoverably "stage struck"—who urged Twain to attend a performance of *Julius Caesar* in which he (the stage-stuck oaf) claims to be one of the actors. This "lumbering, ignorant, dull-witted lout . . . imagining himself to be Othello," stands before a stage bill advertising OTHELLO, with the caption below, STAGE-STRUCK (Fig. 39). Shute achieved the pretentious pose but more importantly captured the "musing" stare which complements the denouement of Twain's story with the actor-fool joyful in his role as a mere "supernumerary" Roman soldier dressed in a nightshirt. Twain's melancholy sarcasm is all the more telling when combined with Shute's contemplative picture.

Fig. 39.
Stage-Struck

When Twain evokes the true-crime style of the *Police Gazette* in his chapter about the "Penitent Thief," complete with thieves' *argot* and irregular spelling, he writes a wandering digression of a letter hoax played out by a Christian-reformed prisoner named Williams. Shute draws the narrative of Twain's tale (Figs. 40, 41, 42 & 43). First the artist portrays the masked burglar Williams in the days he was plying his trade, next he shows the converted-comrade Jack Hunt (supposedly the latter writer) relieving an old woman of her "leather" (512), while on the facing page Shute concocts the scene of Hunt saving the Brown children. On the following page Hunt/Williams is piously

Fig. 40
Williams Plies His Trade

teaching Sunday school. It is
with Shute's final picture (Fig. 44)
that he exposes the "nub" of
Twain's tale. Shute sketches the
convict Williams "penning the
alleged Hunt letter" in jail a full
two pages before Twain reveals
his "word of explanation." A careful reader of the illustration
knows
prema-
turely

that "the burglar
Williams wrote the let-
ter himself" (521). Shute
has pre-empted Twain's
Christian-cynical spoof;
the reader need not
spend the extra time
reading Twain's conclu-
sion.

For another tall tale
an inserted print sets
straight Twain's flight
of     fancy

Fig. 42.   The Crisis

about the Mississippi River's "alligator pilots." Like the illustration in the famous "chamois
hunt" for *A Tramp Abroad*, a
picture holds the truth to
Twain's exaggerated tale.
The print captioned "AN
ALLIGATOR BOAT" (Fig.
45), is let-in the margin

Fig. 43.   Mission Work

where the text describes "an odd-looking craft, with a vast coal-scuttle slanting aloft on the end of a beam" (266). In Twain's prolonged put-on he has a steamboat pilot discoursing on how "A 1 alligator pilots" scoop up the alligators from the river and take them to New Orleans where their hides are made into "soldier-shoes" (268).

The inserted cut of a snagboat, however, signals the truth for any reader with knowl-

Fig. 44.  Williams

Fig. 45.  "An Alligator Boat"

edge of navigation on the Mississippi during the early days.   In the 1830-1840s piloting this waterway was a precarious occupation because of the "planters"— trees that toppled into the river with their roots buried in the riverbed and their tops swaying above the surface—and the "sawyers"—tree roots more loosely set in the stream with their jagged teeth capable of ripping open the bottom of a steamboat. Snagboats (Fig. 46), with their swaying coal-scuttles, picked up these obstructive snags and sawyers and cleared them away.   The river was relatively clean of the largest log jams by 1840.

Twain compounds his stretcher-story when he has

Fig. 46.  The Snagboat *AID*

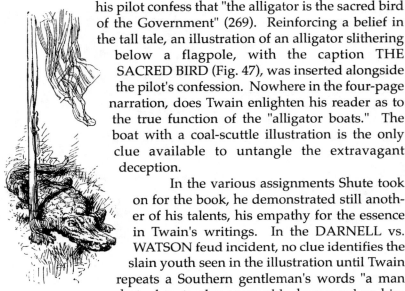

his pilot confess that "the alligator is the sacred bird of the Government" (269). Reinforcing a belief in the tall tale, an illustration of an alligator slithering below a flagpole, with the caption THE SACRED BIRD (Fig. 47), was inserted alongside the pilot's confession. Nowhere in the four-page narration, does Twain enlighten his reader as to the true function of the "alligator boats." The boat with a coal-scuttle illustration is the only clue available to untangle the extravagant deception.

In the various assignments Shute took on for the book, he demonstrated still another of his talents, his empathy for the essence in Twain's writings. In the DARNELL vs. WATSON feud incident, no clue identifies the slain youth seen in the illustration until Twain repeats a Southern gentleman's words "a man shot a boy twelve years old—happened on him in the woods" (286). Ironically, each time Twain refers to the narrator he calls him a "gentleman."

Fig. 47.
The Sacred Bird

However, Shute's picture of the killing placed a page before the narrator's story nullifies the gentleman's flat declaration of the facts. The picture gives a human face to the tragedy. With a murdered, youthful-faced boy sprawled in the foreground and a furtive, backward-glancing killer seen leaving the scene, it is Shute's image that pleads the horror of the feud (Fig. 48).

In a subtle treatment for a wharf scene, Shute again displays a sensitivity for Twain's ideas when the author laments the absence of the once "wide-awake"

Fig. 48.   Darnell vs. Watson

boats and jocund levee hands (Fig. 49). Shute's hard-edged line of

Fig. 49.
A. R. Waud, Looking Toward Jackson R. R. Depot, New Orleans

empty balconies and smokeless stacks for the three, once proud
now "sound-asleep steamboats," parallels the three melancholy and
listless shoreline roustabouts shadowed in the left foreground.
Shute's picture is in harmony with the spirit of Twain requiem for
the steamboat trade (Fig. 50).

Fig. 50.
Sound-Asleep Steamboats

Unfortunately (though understandably) Shute was also
responsible for some offensive ethnic caricatures of both African

Americans and Jews. Several stereotypes appeared in Chapter XXXIII: the hooked-nosed figure in THE ISRAELITE (Fig. 51); a brandy-drinking black in A PLAIN GIL (gil being 1/4 of a stan-

Fig. 51.  The Israelite

dard pint) (Fig. 52); and a tail piece of a smiling black, captioned in the "List of Illustrations" as A WATERMILLION (Fig. 53). All these Shute drawings are, of course, gratuitous cliches clearly prompted by Twain's text.  One full-page print, ELABORATE STYLE, detailing the ornate Sunday dress of the Arkansas Black society, is, however, more sympathetic

Fig. 53.
Tail piece,
A "Watermillion"

Fig. 52.   A Plain Gill

and anticipates some of the later

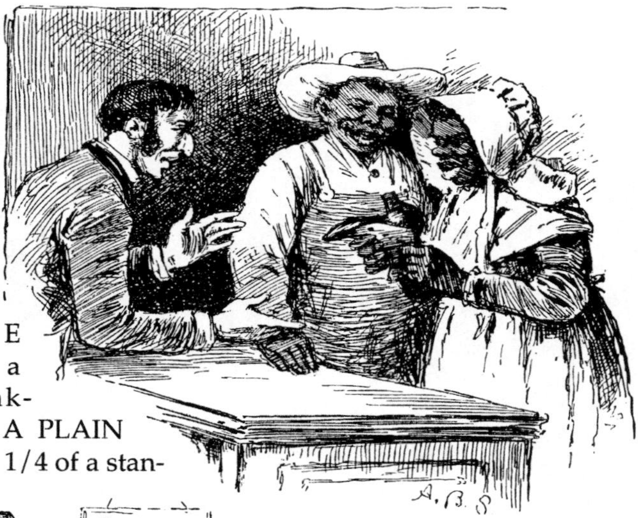

drawings of E. W. Kemble for *Huckleberry Finn* (Fig. 54). Shute signed forty-six of the prints in the book, though he too was undoubtedly responsible for some of the unsigned prints. Because he was a late hire, the majority of his illustrations are in the last half of the book.

In the usual working procedure for Twain illustrators, Harley, Garrett and Shute had the advantage of being able to copy from actual photographs. Twain had asked for and acquired pictures from John Henton Carter, the river editor for the Saint Louis *Post-Dispatch*,

Fig. 54. Elaborate Style

who also wrote and published a humorous almanac under the pseudonym "Commodore Rollingpin." Carter had made it a practice to document the Twain entourage's river journey, often writing in his "River News" column about the tour's progress from updates given to the editor by Twain himself. As writer, editor, publisher, and sometime confidant of Twain, Carter was willing and able to supply many of the required photographs.[31]

One picture Twain considered essential was of a character in *Life on the Mississippi* that Twain ultimately named Uncle Mumford. In his journal Twain had jotted down this reminder: "Make portrait of old Davis," Davis being the chief mate of the ship *John J. Roe*. Apparently, Davis's image was to be the model for an important crew member in *Life on the Mississippi*. At about the same time Twain also asked for a likeness of the cursing "Dad" Dunham of the *Gold Dust*, first requesting this picture from a ship's seaman, Edmund Gray. When Gray inquired whether Twain had received the photo, Twain replied with disgust: "Hang it, *no*! I haven't received Dad's photograph. Maybe it was sent to Osgood, Boston,

instead of to me, at Hartford. Was it?"[32] John Carter, not Gray, finally supplied the Dunham picture. A. B. Shute used Dunham's visual features for his "pen and ink drawing of 'Uncle' Mumford in the
first edition [which] may safely be presumed to be a likeness of

Dunham."[33]  In the meantime, however, Twain had
obviously decided against
naming this character either
"Davis" or "Dunham," and
had      settled      upon
"Mumford."    Shute's full-
page picture was captioned
UNCLE MUMFORD, and
Twain gave the newly-
named Mumford a good
measure of Davis's color-
ful vocabulary—the chief
mate's "regular orthodox
profanity with terms . . . borrowed from a geology
book."[34] Twain's salty, volu-
ble Uncle Mumford is, therefore, a composite character
and one of the more memo-
rable personalities in the
middle chapters of the book
(Fig. 55).

Fig. 55. Uncle Mumford

For years Twain had
harbored ambivalent feelings about another character, a certain
river-boat captain.  But *Life on the Mississippi* was, after all, to be a
"history" of the river, and therefore it seemed obligatory that a picture of this famous captain be included in the book.  Twain requested that Osgood obtain a photo of Captain Sellers's gravesite:

> Won't you please send to Commodore Rollingpin
> and get a photograph of Capt. Isaiah Sellers's
> Monument in Bellefontaine Cemetery, and let our
> artist make a 2/3 or a full-page picture of it.  I
> stole my nom de plume from him, and shall have
> considerable to say about him, for out there he
> was "illustrious."[35]

Fig. 56.
Sellers's Monument

Evidently Carter sent on a picture to Hartford and it was used by E. H. Garrett to create SELLERS'S MONUMENT. Garrett correctly copied the pilot's *bas relief* sculpture into a 2/3 page print, placing Sellers at a ship's wheel with a map of the Mississippi at the captain's feet (Fig. 56).[36]

Carter, or other still unknown sources, also provided the photos of two other men whose portraits were reproduced for the pages of

*Life on the Mississippi.* Horace Bixby's full-page print as THE CAPTAIN (Fig. 57) was probably copied from a photograph of a much younger Bixby. Though this first-edition print is unsigned, it was undoubtedly by the very capable Shute whose similar style is seen in the portrait of Uncle Mumford.

Carter may or may not have provided several other photographs: the picture of the steamboat *Baton Rouge* (used as a model for the frontispiece of the book), the

Fig. 57. The Captain

Fig. 58.   Immortelles

scenes of the IMMORTELLES in Chapter XLII (Fig. 58), as well as numerous other New Orleans sights done by Garrett for these later chapters.[37]

An item from Commodore Rollingpin's *Almanac* was reproduced and used as an illustration for Chapter XVI.   For this chapter Twain, writing of the steamboat-racing craze on the river, argued that the "Eclipse" not the "R. E. Lee," should have the record for the fastest time between New Orleans and Cairo because the Mississippi had shifted, changing the distances traveled in the races (202).   Nevertheless, when a "Time Table" text and an on-the-spot picture of the record-breaking race between the *Robert E. Lee* and the *Natchez* was found in Rollingpin's paper, the two-and-a-half page section was copied and incorporated into the end of the chapter (Fig. 59).[38]

While in New Orleans, Joel Chandler Harris visited the city from Atlanta and Twain took the opportunity to meet the illustrious sage of the South.   Twain described Harris in his text as "undersized, red-haired, and somewhat freckled" (Fig. 60).   A page later Twain recorded a reading by himself, George Washington Cable and Harris, made to a group of school children.   Harris, of course, was known nationwide for his Uncle Remus character.   His appearance brought confusion to the gathering.   The children had expected to hear a lecture by the Black sage of the nation's nurseries and Twain

THE RUN OF THE ROBERT E. LEE.

The time made by the R. E. Lee from New Orleans to St. Louis in 1870, in her famous race with the Natchez, is the best on record, and, inasmuch as the race created a national interest, we give below her time table from port to port.

Left New Orleans, Thursday, June 30th, 1870, at 4 o'clock and 55 minutes, p. m. ; reached

| | D. | H. | M. | | D. | H. | M. |
|---|---|---|---|---|---|---|---|
| Carrollton . . . . . . . . . . | | | 27½ | Vicksburg . . . . . . . . | 1 | | 38 |
| Harry Hills . . . . . . . . . | 1 | 00½ | | Milliken's Bend . . . . . . . | 1 | 2 | 37 |
| Red Church . . . . . . . . | 1 | 39 | | Bailey's . . . . . . . . | 1 | 3 | 48 |
| Bonnet Carre . . . . . . . . | 2 | 38 | | Lake Providence . . . . . . | 1 | 5 | 47 |
| College Point . . . . . . . | 3 | 50½ | | Greenville . . . . . . . . | 1 | 10 | 55 |
| Donaldsonville . . . . . . . | 4 | 59 | | Napoleon . . . . . . . . | 1 | 16 | 22 |
| Plaquemine . . . . . . . . | • 7 | 05½ | | White River . . . . . . . | 1 | 16 | 56 |
| Baton Rouge . . . . . . . | 8 | 25 | | Australia . . . . . . . . | 1 | 19 | |
| Bayou Sara . . . . . . . | 10 | 26 | | Helena . . . . . . . . | 1 | 23 | 25 |
| Red River . . . . . . . . | 12 | 56 | | Half Mile Below St. Francis . . | 2 | | |
| Stamps . . . . . . . . | 13 | 56 | | Memphis . . . . . . . | 2 | 6 | 9 |
| Bryaro . . . . . . . . | 15 | 51½ | | Foot of Island 37 . . . . . | 2 | 9 | |
| Hinderson's . . . . . . . | 16 | 29 | | Foot of Island 26 . . . . . | 2 | 13 | 30 |
| Natchez . . . . . . . . | 17 | 11 | | Tow-head, Island 14 . . . . | 2 | 17 | 23 |
| Cole's Creek . . . . . . . | 19 | 21 | | New Madrid . . . . . . . | 2 | 19 | 50 |
| Waterproof . . . . . . . | 18 | 53 | | Dry Bar No. 10 . . . . . . | 2 | 20 | 37 |
| Rodney . . . . . . . . | 20 | 45 | | Foot of Island 8 . . . . . . | 2 | 21 | 25 |
| St. Joseph . . . . . . . | 21 | 02 | | Upper Tow-head — Lucas Bend . | 3 | | |
| Grand Gulf . . . . . . . | 22 | 06 | | Cairo . . . . . . . . | 3 | 1 | |
| Hard Times . . . . . . . | 22 | 18 | | St. Louis . . . . . . . . | 3 | 18 | 14 |
| Half Mile Below Warrenton . . . 1 | | | | | | | |

The Lee landed at St. Louis at 11.25 A. M., on July 4th, 1870 — six hours and thirty-six minutes ahead of the Natchez. The officers of the Natchez claimed seven hours and one minute stoppage on account of fog and repairing machinery. The R. E. Lee was commanded by Captain John W. Cannon, and the Natchez was in charge of that veteran Southern boatman, Captain Thomas P. Leathers.

Fig. 59.   The Run of the Robert E. Lee

Fig. 60.
Joel Chandler Harris, Sketch

reveals their surprise when they realize, "Why, he's white!" (471), a response that could come from most of the readers of the Uncle Remus tales. The lecture was incorporated into Chapter CXLVII for the book and Harley, in one of his attempts at portraiture, offered a rendition of the well-known UNCLE REMUS, obviously not a likeness of Harris, the venerable storyteller (Fig. 61).

Harris's first collection, *Uncle Remus: His Songs and His Stories*, had been published in 1880—though the folk tales had been running in the *Atlanta Constitution* for two years before. Harley's rendition of Harris's famous character, with his tufts of white hair outlining a broad face, was modeled after the illustration of Uncle Remus by Frederick S. Church, the artist who had drawn the first likeness of this (fictitious) venerable southern negro narrator (Figs. 62).[39]

By January 1883 Twain had finished the manuscript, illustrations were completed, and text and pictures were in page proof. Twain wrote to Osgood:

> In proof-reading I shall cause you no delay—but I don't answer for Mrs. Clemens, who has not edited the book yet, and will of course not let a line of the proof go from here till she has read it and possibly damned it. But she says she will put aside everything else, & give her entire time to the proofs. . . . When you have decided what to condemn in the last batches, run down here with it—no, I'll run up there; it might get lost in transit.[40]

Fig. 61.
Uncle Remus

# UNCLE REMUS

### HIS SONGS AND HIS SAYINGS

#### THE FOLK-LORE OF THE OLD PLANTATION

By JOEL CHANDLER HARRIS

WITH ILLUSTRATIONS BY FREDERICK S. CHURCH AND JAMES H. MOSER

NEW YORK
D. APPLETON AND COMPANY
1, 8, AND 5 BOND STREET
1881

Fig. 62
*UNCLE REMUS,*
*His Songs and Sayings*

Twain's predictions about his wife's careful editing proved only too true. Livy, however, was not the only proof reader to condemn. Joe Twichell objected to one anecdote; Twain had misgivings about several drawings; and Livy demanded that some text and several illustrations be deleted. Osgood ignored most of these suggestions but reluctantly conceded to others, taking out some of the more highly sensitive text and drawings.

Joe Twichell's objection centered on a rather grisly anecdote told to him by a Civil War noncombatant that he had shared with Twain. The author used the incident in a chapter of the book. When Twichell read the story in page proof, he had second thoughts about the "appropriateness" of the material. He voiced his concern directly to Ben Ticknor in Osgood's Boston office:

> I return herewith the proof submitted me.  I do
> not find anything in it to correct in particular,
> since I gave Mr. Clemens leave to tell the story.
> I'm a little dubious as to the propriety of its being
> told, but that is none of your affair, and anyway
> there's no help now for it, I suppose.[41]

The particular episode has never been positively identified, though it was probably the section on "VICKSBURG DURING THE TROUBLE" from Chapter XXXV.  Twichell, who had seen action in the Civil War, had spoken to a man and wife who had survived the seige of Vicksburg.  The man had related to Twichell the poignant details of the siege, and Twichell, in turn, had related them to his friend.  As reproduced by Twain, the long narrative told of "shell-showers," "*iron* litter" in the streets, and life in the caves, concluding with a shocking incident that occurred one Sunday after a church service:[42]

> Coming out of church, one morning, we had an
> accident—the only one that happened around me
> on a Sunday.  I was just having a hearty hand-
> shake with a friend I hadn't seen for a while,
> and saying, 'Drop into our cave to-night, after
> bombardment; we've got hold of a pint of prime
> wh—.'  Whiskey, I was going to say, you know,
> but a shell interrupted.  A chunk of it cut the
> man's arm off and left it dangling in my hand.
> And do you know the thing that is going to stick
> the longest in my memory, and outlast every-
> thing else, little and big, I reckon, is the mean
> thought I had then?  It was 'the whiskey *is saved.*'
> And yet, don't you know, it was kind of excusa-
> ble; because it was as scarce as diamonds, and we
> had only just that little; never had another taste
> during the siege.                          (382)

Twichell had some reason to worry at the printing of the peculiar circumstances surrounding Civil War life in Vicksburg.  The tale was a blend of the Sabbath, rationing whiskey, a dangling bloody stump—and other details that Osgood finally wanted to omit.  Such a story might reflect poorly on the minister of the prestigious Congregational Church in Hartford, where the connection between Twain the author and Twichell the preacher was widely known.

When Twain read the proof he too worried about the retelling of the affair. His concern, however, was more with the content and mood of the illustration that would accompany the text. Twain wanted a guarantee from his publisher on the makeup of cuts to be included. He wrote to Osgood:

> I telegraphed you about that scene in church, because I wanted to make sure to rectify the thing before you get to printing it. You can fill up that space with any kind of cut you please, provided it does not refer in any way to any part of the text, and is utterly without humorous suggestion. I care nothing about what the subject of the cut is so long as it bears no hint of the text, and is not funny. A landscape is a good thing, and can be called, scene in the Adirondacks, or Palestine, or somewhere. The reader can put in such idle time as he may have in trying to arrive at the connection between the picture and the reading matter. This will give him pleasant occupation for an idle week and will cost us nothing.[43]

Twain apparently thought that drinking on the Sabbath and descriptions of bloody stumps could be seen in print, but these touchy topics should not be reinforced with visual humor. In the end the chapter would contain no church-service pictures or peeks at "the pint of whiskey that was saved." However, some rather gruesome illustrations about the Vicksburg "troubles" were included. Drawn by Harley, one cut shows a mother dashing through a shower of exploding shells as she leads her children to safety; another finds promenading ladies, turning and "waiting to make certain" that some detonating shells hadn't landed too near them (Figs. 63 & 64).

Despite Twain's admonition, there is one touch of ironical humor in the text when the Vicksburg citizen talks of his eating habits during this time. While speculating on the starvation of the citizens or subsisting on a diet of "MULE MEAT?" Twain is shown casually taking notes with no comic element seen in the illustration (Fig. 65).

Included at the end of the chapter is a relatively benign graveyard "landscape," with the neutral caption NATIVE WILD-WOODS, perhaps added at Twain's suggestion. The one lonely

Fig. 63.
Bringing the Children

Fig. 64.
Wait and Make Certain

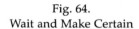

Fig. 65.
"Mule Meat?"

headstone in the foreground adds just a touch of melancholy to give Twain's readers "time to arrive at a connection" between war and death (Fig. 66). Though the author's attitude may have been cavalier about Sabbath Day practices, his concern about the consequences of war—the death and destruction of women and children—worked through the bland tone of his narration. The pictures of fleeing women and children, "shells poised in air," and a quiet Government graveyard, contrasted with a commonplace tone in the discussion about the war. Perhaps, in this instance, Osgood's deleting of some of the more gruesome details and the addition of a peaceful cemetery scene—with Twain's parting remark

Fig. 66.  Native Wild-Woods

"The Government does its work well in the first place, and then takes care of it" (384)—allows for the appropriate irony for Twain's readers.

Twain's directions to Osgood about other illustrations had little to do with propriety, sobriety, or comedy. Twain, as a former river pilot making a new traverse on the river, was both fascinated and appalled when, by an Act of Congress in 1874, the government Light House Board sprinkled beacon lights, day beacons and buoys along the tricky river crossings. In Chapter XXVIII he remarked "This thing has knocked the romance out of piloting" (300). One type of lantern, however, was described in his manuscript: "In the head of every crossing, and in the foot of every crossing, the government has set up a clear-burning lamp" (299). Mark Twain made a sketch of this light, called it a "Crossing Lamp" (Fig. 67), and placed it in the manuscript at page 217 numbering it 217 1/2 and intending his picture to be copied by one of the illustrators. Someone, probably the typist, misunderstood Twain's reason for placing his drawing at this space. He/she added a second sheet into the manuscript with the following inscription: "217 1/2 cannot be, reproduced on a typewriter—H.M.C."[44] Consequently, a picture captioned A GOVERNMENT LAMP (Fig. 68), bearing little resemblance to Twain's drawing, was inserted in the designated space.

The author had also been intrigued by another light during the river trip. He noted in his journal, "Let artist make picture of boat at country landing with

Fig. 67.  Mark Twain, Crossing Lamp

Fig. 68.
A Government Lamp

electric light glaring on trees & white houses."[45] Harley dutifully completed a drawing but his was an urban landing site rather than a country scene, and his light "lit up the water and warehouses" instead of the trees and white houses of Twain's request (Fig. 69).

Twain objected to yet another light. He was afraid that the strong light beam in the artificial-daylight illustration—Twain called it "daylight in a box"—would make it appear that navigating in the fog was as safe and secure as driving a stagecoach. He wrote to Osgood demanding of the

Fig. 69.   The Electric Light

publisher, "Be sure to make this correction. The idea of using an electric light in a fog is a hundred times *too, too*. We should lose the respect of the river-men."[46] Twain directed that the caption also be changed from RUNNING IN A FOG (Fig. 70) to ARTIFICIAL DAYLIGHT, writing his complaint and the caption correction and placing them in the proof sheets at page 301.[47]

Twain's varying attitude about the river lights reveals the frustration in his own mind about the changes on the river. Though in manuscript he was often writing positively about the many current advantages of flood lights and scientific charts that made the pilot's job easier, he just as often objected to adding "too many" illustrations of new safety gadgets. Twain didn't want his readers to think that piloting was easy or effortless; they might get the wrong impression and question the courage of

Fig. 70.   Running in a Fog

the Mississippi river men. Also, as a former pilot, Twain didn't want to downgrade the rivermen's professional skill. Osgood, though sensitive to Twain's requests, was more responsive to mounting costs and closing deadlines.  Neither the picture nor the caption was changed.

In Chapter XXXII, Twain had described the once prominent town of Napoleon, a town which had been totally destroyed by a flood with "nothing left but a fragment of a shanty and a crumbling brick chimney" (363).  Shute's first picture was of NAPOLEON IN 1871, a landing site which had the reputation of being the wickedest town on the Mississippi (Fig. 71).  Alfred R. Waud, a late-hire illus-

Fig. 71.
Napoleon
in 1871

trator for *A Tramp Abroad*, had drawn an on-the-scene picture of the shoreline town for *Every Saturday*, a popular Boston journal, in 1871. Shute used Waud's scene as a model—or the cut was "borrowed" from the journal, with the bottom half redrawn and Shute's signature added (Fig. 72).

Shute provided a second cut for this chapter consistent with his own interpretation of the destroyed town in Twain's narrative

Fig. 72.  Alfred R. Waud, Napoleon

(Fig. 73). In this second cut Napoleon's shops and roadway were flooded out (accurate to the facts), but apparently the artist under-

Fig. 73.   Napoleon As It Is

stood "the crumbling brick chimney" to be separate from the home. Shute's "fragment of a shanty" stood as an undamaged cottage. The house proved not dilapidated enough for Twain. He wrote on the margin of the drawing: "This house is too sound—can't it be turned into a ruin somehow?" But, as Caroline Ticknor later explained, it was "too late to destroy even one of the offending chimneys, and so this last of the shanties of Napoleon must ever remain in the eyes of the reader a trim and prosperous structure."[48] Osgood's reasoning again was governed by time and money; and now even Twain was sympathetic to the deadline pressures. Osgood persuaded Twain it was too late to turn the Napoleon cottage "into a ruin."

Olivia Clemens, while reading proof with her husband, was not as easily swayed. Livy insisted that two illustrations be taken out of the edition. Livy's first objection was to the tail piece for "The Dying Man's Confession," a story dealing with the death of Karl

Ritter. The A. B. Shute tail piece of a withered old man wrapped in a shroud was recorded in the "List of Illustrations" as THE SHADOW OF DOOM (Fig. 74). Twain relayed Livy's reaction to the cut to Hartford: "Dear Osgood—Knock this picture out. The madam's orders are peremptory. She says the chapter is plenty dreadful enough without it."[49] Osgood's decision to retain the print was again probably

Fig. 74.   Tail Piece
The Shadow of Doom

based on time constraints. Publishing deadlines
were too near to have an
illustrator draw a new tail
piece for a page with
only eight lines of
text.

Osgood gave
in, however, to the
second of Livy's
objections—this
protest      much
more serious than
the first.    The
objectionable   pic-
ture    (Fig.    75)
appeared  in  the
proofs  on  page
441 and showed

Fig. 75.   Cremation Scene

A head in profile (an unmistakable likeness of the
author) being consumed in flames; a presage of
possible future punishment which Mrs. Clemens
did not relish, and which she insisted must be
omitted.  This illustration followed the writer's
reflections upon cremation, where he remarks:
"As for me, I hope to be cremated.  I made
the remark to my pastor once, who said, with
what he seemed to think was an impressive manner, 'I wouldn't worry about that, if I had your
chances.'" . . . It was useless for the publishers to
protest that almost the entire edition had been
printed; Mrs. Clemens remained firm in her decision that her husband's profile should not be thus
burned in effigy for the edification of posterity,
and her husband obediently insisted that the "cut
should be cut out."[50]

Hell's fire and cremation were touchy subjects in the 1880s,
especially to a devout Christian like Livy.  Humorous dialogue on
burial practices might slip by Twain's readers—they could rationalize that the writer was just poking fun.  But combining talk about
cremation with a picture of a human being enveloped in Hell's

flames, the human an unmistakable likeness of Mark Twain, that was pushing the subject too far for Olivia and for most of Twain's conservative readers. With Livy's objection fortified by Twain's insistence, Osgood had the press run stopped and the offending tail piece cut out. Thus in most first-edition copies the last half page of Chapter XLIII is blank, the text ending with Twichell's alleged remark and Twain's "innocent" comment upon it: "I wouldn't worry about that if I had your chances. Much he knew about it—the family all so opposed to it [cremation]" (441). Since A. B. Shute had done all three caricatures of Twain in this chapter, it is assumed that he drew the canceled cut. Curiously, there is no caption for this tail piece recorded in the "List of Illustrations" in any state of the first editions. This, however, was not the end of the cremation story.[51]

Twain had been sympathetic with most of Osgood's editing decisions. He wrote the publisher saying: "Make these various changes if convenient, not otherwise. It ain't any matter about the 50,000 already printed."[52] And it was the "already printed" that made the cremation tail piece a bibliographer's dream and a book collector's prize.

It seems in January 1883, Twain had ordered Osgood to run off a large number of copies of *Life*: "make two sets of the plates and dies, and print 50,000 copies of the book."[53] The author's eagerness to have early press runs meant that there were some of the first edition-first state of the book that contained the "Hell's Fire" illustration already shipped to agents. No matter how Livy might have objected to the tail piece in question, collectors have been—and still are—proud to display (and cash in on) first edition copies showing Mark Twain in flames.[54]

One other cut would hold a special interest for Twain scholars. In this case it was the caption, not the print itself, that became (like the picture of Mark Twain in flames) both a first edition-first state point of evidence and a bibliographer's riddle. E. H. Garrett furnished a splendid replica of a many-balconied New Orleans Hotel for Chapter XLIV (Fig. 76). Ben Ticknor, Osgood's partner (who had been instructed by Twain, during the production of *The Prince and the Pauper*, to supply captions himself for the illustrations[55]), had continued with his captioning duties for the Mississippi book. However, it is now believed that Twain himself wrote the original caption THE ST. CHARLES HOTEL and the Charles caption was included in the "List of Illustrations." Twain's

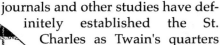

journals and other studies have definitely established the St. Charles as Twain's quarters during his 1882 visit.[56] After a small press run, Ticknor—or someone else in authority at the publishing house—read the text at this point in the book which told of a visit to a "St. Louis Hotel, now occupied by municipal offices" (444). Realizing that the only hotel mentioned in the chapter was the St. Louis, they

Fig. 76.   The St. Charles Hotel

dutifully removed "Charles" and added what they considered the correct caption, THE ST. LOUIS HOTEL.

Twain or Ticknor finally discovered the incorrect caption and, with the press stopped to remove the "Hell's Fire" cut of Twain, it seemed an expedient time to correct the erroneous caption back to THE ST. CHARLES HOTEL.  The chronology for captions in the first-state first editions of *Life on the Mississippi* is:

> The correct first-state copies of LOM, . . . are those
> containing both the St. Charles legend and the cut
> of Twain in flames; the next in order of priority
> are those copies that contain the St. Louis legend
> and the cut of Twain; and, the third, are the copies
> that contain the St. Charles legend but are lacking
> the cut of Twain. All, however, are actually "first
> edition" copies of the book.[57]

As in most of his other travel books, Mark Twain was, of course, often featured in caricature in *Life on the Mississippi*. From Chapter XXII, when a mature Twain takes over as narrator, the author is seen repeatedly in prints drawn by two of the three artists (only Garrett is not represented) as a bowler-hatted traveler. Of the twenty-four illustrations in which an identifiable Twain figure appears, seventeen were drawn by John Harley, the remainder by A. B. Shute.

Fig. 77. James R. Osgood

Harley was also instrumental in portraying Twain's Mississippi travel companions, Thompson and Rogers, who were in real life his publisher Osgood and the secretary Phelps.[58] No known photo to identify Phelps has been located. However, James Osgood (Fig. 77) and Twain are recognizable in the several prints of the trio of travelers in Chapter XXXIII (Fig. 78).

Early in his thinking about illustrations for his travel book, Twain had proposed adding copies of facsimiles. He seriously considered incorporating the following items: a purloined lithograph, a steamer ticket, several pages from various books, and a large-scale map of the Mississippi. The lithograph was one Twain had seen in Mrs. Trollope's *Domestic Manners of the Americans*. Twain also wanted "a specimen-paragraph from her [Trollope's] book—and a facsimile of one of the book's lithographs to

Fig. 78. We Began to Cool Off

illustrate the paragraph."[59]  When this Trollope item was excised from the text at an editing session, at Osgood's direction, the litho-graph facsimile was also eliminated.  Appendix C and many other lengthy passages from the Trollope book, however, were included.

To facilitate his early plans for reproducing a Mississippi steamer ticket, Twain appended a real ticket to a page when he turned in manuscript, intending the coupon to be copied by the artists.  In this section of his text Twain had focused on the issue of scandal and bribery in high places and had directed his readers to see one of the free steamer passes: "Judges of the various Supreme Courts accept passes—and not only that, but with 'Account of Supreme Court' marked upon the face of them. . . . The following is a facsimile."[60] Once more, neither the text about bribes nor a dupli-cated ticket would be used in the first edition. Osgood eliminated this section on scandal—which would have been Chapter XLVIII if retained—to avoid offending Southerners.

Another of Twain's ambitious illustrating ideas would have involved extensive photocopying.  He had written to George Washington Cable in November '82, "Please send me a New Orleans directory of this or last year. I do not know the price but inclose [sic] five dollars at random."[61] Twain had planned a story on white polit-ical liberty to include in his book and wrote to Osgood that four or five pages should be added, "at random, from the city directory for the present year—1882. It 'samples' the book, and affords one a sort of bird's eye view of the nationalities of New Orleans." Cable must have sent on the directory because Twain included the following note to the printer: "(Insert the 4 pages—reduce them in facsimile & crowd them onto a single page of my book, to be read by a magni-fier)."[62]  The idea was vetoed by both Osgood and Anthony—undoubtedly the need to use a magnifying glass to read the names was the deciding factor against including the directory pages.

Twain's most elaborate plan concerned the insertion into the book of a large-scale map of the Mississippi River.  According to Twain's notes in his journal, the map would not have been a simple folded version, like the tipped-in Seller's table-ware guide for the first-edition first-states of *Roughing It*. Twain wanted the printers to photocopy an original map of the Mississippi and cut it "into 20 pieces (full page size) & interleave it along through the book, begin-ning at St. Louis & going down section by section to N. O."[63]

To implement this plan, Twain made several verbal requests

for government maps. He even directed a request to the office of the Secretary of War, and received a positive response.

> On April 11 [1882] the office of the chief of engi-
> neers of the United States Army replied, stating
> that a "copy of Map of Alluvial Basin of the
> Mississippi River, and 16 sheets of the new Map
> of the Mississippi River, has been sent to you by
> today's mail." Many years later Clemens referred
> to "the great War Department map of the
> Mississippi," which was a yard wide and thirty-
> six feet long.[64]

A map allowing the armchair reader to trace his/her journey down the river in the company of Twain and his friends was a
splendid but very expensive and time-consuming idea.
Photocopying and tipping twenty separate sections of a map into
the book's pages would certainly have added bulk—and may
explain why Twain wanted the map included in the first place. The
interleaved-map suggestion, however, never reached the negotia-
tion stage. Not surprisingly, Osgood rejected the plan.

Two much smaller facsimile cuts, however, did make it into
the book. A *Mississippi Steamboat of Fifty Years Ago* (Fig. 79),
appeared on the title page, and COLUMBIA FEMALE INSTITUTE
appeared in Chapter XL. Twain admitted the school cut was "a picture from the advertisement of the 'Female Institute' of Columbia,
Tennessee" (Fig. 80).[65]

Finally, on 15 January 1883, Twain and Osgood declared *Life
on the Mississippi* ready for the public. It was registered with a copyright deposit on 17 May, over a year from the time Twain and
Osgood had stepped aboard the *Baton Rouge*. By subscription standards the travel book was perfect: "a handsome book of its kind, a
heavy volume of 624 pages (sixty chapters and four appendices)
'with more than three hundred illustrations.'"[66] Each full-page print
had a blank verso which was counted and expanded the page total;
there were three hundred and sixteen illustrations. In all Harley
signed seventy-nine illustrations, five full-page prints and at least
one tail piece, though he obviously drew many of the unsigned cuts;
Garrett signed forty illustrations, though many others show his
style; Shute signed forty-six of the prints, though he, too, was
undoubtedly responsible for more. All three artists participated in

# LIFE ON THE MISSISSIPPI

BY

### MARK  TWAIN

AUTHOR OF "THE INNOCENTS ABROAD," "ROUGHING IT,"
"THE PRINCE AND THE PAUPER," ETC.

**WITH  MORE  THAN  300  ILLUSTRATIONS**

*Mississippi Steamboat of Fifty Years Ago.*

[SOLD BY SUBSCRIPTION ONLY.]

BOSTON
JAMES R. OSGOOD AND COMPANY
1883

Fig. 79.
Mississippi Steamboat of
Fifty Years Ago

Fig. 80.
Columbia Female Institute

drawing tail pieces; a few were signed, though most of the work is identifiable only by the artist's particular style. Many of the tail pieces appear to be "stock cuts," not drawn specifically by the artists' commissioned to illustrate Twain's book and often having no relation to the text.

There were several design decisions made by Osgood's house consistent for both *The Prince* and *Life*. The title pages did not record the illustrators, and the "List of Illustrations" followed the "Contents" page. Also, captions for most of the tail pieces were recorded only in the "List of Illustrations," not below the end prints themselves. It seems likely that, as happened in *The Prince*, Twain allowed Ticknor to supply many of the captions—though it is also possible that Ticknor delegated part of this task to his design supervisor, A. V. S. Anthony. In a majority of cases the captions are direct quotes or relate in some way to the adjoining text.[67]

There are, however, a few captions—some mentioned earlier in this chapter—that possibly point to Twain's help in creating captions with extra humor, legends that supply an added dimension for an illustration or extend the comedic elements of his tale. In THE PILOT'S FIRST BATTLE, when cannon balls are bouncing off the pilot house and a frightened man kneels on the floor behind the big stove, Harley has the prayerful gent in front of the stove with a tongue-in-cheek caption MIGHTY WARM TIMES (Fig. 81). For another illustration the caption was taken from a mere phrase in the author's text—"This matter warmed up into a quarrel; then into a fight" (361). Harley draws a tangle of the trio Osgood, Twain, and Phelps and the caption reads WARMED UP INTO A QUARREL (Fig. 82) In another section when Twain is speaking of burial practices, the widow O'Flaherty's decision to have a finer coffin than the one bought by the widow O'Shaughnessy finds an illustration captioned AMBITION (Fig. 83). In a late chapter, when Twain is obliged to speak in a Sunday school, Twain is seen extemporizing to a sea of fresh faces. A sign on the wall reads GOD IS LOVE while the caption for the illustration reads RANDOM RUBBISH (Fig. 84).

With the book out most reviews were favorable, though they tended to harp on the fact—and it really was a fact—that too much of the text was "old material." The New Orleans *Times-Democrat*, however, complimented Twain on his return to his old style. The reviewer, Lafcadio Hearn, dealt kindly with the illustrations:

Fig. 81.
Mighty Warm Times

Fig. 82.
Warmed Up Into A
Quarrel

Fig. 83.
Ambition

Fig. 84.
Random Rubbish

*Life on the Mississippi*—Mark Twain's new production, is a large volume . . . much resembling in
form the famous *Innocents Abroad*, and *Roughing
It*. Like those highly successful books, *Life on the
Mississippi* has been illustrated with humorous
engravings, the spirit of which will be appreciat-
ed by all familiar with the picturesque features of
American river-life.[68]

In an unsigned review of September 1883 in *The Atlantic
Monthly*, the critic was very receptive to Twain's narrative from the
"Raftsman's Chapter," the chapter that Twain had cut from the
*Huckleberry Finn* manuscript and inserted into *Life*:

We are also presented with a chapter from an
unpublished work by the writer, detailing the
adventures of a Southwestern boy a quarter of a
century ago, which places before us in vivid colors the rough, hilarious, swaggering, fighting,
superstitious ways of the bygone raftsmen.
Rude, sturdy, unflinching, and raw though the
picture is, it is likely to stand a long while as a

wonderful transcript from nature, and as a
memorial of the phase of existence which it
describes that will not be surpassed in the
future.[69]

Chatto's London edition, issued days before the American
copy on May 12, was filed in Washington several months after the
date of actual American copyright. It, however, drew less praise for
its text or its radically different design.

Mr. Clemens's new book is a disappointment. To
begin with, it has a vulgar red cover, it is cum-
bered with a quantity of illustrations of the
cheapest and least suggestive American type, its
lines are ungraceful . . . ; it appears at once anom-
alous and offensive, and prejudices its readers
against it as a book even before they get seriously
to work upon it as literature.[70]

The *British Quarterly Review* took the author to task for
unseemly humor and inconsistent style, but the reviewer's comments on the illustrations were favorable, though not enthusiastic:

We are sorry sometimes that Mr. Mark Twain is so
apt to make fun of things pertaining to religion.
Sunday schools may have their faults but they
should not always be laughed at. The illustrations are not equal by any means, but all are
good, and some are deliciously full of humor. For
young people the book will be a treasure; both
letterpress and pictures will suit them.[71]

The English and American editions had radically different
formats (Fig. 85): the British red differing from an American brownish-grey twill cover; the English with a smaller trimmed-leaf size;
561 pages in the British and 624 pages in the American. The Chatto
edition was typeset in London, but for the illustrations the publisher used stereo plates (identical in size with those used in the
American edition) that had been sent from Boston. Since the plates
were identical but the leaf size smaller, placement of the illustrations was often erratic in relation to the text. The English edition
kept the ST. CHARLES HOTEL caption and the "CHARLES" was

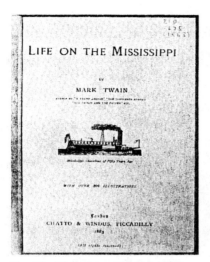

Fig. 85.  Title Page, English Edition
*Life on the Mississippi*

listed in the "List of Illustrations."
As in the later copies of the
American edition, there was no
"Hell's Fire" cremation cut of
Mark Twain in flames.[72]

Despite the negative
English criticism, sales for the
Chatto edition were respectable.
*Life on the Mississippi*, with sub-
ject matter not relevant to the
English, sold 46,000 copies over
the years compared to *A Tramp
Abroad*, a natural winner for the
British, which had sold 174,250.

Unfortunately, the book
did not sell as well in the States
as Twain had hoped.  Since he
had a unique commission contract with Osgood, Twain had
paid out a considerable sum for production, with the result that
there was little left over for profit.

Comparing costs for the printing and publication of a book
published by Bliss with one by Osgood is difficult.  The contracts, a
"royalty" with Bliss and a "commission" with Osgood, the pro-
cedures and the personnel are too diverse.  Moreover, in the Elisha
Bliss "royalty" contract with Twain, Bliss personally handled all
expenditures—while keeping a "double set" of account books in
which Bliss expanded the production costs beyond the true figures.
While Twain realized early that Bliss was inflating production
prices, it wasn't until *A Tramp Abroad* that the author would control
the manufacturing and design costs by having work done in
Europe, much to the exasperation of Frank Bliss in Hartford.  The
"commission" contract with Osgood, left Twain—often through
Webster—to pay the production costs, with presumably no "dou-
bling" of costs.  Therefore, it is impossible to compare pricing
between Osgood and Bliss productions, too many differing contin-
gencies were involved.

An always suspicious Twain requested an accounting in
March of 1884.  Osgood, through Webster, tried to reconstruct the
costs for producing the book.  According to one estimate, an initial

run of 50,000 copies of *Life on the Mississippi* cost $.45 per copy. However, final accounting altered the price to $.60—with higher costs for each item of manufacture. The $.60 per book figure took into account $500.00 paid by Chatto for the electro plates and a $500.00 expense for Anthony as supervisor of design.[73] Osgood added a postscript to the accounting figures to explain the payment to A. V. S. Anthony:

> Anthony's time, and the losses by bad debts are properly chargeable to you both equitably and by understanding. Mr. Anthony's time devoted to the placing and superintendence of the engrav-ings and the oversight of printing was as much a part of the manufacture of the book as the engraving or printing itself. We were authorized to do what seemed best to us to secure a good result.[74]

Later, in order to clarify his role in the production of the book, Anthony wrote a note to Ben Ticknor and asked him to explain to everyone that he had saved them, not cost them, money: "Say to Webster who is here that I saved $600 on the cost of draw-ing by furnishing authorities—That was arranged with the artists—and is a part of my charge for time."[75]

Nevertheless, Anthony's bill continued to rankle in Twain—though it would prove to be a short-term annoyance:

> To approve & "place" 300 pictures, & contract for the drawing & processing of Ms. & suggest things for illustration that seems kind of unnecessary, for the artist could have done that himself. But find out what length of *time* Anthony put on his work & what *system* of charging is.[76]

A larger and more lasting problem was Twain's relationship with Osgood. Twain wrote charitably about his frustration at the unprofitability of *Life on the Mississippi*. "The Prince and the Pauper and the Mississippi are the only books of mine which have ever failed. The first failure was not unbearable—but this second one is so nearly so that it is not a calming subject for me to talk upon. I am out $50,000 on this last book."[77] Interestingly, even at the end of their business partnership, Mark Twain continued to value

Osgood's friendship and in the end absolved him of all blame for money lost on publishing the Mississippi book.

> Osgood was one of the dearest and sweetest and loveliest human beings to be found on the planet . . . , but he knew nothing about subscription publishing and he made a mighty botch of it. He was a sociable creature and we played much billiards and daily and nightly had a good time. And in the meantime his clerks ran our business for us and I think that neither of us inquired into their methods or knew what they were doing. That book was a long time getting built; and when at last the final draft was made upon my purse I realized that I had paid out fifty-six thousand dollars upon that structure. Bliss could have built a library for that money. It took a year to get the fifty-six thousand back into my pocket, and not many dollars followed it. So this first effort of mine to transact that kind of business was a failure.[78]

With two financial failures, Twain recognized that a major change for the publication of his books was necessary. By February 1884, Osgood was no longer selling any of Twain's books through the subscription market. Management of all sales was put in the hands of Charles Webster. Shortly thereafter, Webster and Twain began a new publishing venture; they established the Webster Publishing Company, with thoughts of producing a new Mark Twain book, *Adventures of Huckleberry Finn*.

### Notes

[1] *Businessman.*, ed., p. 207.

[2] *Mark Twain: Mississippi Writings*, ed. Guy Cardwell (The Library of America, 1982), p. 175, n. 217.1.

[3] Horst Kruse, *Mark Twain and "Life on the Mississippi"* (Amherst: University of Massachusetts Press, 1981), pp. 5-6. Hereafter cited as Kruse, *Life*.

[4] Frederick Anderson and Hamlin Hill, "How Samuel Clemens Became Mark Twain's Publisher: A Study of the James R. Osgood Contracts," *Proof*, 2 (1972), 138. *LOM* sales did not reach 50,000 until long after the

Osgood Company filed for bankruptcy in 1885.

⁵ MTLP, p. 158. Charles Webster "had been a business manager and office boy for MT in a number of other enterprises, and had touched on matters of book manufacture when he wrestled with the American Publishing Company and experimented with Kaolatype for MT's books, this letter is the first step in CLW's eventual career as MT's publisher." MTLP, p. 159, n. 1.

⁶ SLC to Howells, 24 [October 1874]. Edgar M. Branch, "Samuel Clemens Steamboats," *Mark Twain Journal*, 24 (Fall 1986), 22, n. 32.

⁷ Judith Hale Crossett, "A Critical Edition of Mark Twain's *Life on the Mississippi*," unpublished dissertation (University of Iowa Press, 1977), p. 691. Hereafter cited as Crossett, *Life*.

⁸ SLC to James Osgood, 31 December 1881, MTLP, p. 149, n. 1.

⁹ Kruse, p. 139, n. 54 and MTL I: 419.

¹⁰ Weber, *Rise*, p. 195.

¹¹ Weber, *Rise*, p. 195.

¹² Fielding, *Dictionary*, 134. Garrett also illustrated books by Keats, Lowell, Dumas, and others. His own books include *Romance and Reality of the Puritan Coast* (1897) and *The Pilgrim Shore* (1897). See also Rasmussen, *A to Z*, p. 163.

¹³ SLC to Osgood, undated, TS in MTP. See also MTLP, p. 158, n. 2.

¹⁴ MTLP, p. 158, n. 2. Twain had early on "planned the use of material from the historians or the river and of travel accounts by foreign visitors." Kruse, *Life*, p. 17.

¹⁵ SLC to Howells, October 1882, MTHL I: 417. See also Guy A. Cardwell, "*Life on the Mississippi*: Vulgar Facts and Learned Errors," 19, *ESQ*, 1973. Only one quarter of the book was from "Old Times," Chapters 4 through 17. The "Body of the Nation" as an Introduction, was copied from *Harper's Magazine*, February 1863 with documentation. The VOYAGE OF THE TIMES-DEMOCRATS RELIEF BOAT THROUGH THE INUNDATED REGIONS, DOWN BLACK RIVER and THE FLOOD STILL RISING were articles from the New Orleans *Times-Democrat* (March 25, 27 & 29, 1882) and appeared as Appendix A with credits. An excerpt from "a now forgotten book which was published half a century ago" was the only citation, appeared on pages 313-320. The long excerpts from Henry Rowe Schoolcraft's Indian Legends, PEBOAN AND SEEWUN and THE UNDYING HEAD, appear as Appendix D, with credit to Schoolcraft. THE LEGEND OF WHITE-BEAR LAKE, is in the final chapter of the book without credit. Laurence I. Berkove speculates in his "Dan DeQuille" and "Old Times on the Mississippi," *Mark Twain Journal*, Fall 1986, pp. 28-34, that DeQuille's sketch known as "Pilot Wylie" may also have been "borrowed" by Twain.

¹⁶ Dewey Ganzel, "Twain, Travel Books, and *Life on the Mississippi*," *American Literature*, Vol. 34, March 1962, 40-41. Ganzel has the most complete listing of Twain's acknowledged sources and of his additions to this article. Hereafter cited as Ganzel, *Life*.

¹⁷ SLC to Howells, 4 November 1882. MTHL II: 418.

[18] *Ibid.*

[19] Osgood to SLC, 5 June 1882. MTLP, p. 154, n. 3.

[20] A. V. S. Anthony to SLC, MTP. The identification of the prints follows from the starting point of Harley's illustrations (Chapter VI) and follows through the chapter with remarks such as "pigs' snouts" and "mules' heads" as evidence of prints referred to by Harley and Anthony.

[21] Moss Engraving Company would also produce the prints for the *Adventures of Huckleberry Finn*. According to accounts for this book, each completed electro cost $1.45. Thanks to Victor Fischer of the MTP for this information.

[22] Anthony to SLC, 5 June 1882, MTP (1883 file).

[23] SLC to Webster, 15 June 1882, MTLP, pp. 154-155, n. 3.

[24] JRO to SLC, 22 September 1882, MTLP, p. 158, n. 3. In his journal Twain jotted down a few ideas for titles: "Title <'Abroad on the Great River.'> <'Abroad on the Father of Waters.'>" "Abroad on the Mississippi." N&J II, 501.

[25] Harley drew all the renditions of the "young cub" and the ship captain. However, they are misleading since Twain was actually 21 years old at the time he apprenticed with Horace Bixby and Bixby was just 9 years Twain's senior. Horst Kruse argues that since Twain was creating a fictionalized autobiographical protagonist, it was prudent for him to make the cub "younger and less experienced than the author himself was when the events actually happened." Kruse, *Life*, p. 23. Harley's cover is a variant of the image of the obsolete woodyard man seen on page 257.

[26] The features in Harley's Bixby do not resemble the features apparent in the older Horace Bixby as THE CAPTAIN (477). THE CAPTAIN was probably drawn by A. B. Shute.

[27] Beard's frontispiece was likely completed without much historical research; it was initially a sample drawing he submitted to Twain when he (Beard) was being considered for the job of illustrating *A Connecticut Yankee*. It seems plausible that he would have referred to the Harley's illustrations in *Life*.

[28] Kruse, *Life*, p. 46. "Of the items not taken from the Grangerford parlor but used in 'The House Beautiful' in *Life on the Mississippi*, the following are mentioned in Cook's book: the 'new and deadly invention' of the coal furnace (p. 11), the bric-a-brac and souvenirs of the family's travels, a shell, quartz specimens, and Indian arrowheads" (101 & 123).

[29] Weber, *Rise*, p. 197.

[30] The lines just preceding this anecdote foreshadow the King and Duke in *Huck Finn* where the pair are acting out a scene from Richard III.

[31] N&J II, 512, n. 265.

[32] N&J II, 509 and N&J II, 509, n. 254.

[33] N&J II, 509, n. 254. The portrait was drawn by A. B Shute. According to Kruse, *Life*, p. 28, Twain used the actual names of the steamer's crew in the manuscript, in incorrect spelling. Mr. Dad Dunham, the second

mate, is called Mr. Dad *Dunn*, Mr. Lem S. Gray, the pilot, is referred to as *Len*. Both spellings are later corrected. "Mr. Dad Dunham was to become 'Uncle Mumford' in the printed version. This change does not appear in the Manuscript." Kruse, *Life*, p. 142, n. 26.

34 See N&J II, 509, n. 254. A Capt. Mumf. Wood was in charge of the tug Wm. Wood in New Orleans.

35 SLC to Osgood, 19 July 1882, MTLP, p. 156-157. "In the space at the bottom of manuscript page 77, which ends with the cue words [required it], Mark Twain wrote 'Copy the photograph.' Another hand, probably the typist's—added in pencil 'I can't, it's Sunday.' No photograph survives with the manuscript." Crossett, *Life*, p. 790. In 1859 Clemens had published a satirical piece signed "Sergeant Fathom" in the New Orleans *Crescent*, burlesquing a Sellers newspaper letter. Sellers never forgave Clemens. The wrangle about Twain stealing his "nom de plume" from Sellers is still under debate. See Kruse, *Life*, p. 83.

36 N&J II, 555, n. 62. The print, SELLERS'S MONUMENT, appears on page 498 of the first edition but does not show the map of the Mississippi.

37 "An illustration of a 'cemetery' on page 430 of the first edition of *Life on the Mississippi* may be the result of the present request [to Osgood]." MTLP, p. 157, n. 2.

38 The picture on page 204, THE RUN OF THE ROBERT E. LEE, has the artist or engraver's signature, F MYRICK, in the lower left-hand corner. The caption appears as RACE OF THE LEE AND THE NATCHEZ in the "List of Illustrations."

39 For further information on Joel Chandler Harris and his illustrators see Beverly R. David, "Visions of the South," *American Literary Realism* (Summer 1976), pp. 189-207.

40 Benjamin Lease, "Mark Twain and the Publication of *Life on the Mississippi*: an Unpublished Letter," *American Literature*, XXVI (May 1954), 249. Partial letter also in MTLP, p. 161.

41 Caroline Ticknor, *Glimpses of Authors* (Boston: Houghton Mifflin, 1922), pp. 138-139. Hereafter cited as Ticknor, *Glimpses*.

42 "Omitted portions of the latter book [*Life on the Mississippi*] included additional passages on Vicksburg during the war." *A to Z*, p. 497. A church scene is also referred to in the "suppressed" chapter of *Life on the Mississippi* and is another possible choice for the incident Twain did not want illustrated.

43 Ticknor, *Glimpses*, pp. 138-139. NATIVE WILD-WOODS appears on page 384 of the first edition and is unsigned though in the style of Garrett.

44 Crossett, *Life*, p. 764. The original Mark Twain sketch is in the Pierpont Morgan Library, MA 677-679. Copy of Twain's sketch is in MTP.

45 N&J II, 472. THE ELECTRIC LIGHT was drawn by Harley.

46 Ticknor, *Glimpses*, p. 138.

47 Caroline Ticknor, "Missing," p. 301.

48 Caroline Ticknor, "Missing," p. 303.

[49] Ticknor, *Glimpses*, p. 138. The illustrations in this chapter are all by Shute. There is a barely discernible "H" in the lower right-hand corner indicating the tail piece may have been drawn by Harley.

[50] See Ticknor, *Glimpses*, pp. 136-137. *The Oxford Mark Twain 'Life on the Mississippi'* reinstates the suppressed cremation tail piece into page 441.

[51] This "tail piece" is used as a verification for four states of the edition. BAL II, p. 198. "The first copies contained a plate at page 441 showing Mark Twain in flames. This was omitted from later issues at the request of the author's wife. Some of the first edition sheets, containing this plate at page 441, were later found and turned over to Webster & Company who issued them with their own title page and substituted their name for that of Osgood at the base of the spine. This later issue does not have the brownish-grey endpapers of the original issue and seems to be trimmed closer." MTB, p. 42.

[52] Ticknor, *Glimpses*, p. 139.

[53] SLC to Osgood, 6 January 1883, MTLP, p. 161.

[54] Ticknor, *Glimpses*, p. 137.

[55] "Put titles under the pictures yourself—I'll alter them in proof if any alteration shall seem necessary." SLC to Ben Ticknor, 1 August 1881, MTLP, p. 139.

[56] "After putting up at the St. Charles Hotel, the visitors [Twain and Osgood] spent the first day riding through the city with Cable as their guide." Arline Turner, "Notes on Mark Twain in new Orleans," *McNeese Review*, Vol. 6, 1954, 10. Also in N&J II, 461, n. 98; and 468, n. 127.

[57] "That Picture of 'St. Louis Hotel' in *Life on the Mississippi*," *Twainian*, VI (September-October 1947), 2. This *Twainian* issue also notes that "Twain himself wrote the line, 'St. Charles Hotel' beneath the drawing of that hotel on page 443; that this line was correctly entered in the 'List of Illustrations.'" The print regardless of caption appears on page 443 of the first edition. See also "New First Issue Point in *Life on the Mississippi*," *Twainian*, IV (November 1944), 1-3; BAL II, 198, and N&J II, 550.

[58] "It is obvious that Thompson and Rogers represent Osgood and Phelps." Kruse, *Life*, p. 30.

[59] *Life on the Mississippi*, Limited Editions Club: Heritage Press, 1944, p. 392. Hereafter cited as *Life*, Heritage.

[60] *Life*, Heritage, p. 410.

[61] SLC to G. W. Cable, 11 November 1882, Howard Tilton Library, Tulane University. TS in MTP.

[62] *Life*, Heritage, p. 416.

[63] N&J II, 455.

[64] MTLP, pp. 455-456, n. 71. Twain would continue with this "map" idea in 1885, "Oct. 3, '85. I think I've struck a good idea. It is to <make> reduce a series of big maps to mere photographic fly-specks & sell them together with a microscope of 1/4 to 1 inch focal distance. By this means I could conveniently examine my <cynchromatic> synchromatic map which is 36 ft. long." N&J III, 196-197.

<sup>65</sup> Twain also included with the illustration a lengthy footnote from *Extracts from the Public Journals*, which contradicted the "southern highest type of civilization" described in the college's prospectus.

<sup>66</sup> BAL II, p. 198.

<sup>67</sup> The "Contents" listed for the chapters and the "Headpieces" on the various pages are curiously at odds with each other.

<sup>68</sup> MTCH, p. 109.

<sup>69</sup> Anonymous review, *The Atlantic Monthly*, September 1883.

<sup>70</sup> MTCH, p. 113.

<sup>71</sup> *British Quarterly Review*, Vol. LXXXVIII, July 1883, 227. Perhaps this reviewer caught the connection between the sign reading GOD IS LOVE and the caption below, RANDOM RUBBISH.

<sup>72</sup> "That Picture of 'St. Louis Hotel' in 'Life on the Mississippi,'" *Twainian*, VI (September-October 1947), 2.

<sup>73</sup> In *Businessman*, p. 244.

| | |
|---|---|
| 50,000 books at 50 cents apiece is | <u>$25,000.</u> |
| At 60 they are $30,000 | |
| — (These cost 60.) | |
| At 45c (what they <u>were</u> to cost,) — | <u>$22,500.</u> |

| | |
|---|---:|
| Paper | .11,581.67 |
| Engraving Plates | .868.79 |
| Sundry Engravings | .133.20 |
| Drawings | .2,437.00 |
| Electros & Compo | .1,766.69 |
| Press Work | .3,900.00 |
| Binding | <u>.13,803.34</u> |
| | 34,580.59 |
| Commission | <u>.4,878.19</u> |
| | .39,458.78 |

There is possibly an overcharge on paper, of $356.50. If my memory serves me, it was to cost 8 cents.

- - - - - - - - - -

By the above showing, these books have cost 60 cents a copy, (instead of 45 or 47)—this *excluding* all items except paper, presswork & binding. Now we are willing to pay 45 for cloth, & no more; the other 7,000 to be paid 35 per vol. extra—say $2000 altogether; so the 39,000 ought to have cost $24,000 instead of $29,284.

| | |
|---|---:|
| Possible overcharge on paper | $    356.50 |
| 310 reams unaccounted | .1,500.00 |
| Electros paid by Chatto | .500.00 |
| Anthony's bill | <u>500.00</u> |
| | 2,856.50 |
| Excess over 45c in cost of 50,000 books | <u>4,500.00</u> |
| | 7,356.50 |

Told me in May, on way to Montreal, books wd cost 45c & maybe *less*—showing skeleton.

[74] *Businessman*, p. 243.

[75] AVS Anthony to Ticknor, 26 March 1884. See also *Businessman*, p. 244.

[76] *Businessman*, p. 246.

[77] SLC to James Osgood, 21 December 1883. MTLP, p. 164.

[78] *Mark Twain in Eruption*, ed. Bernard DeVoto (New York: Harper, 1940), p. 157.

## List of Illustrations

**Fig. #**

# Index